# Weapon of Choice

*One man's journey from false accusation, to unjust conviction, false imprisonment, and beyond.*

Kevin Paul DeCoste

First Edition

PAGE PUBLISHING, INC.
New York, NY

First originally published by Page Publishing, Inc. 2018

ISBN 978-1-64350-486-5 (Paperback)
ISBN 978-1-64350-488-9 (Digital)

Printed in the United States of America

# *Regarding "Foul" Language*

My parents were from the generation that fought in World War II. My first childhood friend, as well as one of my best friends—and one other—their parents were from the generation that fought in the Korean War. What's the difference? My parents basically never used swear words. My friend's parents (with a couple of exceptions) did. A lot. So it was from my first childhood friend that I learned so many of the "bad" words that would eventually make their way into my everyday speech starting in junior high. I'm not proud of that. It's also a very difficult habit to break. I can suppress my "colorful" words until I'm either very frustrated, very tired, or both.

Guys in prison are no different. Many of the men that I have quoted in these pages could out-swear the drill instructor from the movie *Full Metal Jacket.* I deliberated endlessly with myself as to whether or not I should "sanitize" what was said. I finally realized that to do that would be to distort the truth, and since I have basically had my life ruined by a liar, I have decided to accurately write down *exactly* what each person said. I have allowed for only one exception, the use of God's name in vain. As a Christian, that sort of speech is so offensive that I have decided to leave those words, regardless of who spoke them, out of the narrative.

I apologize to anyone offended by what I or anyone else may have said in the pages to come.

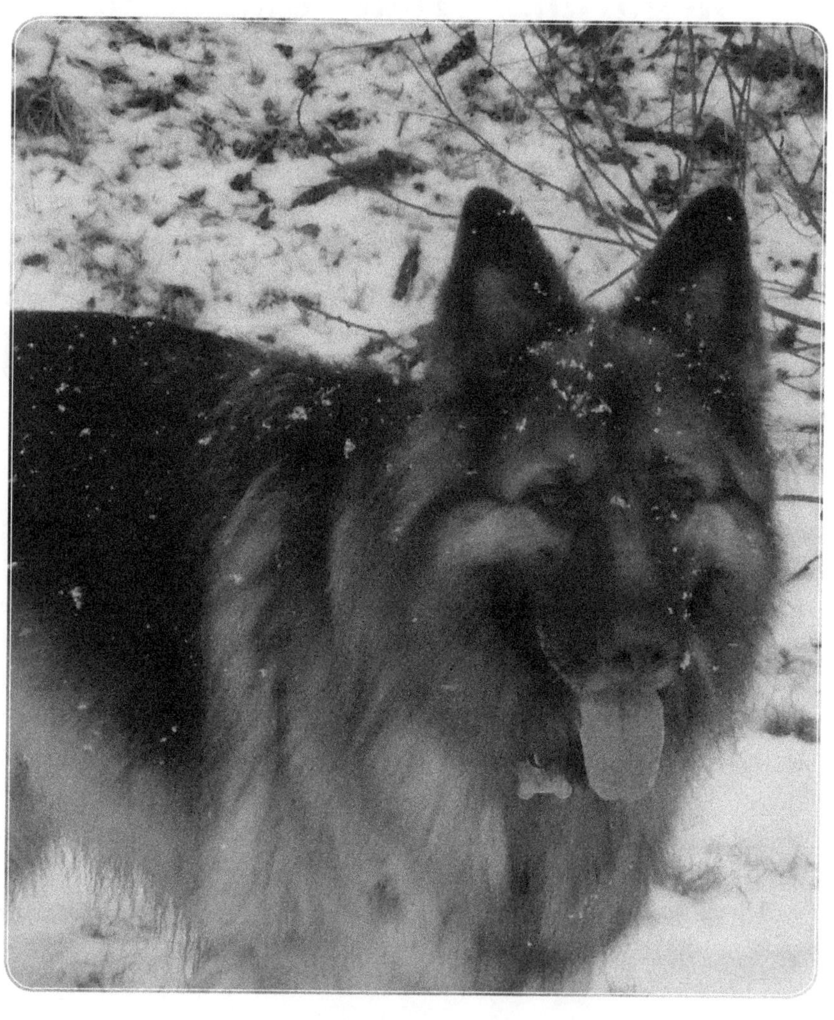

# *Yuri*

## November 18, 2008—December 4, 2016

I have had many great people in my life; however, during the worst of times, my closest "soul mate" was Yuri. When I was hot, he was hot. When I was cold, he was cold. When we lost our home, Yuri was with me. When I was sad, he comforted me. Yuri would never lie to me or about me. Yuri was always happy to see me even when he himself was not feeling well. After he had knee surgery, I would pray when I came home from work that he would not struggle to the door to greet me—but he always did. The anti-inflammatory medication that he was given before and after surgery destroyed his liver. After five hours of surgery to repair his liver, his surgeon told me, "If you don't hear from me until tomorrow, that's a good sign." At 4:00 a.m., she called me, saying, "If you want to say goodbye, you'll have to get here quickly." Yuri died while cradled in my arms. He was barely conscious. Drawing on the words of two theologians—Pope Francis I and Russian Orthodox theologian Father Boris Bobrinskoy—I told Yuri quietly that we would be together again, in a place where the toys never stopped squeaking and the balls never lost their bounce. That in that place, we could play without ever becoming tired. Then Yuri crossed the bridge between my arms and the arms of Jesus, the One who had made him so beautiful. I had never been as close to any human as I was to Yuri. I know that I never will be. We'll meet again, my beautiful puppy!

I sped up to thirty miles per hour then slammed on the brakes. My old Plymouth "K" car came to a skidding halt—within the "safety margin" that I had in mind. True, there were a couple of inches of snow on the ground, but I had made a promise: to take Ray out to lunch as a belated birthday gift.

A week before, I had arrived at work to find Ray sitting alone, staring out a window, and crying. It was his fifteenth birthday and, as with nearly all of the special occasions in his life, his mother had promised to come but never showed up. I felt myself near to crying myself. Ray seemed like a nice kid—easy to get along with. He hardly ever seemed to get into trouble, though the staff members who had known him the longest often labeled him as both sneaky and dishonest. That always angered me. Though I had only worked at the school for three months, I felt that it was simply wrong to attach such labels to kids so young.

I was working at the Lakeside School, a residential school for troubled, abused, and/or court-involved adolescent boys. There were two residence houses: one housing twelve boys; the other, twenty-four. I worked as a counselor at the larger house. Twelve of the twenty-four boys were in the program for adolescent sex offender treatment. Ray, age fifteen, was one of those sex offenders. He had been charged with having sex with a mentally challenged girl close to his own age. As far as Ray was concerned he felt the sex was entirely consensual, not understanding that the girl's retardation made it legally impossible for her to consent.

When I finally arrived at the residence home, the snow had finally stopped falling. Despite the fact that I not only loved snow—

but actually loved driving in the snow—I was happy that for the sake of safety, the roads would soon be plowed down to the pavement.

On entering the home, I asked the assistant house manager where Ray was. "I'm not sure where anyone is right now," Bob replied, obviously having a tough start to his Saturday morning shift. It was amusing—both Bob, the assistant house manager, as well as Roger, the manager, were both accomplished martial artists. Roger held a black belt in the "soft" art of kung fu while Bob held a black belt in the "hard" style of tae kwon do. This led to continuous discussions among the resident boys as to which one would prevail in a fight against each other. I have to admit, at times, the thought of the two of them battling each other played out in amusing ways in my mind as well. However since Bob was kind of a "biker" guy—who had even worked at a biker bar —I always figured he'd come out on top. He was also seemingly more masculine.

Then I saw what had Bob so frazzled. One of the quieter residents, Corey, was in the process of removing the tiles of the overhanging ceiling in what was known as the twelve-man bedroom. What I couldn't understand was that Bob was making no effort whatsoever to stop him. The Lakeside School had a policy of never physically restraining a student. I had worked at two previous programs where a student could be physically escorted to a different area of the school or even physically restrained—essentially held down, like being "pinned" in wrestling—until they calmed down. It was a procedure taught by human service professionals. In my experience, it never caused any physical or emotional harm to the resident involved.

As I usually employed humor in my work, I walked up next to Corey and pretended to be thoroughly engrossed in what he was doing. After two or three minutes had passed, I looked Corey straight in the eyes and asked, "Holy shit, Corey, what are you doing?" Corey stopped, laughed, and replied, "I'm not sure." So I said, "Then maybe you should stop."

At that moment, a clearly agitated Bob called to me, "Kevin! Can I speak with you?" I walked over and, somewhat annoyed, asked him, "What are you doing? I can get him to stop." Bob replied, "I don't want him to stop. I've called for an ambulance to take him out of here. Let him get evaluated at the hospital." "Why?" I asked. "If he stops, it won't be necessary." Bob was clearly frustrated with both Corey and me and barked, "It's your day off. Don't make any decisions. Just go take Ray out to lunch."

I didn't like it. Why subject a kid to being hauled out on a stretcher like some mental patient over something so trivial? He hadn't harmed anyone and was in no obvious danger of hurting himself. Even his "ceiling work" was calm, slow, and methodical. It was a waste of public resources to call an ambulance. In fact, I sincerely believed that all Corey needed was some individual attention. Why not just sit down and have a Coca-Cola with the kid?

Of course, this was a school/residential program based on some obscure Japanese therapeutic model. I never really understood it. The guy that hired me, Leeroy, had given me a book on the subject. The thrust of the book was "OK, your life might suck, but some of it is good, so stop feeling sorry for yourself. Your problems are basically of your own making." My nineteen years of formal education led me to the learned opinion that the book, as well as the entire therapeutic model, was basically bullshit. I was told by an overnight worker that the two men who had founded the school had run a failing furniture store and had come to the conclusion that it might be more lucrative—and easy—to go into human services. All the staff members (except the new guy, me) had been to a one- or two-week "camp" to thoroughly learn this great Japanese system. Otherwise, they had no experience in the area of human services whatsoever. It was funny, despite that, they seemed to believe that they were somehow "junior psychologists" nonetheless.

I finally located Ray in the basement kitchen. It struck me that he was acting strangely. It was as though he wasn't sure if he wanted to go to lunch with me at all. I wasn't happy. This was my day off after all. Finally, he seemed to snap out of it. I thought to myself, *Oh well, if he were 100 percent normal, he wouldn't be here anyway*. We got into my car and left.

Our first stop was Newbury Comics. Ray was in the habit of playing with Magic Cards. I never understood the game—I never wanted to either. However, in retrospect, I do recall a televangelist calling games like the Magic Card game "diabolical." The guy may well have been right.

After Ray got his cards, I (very stupidly) handed him a one-hundred-dollar bill and said, "Bring me back the change." I was shocked when he came back and handed me about sixteen dollars. A word of advice—never hand a fifteen-year-old a one-hundred-dollar bill!

From there, we drove to Staples, as I needed a couple of new ballpoint pens. Without hesitation, Ray handed me a pack of colorful pens that he wanted for himself. This was getting expensive. I left Staples with about seven dollars—hardly enough to buy lunch with. I had always kept a few dollars at home in my desk, so we headed there. At my home, I told Ray, "This will be quick. You can wait here in the car or you can come in and meet my dog." "I'll come in," Ray replied. On entering, my mom was in the living room reading one of her mystery novels. I introduced them, and our dog came out—tail wagging—though strangely, Ray completely ignored the dog. Love dogs or hate them, I've never known a kid to completely ignore a dog.

"Wait here," I instructed Ray as I climbed the stairs to my bedroom. My sister Joan was upstairs and immediately asked, "Who is this?" I turned and was surprised that even after telling him to wait downstairs, Ray had followed me up. But what the hell—I introduced them. They followed me into my room and were both looking at my old army pictures hanging on the wall. I grabbed $45 from my desk and heard my sister say, "That was a few years ago," to which Ray replied, "And a few pounds ago too." "OK, you two that's enough," I laughed. Ray said goodbye to both my sister and mother, and we took off for lunch at China Moon Restaurant in Stoneham, Massachusetts.

After lunch, as we entered the school's city, Lowell, Ray asked if we could stop at McDonald's for a Coke. "You're getting my Coke habits," I laughed. "The program bans caffeine," Ray reminded me. While we were finishing our drinks, Ray asked, "I'm in no hurry to get back there. Can we take the long route back?" I told him that I only knew one way to the school, but he assured me he could show me a longer way. When we arrived at the school, Ray said,

"We should do this again." I said, "Sure, we'll bring a couple of the other kids too." Ray suddenly looked angry and he said, "No! Just us!" I changed the subject. "Make sure someone signs you back into the log book." He waved and went into the residence. I should have gone in and signed him in myself, but I had another motive. It was almost 3:15 p.m. on a Saturday. If I hurried, I could catch the 4:00 p.m. Mass at St. Patrick's Church in Stoneham on the way home. And I did. Yet without knowing it, my entire life as I knew it had just ended.

# The Staff

The Lakeside School staff was easily the strangest collection of people I had ever seen assembled in one place. As I've said, the most "normal" guy was our assistant house manager, Bob. The manager, Roger, was seemingly a total introvert in a position that would tend to require a very outgoing person. After all, half of the adolescent sex offenders had themselves been sexually abused, as had four or five of the non sex-offender students. It often took somewhat of an entertainer's personality to draw some of these kids out of their self-imposed protective shell.

The only thing Roger had going for him was the aura of his being some type of quiet kung fu master. I liked the guy, but I wasn't impressed. He also had the extremely bad habit of criticizing the staff behind their backs —yet within full hearing of the residents. This of course led to the students making fun of the criticized staff members that they didn't like and their running to the staff that they did like to squeal on Roger. I once gently brought the subject up with Roger. His feeble response was that those moments when he was "blowing off steam" regarding a particular staff member helped the students see how we as adults could still work well together despite our differences. I guess personnel management was not covered during the two-week Japanese therapy camp.

Additionally, there were three female counselors and two male counselors in addition to me. Two of the women seemed to be friends, and they both sort of "tolerated" the third. Sadly, I forget two of their names, yet the girl who was on "the outside" of the counselor group—Gail—seemed to be a somewhat spiritual person and a devout Roman Catholic. She was never loud but tended to reach out to the students in a quiet, personal way. As much as I liked her, there was no way to really get to be friends with her. She possessed simply too quiet a personality. The other two girls were quite aloof. They had all the answers; after all, they had attended the two-week camp-style training. During the hours when the kids were active, they were simply quietly present. They didn't really bring anything to the counseling environment. They could bark orders at the kids, eat with the kids, even organize games for them, but they only related to the residents on the most superficial of levels. "Do this, don't do that, clean the table, catch the ball."

The other two male counselors, Gordon and Steve, were unlike any guys I had ever encountered. They were two similar personality types—somewhat loners, very quiet, seemingly introspective, and neither struck me as particularly masculine. I'm not saying that all guys should be like Rambo, but these guys seemed to be neither masculine nor feminine—neutral, if that's possible. You couldn't really relate to them on any level; they let no one get close to them. And by "getting close," I'm talking just even having a cup of coffee or a glass of soda with either one of them. These two let no one into their separate private little worlds.

Yet by far, the most colorful characters in the entire school were the head therapist, Tyler Cohen, and another therapist named Jane. It was the first time in my life that I had ever met a woman named Tyler. Tyler was a forceful person seemingly very used to always being "right" and always getting her way by the force of her own personality. As time went on, I found it impossible to like her. Jane, on the other hand, was a warm-hearted, kind sort of woman—most likely the one who should have been in charge.

Tyler was the head of both the kid's sex-offender treatment group, called the Sexual Issues Group, as well as the group for the boys who had been victims of sexual abuse, called the Sexual Survivors' Group. (Ray was in both groups.) One of Tyler's cardinal rules was that nothing said in either group could be discussed with anyone outside of the group—and that included the rest of us on staff. It wasn't a particularly helpful policy. Often, when a student seemed either severely depressed or highly agitated, one of the kids in one of the two groups would tell me that the depressed/agitated resident had just been the subject of one of Tyler's rant sessions in the offender's group or had been "interrogated" by her in the survivor's group. And there was nothing I could do about her actions without totally screwing the kid who had passed on the information to me in violation of Tyler's "gag rule." Quite simply, when it came to Tyler's sexual groups, she had no supervisor. Not even the school's director dared challenge her—and how could he? The groups were cloaked in total secrecy. Tyler was the Saddam Hussein of the sexual therapy groups, and she would figuratively cut off the head of anyone—staff or resident—who challenged her.

# My Winter of Discontent

The Lakeside School was my third employment at a residential program. My first program was at Northeast Family Institute's (NFI) Alliance House for court-involved boys in Stoneham, Massachusetts. The second was the Wreath School, then in Middleton, Massachusetts, for boys both court involved and others who simply had social services involvement. The first two programs had, with a couple of exceptions, great staff members. They were regular guys and young women who were well-educated and fun to work with. These staff member's greatest personal asset was that they did not take themselves too seriously nor see themselves as the center of the universe. They were outstanding role models for adolescent boys since they worked hard, played hard, and enjoyed life to the fullest—all without alcohol or drugs. When differences did arise between them, they were always solved through peaceful (though at times loud) dialogue. In short, for most of the kids, these counselors were everything their fathers—or mother's boyfriends—were not.

The Lakeside School could not have been more different. The Lakeside boys disliked most of the staff with the exception of Bob, Gail, and myself. Some of the kids, who were impressed by Roger's frequent demonstrations of his kung fu moves, liked him as well. The kids seemed neutral when it came to Jane, and I never understood that. It's possible some of them were disappointed that she did not stand up to Tyler, but trust me, doing that would have been employment suicide.

Things at first went quite well. One student in particular, Erik, seemed happy that, as he put it, I "never judged him." One night I was asked to stay overnight—do a double shift—with an overnight counselor who's name was also Kevin. (Kevin was the staff member who knew how the school was founded by, as he put it, "failed furniture salesmen." In fact, he was somehow a relative of one of the founders.) In the morning when the kids were getting out of bed, Erik began questioning why I had been there all night. At that point, the other Kevin interrupted our conversation, saying, "Don't get too friendly with Erik. He's a sneaky German, straight from Germany. You can't trust him." I was totally shocked! Not only was it a rude, vicious comment to make about a thirteen-year-old but he also said it right in front of the kid! Erik seemed crushed. I quickly said, "I make my own decisions about people. I don't need any help."

In fact, Erik was from Germany. Sexually abused by his father from an extremely early age, he went on to sexually abuse his own younger brother and sister. All moral questions aside, Erik was doing exactly what his father had done to him. He had learned his "behavior" from one of his parents!

That was the beginning of a bad day for Erik. He couldn't forget the incident. He acted out in class and was sent to the separate class run for kids who were presenting problems for the "regular" teachers. Roger was often part of the two-man team that supervised that class. When I arrived back at work for my 3–11 shift, Roger had already convened one of the Japanese-style therapy group meetings. I walked in and sat down. Roger was going around the room, asking each student what they were grateful for and what they were sorry for that day. When Ray's turn came up, he said he was grateful for the "understanding nature" of the staff and that he was sorry that the day before, he had "given Kevin a bad time." Ray looked at me and said, "Sorry." I had absolutely no idea what the hell he was even talking about! "OK, thanks," I muttered. It was too weird; he hadn't given me any kind of trouble whatsoever. I wondered, was he just trying to impress Roger, or had he actually believed what he was saying? I decided to just let it go. Perhaps I should have questioned him in front of the entire group. We'll never know.

Then Roger moved on to Erik. "Erik, what are you grateful for, and what are you sorry for?" Erik replied, "I don't want to talk. I'm depressed." Roger exploded, "That's because all you think about is yourself! Why don't you think about the two people you raped?" Erik started to cry, and Roger abruptly ended the group. All I can say is, if that's how this particular Japanese therapy is conducted—it's stupid and worse—it's abusive.

The following day we had a staff meeting regarding the Christmas holiday and where each resident would be headed for that day. Every resident got to go home to whatever they had for parents. Ray was going to stay with his mom in Lawrence. She lived in a tough public housing project. When the subject of Erik came up, Tyler said, "I want him to go home—I want him to have just enough rope to hang himself." That angered me, but to be cautious I simply asked, "Hang himself?" She answered, "Give just enough freedom so that he'll screw up." I decided it wasn't worth pursuing. Even if Tyler was Jewish, wasn't there some kind of holiday spirit in her heart? Like anyone, didn't she simply enjoy a few days off?

When we got back, a really unique situation arose. The kids were on a "point system." There were basically three possible levels they could be at. It was all behavior-based. The top-level kids got to stay up later and watch television. The middle level went to bed somewhat earlier. They both got to have a snack with juice at night. The lowest level had to go to their bedrooms around 8:00 p.m. They had to be in bed earlier, watched no TV, and received no snack or juice at night. Only a complete idiot would have come up with that system. First of all, sending kids to bed early as punishment. Many of these kids had been sexually abused in their beds, at bedtime. So being sent to bed (early) as a punishment simply reinforced their mental concept that bed and bedtime were "bad things." Over time, this could lead to lifelong sleeping disorders as well as relationship problems in their later adult lives. And using food and drink as a tool of punishment—even though it was a snack outside of their regular three meals—that's just both cruel and immoral.

But a "unique" situation arose over another punishment. The lowest tier of the three levels were not allowed to participate in the very popular outside physical games. One of the very youngest—and most intelligent kids—who was at the lowest level, addressed that restriction during a "house meeting" between residents and staff. (Minus the therapy staff.) Chad got up and with the eloquence of a seasoned trial lawyer made the case that what the school was, in fact, doing was denying the lowest level kids of, as he put it, "their legal right under state law to participate in physical education." Well, this threw Roger off his game for just a few minutes. I had no idea what had entered his mind, but when Roger's facial expression transitioned from one of worry to one of complete satisfaction, I knew something bad would result.

The next day, after the classroom work was finished, all the "level 3" kids, Gail and I were loaded into a school van and driven by Roger away from both the school and residence home. At some remote point, Roger stopped the van and told everyone to "get out." We all stood there in disbelief as Roger said, "The house is three miles down the road that way. Start walking. This is your physical education." It was the winter of 1995–1996, one of the coldest and snowiest that I could remember. As we started the walk back, I was angry at Roger, but some of the other residents started, one by one, saying, "Thank you, Chad." In a rare angry outburst directed at the kids, I yelled out, "Shut the hell up. This isn't his fault." At that point, Chad decided to walk next to me. It was very cold, but there was a worse problem, the streets were plowed—but not down to bare pavement. The sidewalks were not uniformly shoveled, so at times we had to walk in the street. The cars at times literally came within inches of all of us. Gail was totally silent. Chad was genuinely afraid of being struck by a car.

When we got back, I should probably have immediately launched into a tirade over safety concerns. My ego, however, got the best of me. I was determined not to let Roger enjoy the moment. When he asked with a jackass grin how our "walk" was, I simply faked a smile and replied, "Refreshing." I would be assigned to "the long walk" every day for as long as it took place. After three such hikes, Roger asked me, "Do you hate these kids yet?" I told him, "I'm not in the habit of hating kids." Roger smiled and said, "A few more weeks of this and you'll hate the level three kids more than anyone." "Don't count on it," I snapped back.

Thankfully, our attorney, Chad, finally got the ear of the school's director. And from what I heard, Chad gave him an earful, including his threat that he—Chad himself—would "own" the entire school as well as the director's house if he got even slightly injured during one of Roger's long walks. After two and a half weeks, the "long walks" abruptly ended.

After another winter weekend during which all the residents got some time back home an event took place that, while it shocked me, it didn't seem to surprise any other staff member. Just before the residents left for the weekend, Ray got into the house safe. Each resident had an envelope with either money he had been given by his family or that he had earned doing different jobs around the school. Ray had stolen every other kid's envelope, and he claimed that he had spent it all during his weekend at home. Ray was grilled by both the staff and his fellow residents during an hour-long house meeting. Ray astonished me—he just didn't care what he had done, didn't feel sorry for the kid's whose money he had stolen, and he said so with such a cold demeanor that it absolutely blew my mind! Had I been wrong in thinking that Ray was a "nice, quiet, cooperative kid"? Was his "good behavior" all an act—a very shrewd way of "getting by" in the program?

I should have learned from that episode, but my religious orientation and education took over. I believed that anyone as young as Ray could be "reached"—even completely "transformed"—by patience and kindness. I was a fool.

Ray immediately joined the level three group. He responded by either reading books in the dark or by just going to sleep early. He never complained. He never caused any further trouble—he knew that with quiet cooperation that his "point level" would pretty much automatically rise. And it did.

In late February, Roger told me to take six of the students, including Ray and Erik, to a local hill to go sledding. I wasn't exactly happy. I felt that with six kids on a large-area hill, there should have been at least two staff persons. Supervising six residents in a confined area—such as the YMCA gym that we used was one thing—but these six would be all over that sledding hill and it would become difficult to separate the Lakeside kids from the fifty or more other local kids on that hill. But I knew that to argue with Roger was a pointless exercise.

When we got to the top of the hill, four of the boys immediately jumped on their plastic coasters and sailed on down the hill. The hill was incredibly steep and the speed that those plastic coasters—and one huge tire tube reached was breathtaking. When I was very young, everyone used wooden sleds that featured steerable metal runners. We had a lot of control over where we were going—these more modern—and much cheaper -made, coasters were just barely controllable. (Where was Ralph Nader when these things came on the market?)

I turned back from watching the four take off down the hill only to see Erik and Ray standing in front of me, looking far more serious than I had ever seen before. "What?" I asked. Erik spoke up, "We need to know something right now. Which one of us do you like the best?" Startled, I quickly said, "I like everyone here the same." "Bullshit," Erik said. I was going to have to tread very carefully here, yet I had no idea what to say. I decided to try and bury both of them intellectually with a real long-winded speech. That was a disaster. I started out with, "Well, Erik, you and I have been through a lot together." I never got any further. Ray took off back down the hill on foot and threw his coaster over a fence out of the park. I resisted the impulse to chase him down and talk to him—and that too was probably a huge mistake. Ray just sat near the school van, looking angry.

When our time on the hill was over, I asked Ray to go around the fence and retrieve his coaster. At first he refused, but most likely fearing a reduction in his point level, he eventually did go and get the sled.

Back at the residence, I most certainly should have brought what happened to the attention of Roger and Bob—but for some reason, I was embarrassed at how I had handled things and I said nothing. The following day, there was going to be a daytime school field trip. Roger announced that those residents who had money in the safe would be allowed to buy lunch—those who did not would have to eat whatever the overnight shift made for them. Roger then took out the money envelopes and told each boy how much money he had. Ray had nothing. I walked over to Roger and gave him six dollars for Ray. At that point, Ray yelled out, "I don't want your fucking money!" Roger, remembering Ray's earlier theft, quipped, "You had no problem taking your fellow *resident's* money a few weeks ago!" Roger took the six bucks and placed it in Ray's envelope anyway. After a couple of more days, it seemed that Ray had gotten over his anger toward me, but then he began something entirely new—Ray asked me to volunteer to either adopt him or become his foster parent.

I enjoyed working with nearly all of the Lakeside School kids—including the often unpredictable Ray—but becoming a foster parent of a deeply troubled kid? I wasn't qualified nor did I have any desire to do it. Now how would I gently but firmly explain that to Ray? I started out on very practical and very true grounds. I said, "Ray, I don't own my own house or even have my own apartment. Right now, I'm back living at my parents' house, and on my salary, I really can't afford a place of my own. Plus, I work five days a week on the 3 to 11 shift—who is going to supervise you during those hours? To be honest, the state will never allow it. And if an opportunity comes up to serve my church, I'm going to take it, no matter where in the country that is. Ray, it just won't work." Ray went silent, yet he would bring the subject up every day for nearly a week. Finally, he just stopped talking about it.

Another bizarre moment of February came one afternoon. I came into the residence after the kids in the two "sexual issues" groups had just come up from a rare combined meeting. They all had printed handouts. They all looked quite shocked. I asked one student if I could see the papers he was holding. It was all about the Holocaust—complete with some of the most graphic photos I had ever seen. If these photos, along with the accompanying descriptions had been passed out in a local high school, there would have been an enormous and very negative public reaction. And some of these kids were junior high age! Although I had no doubt as to their origin, I asked where these handouts had come from. Almost in unison, the kids answered, "Tyler." What the hell was she thinking? Of course the Holocaust needed to be taught in our history classes, but this was not a history class, and Tyler was not a teacher. Further, these were, in fact, troubled kids for many different reasons. Most of these boys should not have been exposed to what amounted to excessively violent crime scene–like photos. I was disgusted. Even as I write this, I recall how emotionally and physically ill I had felt just watching the movie *Schindler's List*. These handouts in both words and pictures were, at minimum, "R-rated." None of the residents at Lakeside were equipped to process such violent images and descriptions. This is what happens when a person's job becomes their unsupervised, impenetrable kingdom.

As the winter went on I began to notice something odd. Regardless of Ray's point level, whenever there was a snowstorm, he was picked up at night by the daytime cook who plowed snow on his time off. The cook's name was Thom, pronounced "Tom" despite the spelling. No one said a single word about this arrangement, not even Roger, who had been there countless times when Thom pulled his red truck into the driveway, and no matter what Ray was doing or how low his points might have been, he simply got up, grabbed his coat, and took off with Thom. He would return one or two hours later. No entry was ever made in the house logbook of either his coming or going. I thought it was especially strange since it was very apparent that Thom was not particularly bright mentally. Thom was, however, somewhat popular with *some* of the kids. Since he controlled the kitchen and hence the food, he would often pick a few kids to assist him with meal preparation. It was always the same kids, and Ray was always one of them. The benefit of helping Thom out with the cooking was that he gave you extra food, and these kids were seemingly always hungry.

One morning, after I had again been forced into a double shift (3:00 p.m.–7:00 a.m.), I was driving one of the vans taking the boys to the school building for their classes after breakfast. I was the last van to leave. I was waiting for Ray, who again was assisting Thom with the clean-up after breakfast. At last Thom and Ray came out of the basement. Thom said to me, "Kevin, I've got Ray." I assumed that meant that they had more cleaning to do and that Thom would drive Ray to school when they were finished. Still, I didn't like it.

Damn it all—it was Thom's job to cook and thus to clean up the kitchen afterward. Of all things that could be "cut," educational classes should not be one of them. Still, I had in mind the enormous freedom of access that both Roger and Bob—and thus, by extension, the school's administration—gave Thom when it came to Ray, so I just shook my head and took off for the school building.

It was rare that I ever spent any time in the classroom building, so when I got there, I took my time and just watched how the classes got going. Roger and some other guy already had a "disciplinary" classroom with two kids in it—they had been kicked out of their regular class for acting up, and the school had only been in session for about twenty minutes. I walked by the "forbidden file cabinet" and I had to laugh. The kids had two files on them, one very brief file at whichever residence home they lived in (there were two homes) and this "therapist" file at the school. Roger would often tell the counselors that we should read these more extensive files at the school, but the therapists, particularly Tyler, made it quite clear that only the therapists themselves were welcome to view these records. I never went near them.

Soon, exhaustion started to get the best of me, and I decided to return the van to the home, get in my car, and go home to bed. It had been about forty minutes since I had left the residence home with the students. When I pulled into the driveway, I was startled to see Thom's red truck still parked there. Had he already dropped Ray off at the school? Did we miss each other in transit and at the school building? I went into the basement kitchen/dining area. The kitchen was clean, and no one was there. I went up to the first floor, and something strange was happening. Roger's office had really loud rock music coming from it, yet I had just left Roger back at the school. I thought to myself, *What idiot used Roger's office and stereo and then forgot to turn it off?* I went to open the door, but it was locked. I knocked on the door as hard as I could without breaking a bone in my hand, but there was no answer. For some reason, I decided to search the building—had someone broken in? I checked every room and closet from the top floor all the way to the basement. No one was around, and nothing seemed disturbed. Still, where the hell was

Thom if his truck was still parked in the driveway? Did he catch another ride? Again I returned to Roger's office. I tried to force the door open but couldn't. Finally, I just got in my car and drove home.

I have been somewhat haunted by the memory of that day ever since. As time passed, I have wondered, was Thom in Roger's office and ignoring me? Worse yet, was Ray with him? If they were together, what were they doing? And if they were doing anything inappropriate, why hadn't Ray ever said anything about it? Further, if Ray was there and arrived at the school building quite late, why was there never any discussion of it. Could a student, in what the state called a staff-secured environment, simply show up at the school building more than an hour late with no questions asked? Finally, why did a guy employed as a cook have such unlimited access to one particular student? Should I have called Roger? the police? Sadly, there were only two people in this world who knew where Thom and Ray were that day: Thom and Ray.

# War with Tyler

Early in March, Erik came to me with such a serious look that it instantly grabbed my attention. "What's going on?" I asked. This was different; Erik was a fairly tough kid. In his interactions with his fellow residents, no one, not even the older guys, messed with this thirteen-year-old. It's possible that some of his bravado was an act, but not all of it. This was the first time I could remember that he actually looked scared. Erik began slowly. "You know Tyler's two groups, right?" I was already concerned. "Yup," I replied. "Well," Erik continued, "She's tearing you apart in both groups." "About what?" I inquired nervously. Erik went on, "She's saying things like you're trying to set us up." I was now white-hot with anger. "Set you up for what?" I asked. "That's just it," Erik continued. "She's just leaving it like that. Like we're supposed to know." I was near blind with rage, and yet, knowing Tyler's ruthlessness, I was also worried. I looked at Erik and asked, "Anything else?" Erik just shook his head.

It's always possible that residents in a structured program would like to set one staff member against another for a variety of reasons, but this didn't feel like that. I didn't know what to do.

I sought out Ray. I asked him, "Is Tyler bad-mouthing me in your therapy groups?" Ray nodded. I then asked, "Should I be offended?" Ray replied, "Oh yeah." Now I know I should have asked Ray more exploratory questions, but I was too angry and too worried to think. Was Tyler trying to get me fired? Why? I had witnessed firsthand how ruthless Tyler was when she decided that she didn't like a student then went after him. This was not good.

I eventually decided to seek counsel from Bob. I told him the whole story. I wanted his advice; I did not want him to actually do anything. However, at the next schoolwide staff meeting Bob brought the whole issue up in front of everyone. Tyler was outraged and denied ever even using my name in either of her two therapy groups. However, what Tyler was most insanely angry about was that someone in one or both of her groups had spoken to someone who was not part of either group—me. I refused to tell her my sources. Unfortunately, I had told Bob, and he told the entire staff.

From that moment on, Tyler was on a mission: to punish both Ray and Erik for talking. She called a meeting of Ray, Erik, me, and her in her tiny in-house office. Steve, Ray's advocate, also asked to sit in. We were stuffed into this tiny closet-like room, and it was unbearably hot in there. To make matters worse, Tyler closed the door. From the very beginning, it was clear that all Tyler wanted to discuss was Ray and Erik's talking to someone outside the group. That she had been accused of trash-talking me was not even an issue for her. Erik, however, wanted to make it all about her trashing me in front of the kids. Erik got angry and said, "Just let me hear you say out loud, right now, that you haven't been talking about Kevin in both groups." Tyler got quiet and, in an almost diabolical way, switched tactics. "Erik," she began coldly, "you wanted to be home before next Christmas, but I can see now that you won't be ready." Erik looked as though he had been hit in the face with a sledgehammer. "And, Ray," she went on, "you're fifteen. I can legally keep you here until your eighteenth birthday." It was blackmail time! Then Erik really shocked me. He said, "I would say that he *did* do something to me just to get out of this." That could only mean one thing! Tyler was trying to get the kids to accuse me of something! Apparently anything! Why was this evil, dictatorial shrew after me? I had done nothing whatsoever to piss her off at all, but here she was apparently trying to get some of the students to deliberately make false accusations against me. It was simply too much.

I kept all these things turning over and over in my mind for a week. One night during dinner at the school, all the staff members were seated at their assigned tables, which were also specifically assigned to certain residents. Before the food was served, Ray got up from his assigned table, walked over, and sat at mine. Roger instantly ordered him back to his designated table. Ray started to argue. I spoke up. "Roger, I don't care if he sits here or not." Roger replied, "I care. Ray likes you too much."

After dinner, I got Roger alone and asked, "What do you mean Ray likes me too much?" Roger became extremely condescending. "Kevin, you have to stop treating everything people say as some kind of intricate puzzle that you have to analyze."

That was it. I had had enough. The next day, I wrote up a resignation letter and sent it to Leeroy via Express Mail. I forgot I still had a set of house keys. A couple of days later, I drove to the administration classroom building and gave the school's secretary the keys. It was awful. The school secretary was an extremely pleasant woman, but when I came in to hand her the keys, she acted like I was the world's most notorious terrorist or something. Her complete personality change both shocked and saddened me. I couldn't get out of there quickly enough.

# How Did I Get Here?

Ever since I was a little boy in St. Mary's School in Melrose, I had sort of wanted to be a priest. Though in elementary school, I often wanted to be something different with each passing week. As time went on, I often would think about the priesthood but always sort of "forced" the thoughts to the back of my mind. In 1986, I gave up everything: my apartment, my job, and the best roommate in history (two years at Westfield State University, six years afterward) and traveled out to the University of Notre Dame's Moreau Seminary. I entered the "candidate class" for the Holy Cross Fathers who ran Notre Dame. It was a personal disaster. At the time, the Holy Cross Fathers admitted around thirty to forty men as "candidates" for their Order. What the vocation directors never told the guys they recruited was that when all was said and done, one to six years after all those guys were "accepted" as candidates, they would allow only three or four to take "perpetual vows" and be ordained as Catholic priests. Had I known those grim statistics, I would have never in a million years have given up all that I had and gone out there. There had been many other religious orders that had expressed interest in me, but none pursued me with the vigor of the vocations director of Holy Cross Eastern Province. I've known many military recruiters—I even briefly served as a recruiter for the Massachusetts Army National Guard myself—yet none were as tenacious as this one priest.

Early on, there were warning signs. During the first week of orientation at a rural camp in Deer Park, Maryland, I overheard a second-year seminarian say to a priest, "A lot of conservatives is this year's candidate class." To which the priest replied, "That's OK. Either they will become liberals or we'll get rid of them." I was what might be called a conservative Catholic, but more correctly, I was an orthodox Catholic. (Not to be confused with Eastern Orthodoxy.) What I strongly object to is the asinine notion that an orthodox Catholic somehow is a person without compassion. Saint Pope John Paul II was an orthodox Catholic that many called a conservative, but he was a man of limitless compassion. (Very few "mean" people end up being canonized a saint.) Being "orthodox" in a Catholic sense means accepting without question the "Teaching Authority" (Magisterium) of the Church. It means accepting dogma without question and questioning doctrine only with the greatest of caution.

There were three people in charge of the candidate class: two priests and one lay woman. Early on, I could tell that one of the priests, John Rossi, didn't like me. One day at orientation, while teaching a class on "The Divine Office," he asked me not to talk. He said, "You don't have a loud voice, but it fills the whole room." Thanks, John! (I refused to call *Father* any priest that I had lost all respect for. Humorously, at Moreau Seminary, all the priests *insisted* that everyone call them by their first name and never address them as *Father*.) When he told me not to talk as I said, he was supposed to be teaching us about the daily cycle of prayers—"the daily office"—but what he was really doing was holding a "change Sacred Scripture" session. He had us go to hundreds of places—mostly in the Psalms—and he wanted us to cover up all references to God as a "male" with a black pen. I was extremely uncomfortable marking over Sacred Scripture, so I was using a yellow highlighter to mark the places that Rossi, and apparently the entire Holy Cross community, believed were "offensive to women." At one point, one of my fellow candidates looked over at my book and asked, "Why are you using a highlighter?" Rossi, aware of what I was doing, sarcastically said, "He wants to keep the book as it is for when he uses it in another community." What a prick.

Next was a priest named Bob. He just plain frustrated the hell out of me. Nothing anyone said or did was ever acceptable to Bob. One day, after a bruising talk session with Bob, I left his room fit to be tied. I ran into one of the priests/professors on the university side of the campus, and the priest stopped me and asked what was wrong. Halfway through my explanation, he exclaimed, "Bob *********!

He's on the seminary staff? You're kidding me—he's a total mental cripple!" Another priest later told me, "I really feel sorry for you guys at Moreau. You see, when the community (order) has a priest who's a complete loser, the only place to assign him is to the seminary. If they went to a parish, the people would run them out of town, and God knows their too incompetent to teach, so sadly, you guys in the seminary get saddled with them."

Bob would often be seen trying to overhear the private conversations of other people. And he was always hanging around the seminary mail boxes. I wondered why until once, just a few days after I had received a letter from a personal friend—who happened to be a Russian Orthodox priest—Bob came to my room, sat down at my desk, and said, "I think we have a problem with you and the Eastern Church." I should have thrown him out of my room! Did he just look at the envelope, or had he opened and read my mail? Later that day, I told yet another priest/professor that I should go and "kick Bob's ass." The kindly old priest calmly said, "Dear God, Kevin, that would be like hitting a girl." Bob was a weasel, a sneak, and a coward.

Finally, there was the lay woman. The candidates were told that she was there to teach us "how to keep our vows" (poverty, chastity, and obedience). Only toward the end of my four-month stay there would I learn that that lay woman was an ex-nun who was married to an ex-priest. And she was going to teach *us* how to keep our vows?

To make a long story short, the seminary staff at that time was anti-Church and anti-Pope and often vilified the local bishop. One day, three Holy Cross nuns came to one of our candidate classes to ask how many of us supported the ordination of women. No one spoke up. The priest teaching the class looked at me, so I said, "It's fine with me as long as it's approved by Rome." The nuns then looked at a classmate of mine—a great guy named Mike—and very slowly, Mike said, "I have to agree, the change is up to Rome." The nuns were outraged! "I never thought we would be treated like this in any class at Moreau Seminary!" one of them yelled. They stomped out of the room. It probably wasn't really what Mike and I had said but, rather, the fact that none of the other guys spoke up and either disagreed with us or simply stated their being in favor of women's ordination. But seriously, if not approved by Rome, what were they looking for? Did they want some Catholic bishop to ordain them as priests in defiance of Church doctrine? That bishop and the females he ordained would all be excommunicated. There are other churches that the Catholic Church recognizes as having valid orders. In other words, the priests these churches ordain possess the ability to *validly* administer the seven Sacraments. Of course, the largest of these churches are Eastern Orthodox. Yet there are many, many smaller valid churches such as the "Old Catholic Churches." Here is a quick course in Catholic doctrine regarding these valid bishops. Let's say that the Old Catholic Church consecrates a new bishop on Friday. On the very next day, Saturday, that bishop is going to ordain four new priests—three men and one woman. First he ordains a man. The Catholic Church holds that that man is a validly ordained priest. The bishop then ordains the woman then the last two men. The Catholic Church holds that the woman is not a priest, nor are the two men ordained after her. And no person that bishop will ever ordain will be considered a valid priest. So seriously, what were they looking for? A new church schism?

Toward the end of the fall semester in 1996, it became apparent to me that the order did not want me to continue there. I wasn't happy, and if allowed to stay, I would have. It would have been a huge mistake. Remember my friend Mike? Well, Mike stayed there for all six years, and in the end, the order refused to allow him to take his final, perpetual vows. They stole six years of Mike's life. At the end of time, may God in his justice punish them for that.

One day, a priest at Moreau told me, "You know, if you weren't more Catholic than the Pope, we'd probably be really good friends." I really didn't need friends like that. At my exit interview, the rector brought up my close relationship with Fr. Charles Weiher. Father Weiher had not been on the "approved" list of spiritual advisors at the beginning of the year, and though I did have to chose an approved advisor, all my spiritual advice came from Fr. Weiher. I was able to tell him my deepest and most personal thoughts without fear of the kind of reprisals that could result from speaking to one of the approved guys. Anyway, toward the end of the interview, the rector said, "I'm very happy that you met Father Weiher, otherwise you may have lost your faith in the Catholic Church." "That would have been impossible," I replied. The rector asked, "How is that?" And so I told him, "I don't consider any of you to be Catholic." He took that well, at least while I was in the room. One year later, every priest on the seminary staff was replaced.

After Moreau and Notre Dame, I worked in a program called Alliance House, for kids involved with the juvenile courts. It was an OK job. In 1989, I was hired as a campus police officer at Emerson College in Boston. Those running the department were a little "too intense" for me, but they meant well—I guess. The other officers I worked with were awesome, until for some reason, the college lowered their hiring standards. When I was hired, you had to have a bachelor's degree. An exception was made for a person who had an associate's degree in criminal justice while also holding certification as an emergency medical technician, or EMT. There were two guys in that category: one worked out; the other did not.

One officer, a supervisor named Jeff, was a great friend to me. I say "supervisor" because every time the chief tried to promote him to sergeant, he refused. Finally they gave him a badge that read "Officer-in-Charge."

While at Emerson, I decided that I wanted to earn a Master of Divinity degree. I was looking at some local divinity schools—in particular, Andover-Newton Theological School and Gordon Conwell Divinity School. When I told Jeff, he nearly exploded. "What!" he exclaimed. "Who ever heard of those schools?" I assured him that both schools were very well-known in the Boston area. Jeff went on. "No. You need to check out places like BU (Boston University) or Harvard. I don't want to hear anymore about those other places." The way Jeff was speaking was a reflection of his great sense of humor, but the content of what he was saying was 100 percent serious. I checked out BU School of Theology, applied, and was accepted. I sincerely think Jeff was as happy as I was. (Jeff was working on a master's in criminal justice at BU.)

Because I was working at Emerson full-time, the admissions director at the school of theology wanted me to attend part-time. I insisted on being full-time. We sort of compromised by my taking a full-time load but with one class less than normal each semester. It was a brutal grind. Jeff eventually went on to the Milwaukee Police, and I was later promoted to corporal. A corporal at Emerson College is a supervisor with all the responsibilities of a sergeant. The only difference? Less money.

Here is the schedule I eventually worked my way into. I supervised the 11:00 p.m. to 7:00 a.m. shift. If it were possible, I would occasionally sit at dispatch, and while handling the phones and radio, I'd read my text books. However, I really liked being out on the street, so I did that infrequently. When I got out after 7:00 a.m., I drove the half mile up Commonwealth Avenue to the School of Theology building. There I proceeded to the theology student lounge, set a timer on my watch for thirty minutes, and went to sleep. When the alarm went off, I got up, went to the Student Union building next door, and either got breakfast and a Coke—or at times, just the Coke. Then I attended classes until noon, 1:00 p.m., or 2:00 p.m. After that, I drove home and went to bed. I got up at around 6:00 p.m. and drove to the local McDonald's for a Coke. I would sometimes grab a burger there or eat something quick when I got back home. I would then study until around 10:00 p.m. then head back to work and start the cycle all over again. A year or two after graduation, I would hear that a BU professor had said that I "was not a great student." If only that professor had known what I was going through. (Out of a possible 4.0, I got an associate's degree in criminal justice, finishing with a 3.97 average. I finished my bachelor of arts degree in political science with a 3.71 average.

My MDiv. degree came in with cumulative average of 3.05. Yes, I'm embarrassed, but if I didn't have to work full-time, I think the final average would have been somewhat higher (I did not work during the school year while earning those first two degrees).

Eventually, in their quest to hire a more diverse campus police staff, the college completely dropped nearly all the educational requirements. A minority male officer as well as a white female officer were hired possessing only their GED. In four years, the college went from requiring officers to have a bachelor's degree to hiring high school dropouts! I remain convinced of two things: First, it was a control issue. The dumber they were, the easier they were to order around without the person asking any questions. And second, the college personnel folks were either incompetent or lazy. If they had sent *me* out to recruit officers who were female or members of a recognized minority group, I would have brought in stellar candidates! Boston is a college town, and the students are highly diverse. Many criminal justice students would have jumped at the opportunity to "get their foot in the door" as campus police officers.

Eventually, a well-liked lieutenant would lose his bid to become the deputy chief to one of those incredibly unqualified candidates. The lieutenant had a BA in criminal justice from Northeastern University. The person who got the job had their GED. At that time, we also tried to unionize the department and lost by one vote. It was too much for most of us, and the well-educated officers began to leave. (An officer named Craig once lamented, "At one time, we had a really smart department." Craig was one of the first to leave.) I eventually left for a campus police dispatch job at another college. The job sucked, and I quit.

I got a job as a counselor at the Wreath School in Middleton, Massachusetts. It was a boys' school. A small number of the kids had some court involvement. Most simply had family issues or had behavioral issues at school, home, or both. They were, for the most part, some of the nicest kids you could ever find. It might sound racial, but there were black counselors and white counselors. The black counselors were the brightest and most effective youth counselors that I had ever worked with. Some of the white counselors were OK and some of them were backstabbing pricks. I became very close friends with the black counselors. Trust is everything, and I trusted those guys 100 percent. (OK, I know it's fashionable to say *African American*. I'll start using that term as soon as I'm referred to as *European-American*.) I worked at the Wreath School from 3:00 p.m. to 11:00 p.m., five days a week. I have no idea how I managed to get my schoolwork done, but with God's help, I did. Sadly, the school in Middleton is gone. I believe another branch of that school may still exist in New Hampshire.

Eventually, I applied for admission to Saint Gregory's Melkite-Catholic Seminary in Newton, Massachusetts, and was accepted. I said goodbye to the Wreath School kids and moved into the seminary. I had one year left before graduating from BU. I was told that I would need to complete two years at St. Gregory's before being ordained a priest. (I would be ordained a deacon a few months before the final ordination.) The Melkite Church is one of the Eastern Catholic Churches. It's an oversimplification, but for the sake of brevity, the Eastern Catholic Churches were (and are still) located in the same countries as what are now Eastern Orthodox Churches. When many churches in the east decided to sever ties with Rome, the Eastern Catholic Churches did not. They remain in communion with the Roman Pontiff though their liturgies, canon laws, and theology are nearly identical to those of the Eastern Orthodox Churches.

The rector of St. Gregory's was an exceptional priest named Father Paul Frechette. Father Paul was absolutely perfect for the position of rector. He had an academic way about him. Even after completing his studies at Boston College, he continued to do theological reading and research. I never once had a question about Byzantine theology, church history, liturgical directions, or any other question that Father. Paul could not answer. Most importantly to me, he liked to teach, and he taught with great patience.

Shortly after my acceptance, a decision was made to move Father Paul to a local parish and to replace him with a priest from Rome named Father John. I hadn't even moved all my stuff in yet! I was thoroughly devastated despite being told by a classmate named Justin that Father John was an OK guy. Father John was formerly part of an Eastern Catholic Church known at the Italo-Greek Catholic Church. As that church no longer exists, Father John was brought into (incardinated) the Melkite Church. (All Eastern Catholic Churches can be called Greek Catholic. They are not Greeks, but in many cases, it was the Greek Church fathers who brought the faith to the nations that these churches are located in.)

From the beginning, I could see a serious problem. There are eight "tones" used for singing the prayers in the Eastern churches. Each week uses a different tone. It's hard to explain, but Justin could sing the song "Happy Birthday" with eight different "melodies" using the eight tones. What made it more difficult was that the Melkite Church arose in the Middle East, in Arab countries. Music from Arab nations is very different from Western music. For me, that meant that it was exceedingly hard to learn. (The tones in Slavic Churches are a bit easier on the Western ear.) Each week, I drove to and from BU while listening to a tape—a very bad tape—of a priest singing that week's tone. The serious problem? Father John knew when we students were not properly singing one of the tones. However, Father John could not sing the tones himself! He could not teach anyone the tones because he couldn't use them himself, yet he could tell when anyone else was not singing the tone properly, and that would frustrate him and even make him angry. Justin, on the other hand, was an expert with the tones and had an extremely good singing voice. (Though once, when Father John was away, Justin ran the prayer services, and he had even less patience than Father John! He had an angry outburst after one such service and let me and the other student, Hosni have it "full force." I wanted to thoroughly kick Justin's ass, but instead I got in my car and drove to my family home for the night. I was later asked by a priest why I left for the night, and I told him, "So that I wouldn't kill Justin." The priest replied, "Oh, then I guess it was a good decision.")

Hosni, the other seminarian, was a young guy from Syria. He was a pretty smart guy who was fluent in both Arabic and Italian. His English was just OK, but he was really just beginning to learn our language. It was annoying, but Father John and Hosni carried on the bulk of their conversations in Italian. As the school year progressed, the two seemed to have far more heated arguments than conversations. One day, when it was my night to cook dinner, Hosni came into the kitchen and picked up the small meatloaf seasoning packet that I had purchased on the way back from school. "Where did you get this?" he asked. I told him that I had stopped at the local market on the way back from BU. "So you paid for it?" he went on. "Yes," I told him, "but it was only a couple of dollars." Hosni held the package way above his head and yelled out, "Then I shall obtain justice for you!" There was no time to even attempt to stop him.

He then raced up the stairs to Father John's office, and soon I could hear a very loud argument taking place. After a few minutes, Hosni came down to the kitchen and slammed two one-dollar bills on the counter in front of me. "Now there is justice!" he exclaimed. I was speechless. All I was hoping was that Father John didn't think that I had complained to Hosni about the two dollars—or worse yet, sent him up to get the money from him! Humorously, I later told a visiting priest of American descent about the incident. He laughed and said, "They're all like that! That's why there will never be peace in the Middle East."

Each and every time that we had chapel at St. Gregory's, Hosni would go out of his way to get there before anyone else. He had this "thing" about the candles—he felt for some bizarre reason that only he should be allowed to light them. What the hell that was about, I was never able to ascertain. At the end of any service, I would occasionally blow out a couple of the candles. That seemed to really annoy Hosni, and to my discredit, I kind of enjoyed that. Every Sunday, we visited a different parish for the Divine Liturgy and the coffee hour that followed. One particular Sunday, we made the long trek down to Saint Anne's Parish in Danbury, Connecticut. Before the liturgy began, I happened to look around only to see what looked like Hosni arguing with the sole altar boy. As I walked over, it was clear that the kid was only ten or eleven years old. I had a strong feeling that whatever was taking place, the altar boy was not at fault. I looked at both of them and simply asked, "What?" "He won't light the candles," the boy told me. "Why don't you light them?" I asked the kid. The boy went on to explain that his parents were deathly afraid that if he lit the candles that he might accidentally catch his robe on fire and be seriously burned. So I turned to Hosni and said, "So light the candles!" I couldn't believe his reaction! He put a look on his face—the kind Donald Trump might put on if a waiter told him that his credit card had been declined. He then turned away so as not to look directly at either the kid or myself and, with an incredibly arrogant tone, said, "It's beneath my dignity."

I was thoroughly beside myself! That arrogant, self-centered bastard! However, we *were* in church, so I just reached out and took the lighter from the altar boy. As I turned, I saw that there were an absolute ton of Icons around the church, each with its own candle. I turned quickly back to the kid and asked, "You want all of them lit?" In pure comedic relief, as only a ten- or eleven-year-old could pull off, the altar boy let out a long, loud sigh and said with total frustration, "They must *all* be lit." I cracked up laughing, which seemed to double Hosni's anger, then I lit all the candles. Later, Justin and I howled laughing as I told him of the kid's saying "They must all be lit." However, we both realized that Hosni had some kind of problem. Without overanalyzing it, I simply concluded that Hosni was somehow seriously overimpressed by what he believed was his own importance. (The Melkite Church in America is predominantly made up of people of Arab descent. However, there are quite a few non-Arab families and individuals who belong to the Church as well. I later wondered if Hosni's problem with that altar boy was that he was a blond-haired, blue-eyed "American" kid. We'll never know.)

Hosni was not engaged in theological studies. His only "job" was to attend a language school in Boston in order to become proficient in English. Then he could study theology. Justin attended Holy Cross Greek Orthodox School of Theology in Brookline, Massachusetts. It will probably seem rude, but academically speaking, Holy Cross was a "high school" when compared to the academic rigors of Boston University. Make no mistake about it—I'm comparing schools only because in actuality, Justin is a hell of a lot smarter than I am. What I am saying, though, is that I had ten times more reading and studying than Justin and a thousand times more than Hosni. As the year went on, it became harder and harder to balance the time requirements of St. Gregory's and the huge amount of reading, studying, and writing that BU's School of Theology required. And that was utterly amazing when you recall the balancing act I had to perform while both working full-time and going to school full-time.

Every morning, there was morning prayer. On Wednesday and Saturday mornings, the Divine Liturgy. That was followed by school. Then there was an evening prayer either before or after dinner. Dinner itself was a somewhat prolonged affair, usually lasting an hour to an hour and a half. Once a week, I had to cook dinner, so that took at least an hour of the afternoon. One night a week, it was my turn to do the dishes—another hour gone. One night a week, the bishop came for evening prayer then stayed a couple of hours "teaching" us about the Melkite Church. When he left around 9:00 p.m., I couldn't ever get my studying going. Father John could never understand that while Justin and I had "seminary and school," he only had the seminary. In a more negative sense, we had many things to concentrate on—Father John only concentrated on us.

One weekend, Father John had scheduled a Saturday/Sunday retreat at the seminary with a Dominican Father. I needed both days to study! To accommodate the visiting priest, I had studied from 7:00 p.m. Friday night until around 1:00 a.m. The next morning, Justin, Hosni, and I sat in the seminary's living room while the visiting Dominican did his talking. At one point, I looked up and the priest said to me, "If you're that tired, I'm sure God would want you to go to bed." Unbeknownst to me, I was breaking up the retreat with my snoring! There was simply nothing I could do! I was dead tired, and my damn schoolwork had to be completed! The same thing happened on Sunday. Funny thing, though, when I left to go sleep, Hosni took the initiative to go back to his room as well. Apparently he had been up late too—watching TV.

One night, I was in my room studying. Around 9:00 p.m., Father John could be heard calling all of us to come downstairs to the kitchen. I got there just after Justin. Father John was holding a loaf of bread in his right hand. In all, there were four of us "in the seminary," but there was one other priest that lived there, though we hardly ever saw him. Additionally, there was a BU graduate student living there. He was from Romania. (He ate like a hog—he actually ate most of every loaf we bought.) With six guys, you can imagine that when we bought a loaf of bread, we bought the longest loaf possible. Once Hosni arrived, Father. John began a "speech" with his moderate Italian accent. "A, gentlemen, I am, a, concerned that the, a, bread has a tail." The three of us students all looked at each other with that "What the hell?" kind of look. Father John continued, "As the bread is, a, used, the tail of, a, plastic gets, a, longer and, a, longer. So from, a, now on, after you, a, seal up the, a, bread, take a pair of, a, *sissors*, and, a, trim the, a, tail to exactly, a, three inches." And with that, Father John picked up a pair of "sissors" and cut the excess plastic off the bag of bread. Then with a forced smile, he looked up and said, "That's, a, all, gentlemen." From that point on, I seriously doubted that Father John was "the picture of mental health."

My studying time problems began to increase during the final months of my final semester. In one of my classes, there was a young Greek Orthodox priest who was working on his doctorate degree. Since the services used in the Melkite Church are identical to those used in Orthodox churches—and he held some type of faculty position at Holy Cross—one day, I showed him St. Gregory's chapel schedule. He looked astonished! He turned toward me and asked, "How in the world are you getting your schoolwork done?" Sadly, I told him, "That's just it, I'm not."

This was damn serious. I was paying for my education, not the church. Yet it was now the church that was threatening to cause me to fail. It doesn't matter if you were in your first year or last year at BU's School of Theology—if your grade point average dropped to C+, you were finished. You couldn't complete your degree; you couldn't "make it up." You were out. Oh, and you would not be readmitted. I couldn't lose all the time that I had invested in my education. I went to tell Father John that I would have to go home until I completed the semester. He erupted in anger. I stayed calm, but it was clear that he couldn't be reasoned with. I left his office, packed all my belongings into my car, and went home.

I was scheduled to spend the summer at St. Anne's Parish in Danbury. The pastor, Father James, was an awesome guy, and he was on the seminary's board. Justin was ordained a priest at St. Anne's. I attended and stayed at the parish overnight. I wasn't "out" of St. Gregory's at all. Father James and I sat talking in the rectory living room. He was reading my BU transcript. He told me he wanted me to complete some "directed reading" aimed at increasing my knowledge of things related to the Eastern Church. Then he told me that he wanted me to take a course on the Psalms at the Western-Jesuit School of Theology in Cambridge. I asked him how I was supposed to pay for the course. I never really got an answer. He also told me that Hosni was asked not to return to the seminary.

Once back home, I really started to worry. I had watched for eight months as Father John spent hours every day just blasting Hosni for one thing or another. (Since they argued in Italian, I have no idea what the actual "issues" were.) I also realized that Justin had truly acted as a "firewall" insulating both Hosni and me from the unpredictable Father John. I thought of the "bread-tail" incident. All I could think of was the idea of my being the sole focus of attention for Father John for eleven to twelve months. I told the Church I wanted to take a year off. I was thirty-nine years old, and in those thirty-nine years, that was the single most stupid decision I ever made. Without knowing it, I had just traded a year with Father John for three years in prison, five years of probation, and a lifetime of abject misery.

# A Knock at the Door

On a warm day in the spring of 1996, I was getting ready for a job interview in Boston. Since I had experience in both the Reserve Military Police as well as having been a corporal with the Emerson College Campus Police in Boston, I felt my chances were quite good to land the Assistant Director of Security position with a prestigious Boston hotel. I was hurrying around the house gathering up all my papers as I didn't want to be late catching the train to Boston. Suddenly there was an (unnecessarily) loud and continuous knock at the front door. I looked at my sister Joan as if to say, "What the hell?"

I opened the door only to find a short, mustached, well-dressed guy. "Yes?" I asked impatiently. "Kevin DeCoste?" he inquired. "That's me," I answered. "Could you put your dog out back somewhere?" I answered, "No." He asked, "Why not?" "Because it's his house," I replied. That seemed to frustrate him. Then the guy opened up a notebook, the front of which had the words "Melrose Police." He slowly introduced himself as Detective Ron Callahan. Yet all the while, he kept moving his notebook like a man trying to catch a ray of sunlight with a signaling mirror. My attention was drawn to his pad of paper in the notebook, and in large block letters, I read the name "RAY SWANSON." As I said before, the Lakeside School was the third residential program that I had worked at, and in so many cases, when a kid would "run away" (escape) from such a program, they would either flee to their parents' home—or to the home of a trusted counselor. Sounds strange, but it happened all the time. And so I was very concerned, and I immediately asked, "Is Ray Swanson OK?" At that exact moment, the detective smiled slightly and said, "Let me read you your rights."

I was completely stunned—numb even. I muttered, "I've been a cop, I know my rights." He replied, "I have to read them." All I could think was *What the hell is this about?* Then he finished his "reading" and said, "Ray Swanson said that while he was with you here and"—at that point, he motioned toward my car without saying anything, then he continued—"that you sexually abused him." I said what came immediately to my mind: "Nothing like that ever happened here!" Again the guy motioned toward my car. "Or there!" I added. Then the detective said, "Look, you will probably be indicted—you *will* be indicted. It will be your word against his. You need to hire an attorney right away." Then he handed me his business card and added, "If you want to talk, give me a call." And with that, he got into his unmarked car and left.

In a complete state of shock, I slowly reentered my home, looked at my sister and said, "Life as I have known it has just ended. No matter what happens, nothing will ever be the same." My mom was there, and she asked what had happened. As I told her, she said, "What a rotten kid! You were never even alone with him!" All I could say was, "I know." I sat down then asked my sister to call the hotel and cancel my interview. I must have sat there for a couple of hours just looking at the television screen without even realizing what was on. After a while, I got up and noticed my mom sitting at the dining room table, carefully going through the local Yellow Pages. She was searching out attorneys. "Here," she said finally, "this guy specializes in this sort of thing." I made the call. Attorney John Kaufman's secretary went through a seemingly memorized spiel. "Do not say anything to the police. Do not talk to reporters. Come here at 3:00 p.m. Remember, speak to no one about this until you meet with Jack." *Jack?* I thought. I guessed there would be no formalities.

* * *

Attorney Kaufman's office was in an old building in downtown Malden, Massachusetts. The building was old, the interior was dark and, well, old. I felt very uncomfortable. Finally a guy came out. I thought to myself, *Must be the day of the mustache.*

Kaufman introduced himself, adding, "Call me Jack." It was hard not to instinctively call the guy "sir," but I tried my best. I told him that I was innocent and that if he believed me—OK, if not, I needed someone else. "Tell me the entire story, and I'll tell you what I think." He never did. What he did tell me was that he had never lost a sexual abuse case. However, he added that he had founded the Middlesex County Sexual Abuse section of the prosecutor's office and that he was once a prosecutor. He also said that whomever was assigned to prosecute my case would be a former colleague of his. "Are you comfortable with that?" he asked. I'm not sure I made the right decision, but in my mind, his experience as a prosecutor might just help him to better defend me. After all, he would at least be very familiar with his former colleague's tactics. I agreed to hire him.

When I got home, I again fell into a stunned silence, yet I felt like I was under enormous stress. I got the same kind of feeling one gets while waiting in line for a scary amusement park ride—but after a few hours, that "frightened" feeling wouldn't go away. I remembered that a year or so before, I had had a severe case of insomnia while in graduate school. A doctor had prescribed the tranquilizer Xanax. It had broke the sleepless cycle for me after only a couple of nights use. Would it make this "fear" sensation go away? I went upstairs to my desk and located the bottle. There were a dozen tablets left. *Really bad day*, I thought, so I took two tablets. I returned to the living room, sat down on the couch in front of the television and fell into a deep sleep.

# Descent into Hell

I woke up to my mother's voice telling me that the eleven o'clock news was on. "You want to watch it, don't you?" she asked. "Of course," I answered. We watched the news together, followed by David Letterman's show, then like always, we went to our bedrooms. I was now wide awake, and my head was spinning with horrific thoughts. *If you get convicted,* I thought to myself, *you'll go to prison marked as a child molester. What if someone you picked up on an outstanding warrant while at Emerson College is there and fingers you as a former cop? God, what if there is someone there who just remembers seeing you driving a police cruiser?* There was no way I was going to sleep. I got up, got dressed, and went to a twenty-four-hour McDonald's on Route One in Saugus. I bought a large Coke and returned home. I got back into bed and switched on the TV, finally settling on a History Channel program. Then I remembered the Xanax. I retrieved the bottle and took a tablet. After another hour or so, I was still awake. So I took two more tablets, and eventually, I must have passed out.

As bad as what I had done with the Xanax was, I woke up the next morning and discovered yet another "benefit" to the drug. I must have slept ten times more soundly than I would have normally because I hadn't ever woken up so thoroughly refreshed in my entire life. I went to an early-morning weekday Mass at my parish. I fervently prayed for God's help in making the truth known. I even prayed that Ray himself would realize the evil in what he was doing and would decide to tell the truth himself. Then I thought about, well, everything. How could Ray tell such a vicious lie about me? I was the only counselor at Lakeside that actually thought he had the potential to be a good kid. I had stuck up for him in countless staff meetings and countless house meetings when all the residents were present. I was the only staff member who didn't harangue him endlessly after he had stolen all the other kids' money from the house safe. And then I got very depressed, and once again, that brutal anxious fear returned. I needed to see a doctor about this.

* * *

I had been out of work for a short time, but my health insurance was gone. I went to the Melrose-Wakefield Hospital and told them of my plight. The hospital very graciously had me fill out an "application for free care," and they scheduled an appointment with a staff psychiatrist.

I met with Dr. Markos the same afternoon. Markos was a big guy—again with a mustache—and to be perfectly honest, he looked like a twin to a guy who ran a Melrose pizza shop. "What are you taking, and how angry are you?" he inquired. I told him Xanax, and I added, "I'm not really angry, I'm profoundly sad." "Ah," he said, "so I'll refill your Xanax and prescribe an antidepressant! However," he continued thoughtfully, "I think you should stop being sad and get angry. Really angry. You should want to kill this liar!" In disbelief, I asked, "Kill?" "Well," he continued, "I don't mean to say that you should go kill someone, but that that's how you should feel right now." He then broke out his prescription pad, wrote two out, and handed them to me. "I'll see you next week. And work on your righteous anger! Oh, and here is a list of therapists—make an appointment with one of them." "Why?" I asked. "I'm seeing you." "Sometimes it helps," he said and ushered me out of the office.

The next day, I met with a female therapist on Rowe Street, just behind the hospital. I sat and explained my situation. The therapist then said, "I know, I read about it in the paper." I instantly knew what she was talking about. The local paper, the *Melrose Free Press*, had run a story about my being indicted on the lower left hand corner of page 1. It featured a quote from some spokesman for the Middlesex County Sheriff's Department, who stated what Ray was saying as though it were an absolute indisputable fact. The last line said, "Mr. DeCoste's attorneys had no comment." "My attorneys?"

While the sign did say "Kaufman and Kaufman," there was only one Kaufman actually working there.

What actually bothered me was I could tell that if this "therapist" was keeping an open mind about my case, she certainly could have fooled me. Then I realized that this is exactly how most people viewed newspaper accounts of either arrests or indictments—guilty until proven innocent, and even then, probably guilty. Often you hear, "he or she was found guilty." But on the flip side, when a person is found not guilty, we often hear people say, "He or she 'beat' the rap"—meaning they somehow "got away with it." Many people who work in the criminal justice system are highly practiced at virtually "singing" little "songs" like "innocent until proven guilty," but few of them actually believe those words. (Another favorite "song" of people who work in the system—in fact, by far, their most favored one—would turn out to be "Well, a jury of your peers found you guilty, so you have to be guilty." I just had not as yet heard that one.

This "therapist" was, as are most psychologists and psychological therapists, utterly useless to me. I was trained as a pastoral counselor at Boston University's School of Theology, and I can tell you that while talking about your "problems" may be beneficial up to a point, I honestly do not believe that continuous blabbering about some personal issue is a very effective way to overcome your problems with that issue. Most therapists simply want to keep you returning in order to keep up their revenue stream. It is helpful to talk to someone about a complex problem—maybe a couple of times, but then you need to come to a concrete decision as to how you will address that problem, with an eye toward solving it. On the other hand, my problem was having been falsely accused of a crime that I didn't commit. The only solution to that problem would be a court acquittal. The resultant depression and anxiety could be temporarily addressed with medication. The more serious problem was that I was becoming highly addicted to one of those medications.

Eventually, I grew weary of Dr. Markos and the therapist, and I dropped them both. I then turned to my primary care physician for continuing my prescription for Xanax. However, a new situation would arise that would cause me to double my Xanax intake. That situation would be witness intimidation—by the police.

* * *

My family home was situated on West Emerson Street at the intersection of Charles Street. Charles Street was a long, steep hill ending at West Emerson. If you could continue driving after reaching the top of Charles—and you'd need a tank to do this—you would climb the steep stairs to our home's front door. You would then drive through our living room, through a wall into the kitchen, then out into the backyard.

As it happened, I was watching the end of the NBC Nightly News when I could see two Melrose police cars very slowly driving up the hill. One car was behind the other but in the other "lane" so that both cars were visible. They both had every single emergency light either on or flashing—the blue lights, the alternating headlights (called wig-wag lights), the super bright "take down" lights, and the side-mounted spotlights. After they reached the top of the hill, they both turned right and they both turned off all those lights. I would like to say that I'm a much stronger person than this, but I was totally unnerved. I quickly got my bottle of Xanax and downed three one-milligram tablets. I'm not entirely certain of the exact order of my thoughts, but high among them was this: *What are the neighbors thinking?* I spent the rest of the night in a drug-induced stupor.

The next day, I went to Jack Kaufman's office without an appointment to tell him of the previous night's police antics. He said he would "take care of it." That exact tactic was never repeated; however, shortly after that, one cop would drive by four or five nights a week, and turning on his side alley light, he would slowly allow the illuminating light to pass the front of my house like a barracks building in a prisoner of war movie. If this was done by anyone other than the government (police), it would constitute the Massachusetts crime of witness intimidation. The prosecutor was aware that I planned to testify in my own defense and this was a clear attempt to try and coerce either a plea agreement or an outright guilty plea out of an innocent man. Further, I'm certain that Mr. Kaufman had complained to *someone* after the first incident—only he knows whether he complained to the police, the prosecutor, or both. So who orchestrated this witness intimidation? The detective on the case? Individual police officers? Or was the prosecutor on the case involved as well? I strongly doubt we will ever know. Well, we will know on the day of God's final judgment.

* * *

Eventually, the day of arraignment arrived. I got a call from Jack Kaufman just before I left for court. "Kevin, Jack here," he began. "I'm going to be a little late. At court, you'll see a gentleman with gray hair and a beard. That's Kevin Johnson, the ADA [assistant district attorney]. Tell him I'll be along shortly." I thought to myself, *Oh great! I have to meet and talk to the prosecutor without an attorney present.* I wasn't happy at all.

At the Superior Court in Cambridge, Massachusetts, I got to the courtroom and saw a guy matching the description that Jack had given me. I walked up behind the guy and said, "Excuse me, Mr. Johnson?" He turned around and nodded, "Mr. Kaufman says he's going to be a little late." Again, Johnson nodded without so much as a single word. It was obvious he didn't like dealing directly with me; he probably didn't like me either. Johnson was dressed OK but nowhere as well as I had seen Jack Kaufman dress. I guess private practice has its rewards. However, what surprised me was the guy's beard—it was all over the place. Apparently, trimming the damn thing wasn't high on Johnson's to-do list.

Soon after, Jack arrived. He told me to say "Not guilty" when asked and to say nothing else. I did as I was told then the judge asked the two of them about bail. Of course, Jack asked that I be released on my "own recognizance." What startled me was that when the judge looked at ADA Johnson, he said, "Your Honor, this is an old case. We have no objection to the defense request." And that was it. We were done for the day, Jack got paid five hundred dollars for ten minutes' work, and I was free to return home.

Years later, I would wish that the trial had begun that very day. I was feeling good and highly alert despite being somewhat medicated. It would be the nearly year-long wait for the actual trial to begin that would cause the most damage or, should I say, allow me to do the most damage to myself.

* * *

Two things were now certain, first, the trial was quite a few months away. Second, I needed some type of income. Strangely, I applied for and was hired to work part-time in the neighboring town of Wakefield, at Blockbuster Video.

I have often said that if only Blockbuster paid a "living wage," I would have loved to work there for a very long time. The employees were great, the customers were great, and I really enjoyed helping people—especially older folks—to find just the "right" movie. Even the building cleaning at the end of the night was somewhat enjoyable. Well, it wasn't difficult. If you look at many minimum-wage jobs—especially in the fast food industry—you'll see the supervisors there pushing the employees hard. Any spare time is spent endlessly cleaning up the store. That wasn't the case at Blockbuster. When things were clean, returned movies put away and a break in the flow of customers occurred, they really didn't mind if you grabbed a snack and just watched the film that was playing on the store's big screen at that time. It was a very relaxed atmosphere.

The only really bad day at Blockbuster, at least in the beginning, happened early on. One day, I came to work, and there was, as always, a stack of free newspapers near the door. This was a new start-up paper, and they simply gave it away—making their money off advertisers. However, on this day, I saw that the paper had a small article on the lower front page—about my indictment. I immediately made a move to grab the entire stack when one of the assistant managers came over and started talking to me. I kept repositioning my body in the hope of blocking her view of the papers. When she finished talking, I again turned toward the stack of papers when a young employee named Peter called over asking me to help him stock the beverage cooler. It took me nearly two hours to get the chance I needed. When dinner time came, I volunteered to go pick up the food—something I hated doing. (Making separate change for four or five employees was not my idea of a good time.)

As I was leaving for a local takeout place, I grabbed the entire stack of papers. Just then, an assistant manager called after me, saying, "Kevin, wait! Peter is coming with you!" Peter ran out and jumped into my car. He immediately looked at the stack of papers and asked, "What the hell, your picture in there or something?" I was blown away. I liked this kid. Despite the appearance of being eighteen or nineteen years old—not to mention being 6'3", Peter was fifteen, the same age as Ray. For some reason, I decided almost instantly to tell him the truth.

"About three months ago, I was working at a residential school for kids who are sex offenders. I quit last March." Peter had become extremely quiet and he was concentrating very hard on what I was saying. I guess he could tell that this was deadly serious. I continued, "About a month after I quit, this kid told his sex therapist that when we had gone out to lunch one Saturday, that… that we had sex with each other. Peter, this will sound weird, but I've never had sex with anyone." Peter instantly exploded in anger, "Of course you didn't have sex with him! What a fucking asshole! How are you going to fight this?"

I was blown away. He believed me without any hesitation whatsoever. I began to answer him. "Look, the news is full of this sort of thing right now. It's going to wicked hard to get a jury to believe me—even though I'll tell them the absolute truth. I'll probably end up in prison." Peter seemed to get angrier. "You can't just think that and give up! You have to fight. You have to." Peter stopped. We arrived at the restaurant and picked up everyone's food. On the way back, we were both silent. When we got to the Blockbuster and parked, I said, "Peter, no one else here knows." He cut me off. "And they're not going to," he said.

The shift went on without incident. Because of his age, Peter had to leave work at 9:00 p.m. The state had rules. When his father came to pick him up, Peter walked over to me and, looking incredibly serious, said, "You have to fight." I almost started to cry. "I will," I told him. He smiled and left. Later that night, while I was saying my final night prayers, I thanked God for Peter. For his support and his belief in my innocence. I prayed for Peter and his family. Then I did cry.

Peter was an expert at computers—even Blockbuster's computers. When you're young and really smart, sometimes temptation can get the best of you. And no matter how good you are at something, there is almost always someone who's better. The store manager was that person. Peter had used the store computer to cut himself a few breaks in renting films. Actually, he had cut himself quite a few breaks—and he had around fifty tapes at his home. Even though he returned the tapes, the manager fired him. I still think he should have caught a break. He was an excellent worker and had a great rapport with all types of customers. He always volunteered for the hard jobs and was the first to help the rest of us whenever we had a difficult task to perform. When he was in the middle of something and his shift would end, he would usually stay a few minutes off the clock so that the rest of us wouldn't have to finish what he had started. No one else ever did that, not even me. Most importantly, he looked eighteen, but he was fifteen—just a kid. If they had kept him on, I know he would have learned from the experience. I saw Peter again four years later. He was still the great kid that I had worked with during the summer of 1996.

* * *

As the summer wore on, my fears steadily increased. I had frequent discussions with close friends. They were very supportive. However, I was starting to worry about the trial, now scheduled for a couple of weeks before Christmas. When I first met with Jack Kaufman, he had said, "You have a very strong case." However, each subsequent meeting brought steadily diminishing statements from him. "You have a good case" came next. That was followed by "You're going to have your day in court," and near the actual trial date—which would be delayed until February of 1997—Jack told me, "You know, whether a person is guilty or innocent, they have a fifty-fifty chance of being found guilty." I don't know who had the lower expectation, me or Jack.

I had met with my pastor. I was expecting spiritual support. He was useless. After one meeting, he asked me to use a different door to leave by. When I realized that he had said that so I would not come into contact with some kids in the church hall as I left, I stopped seeing him. My greatest spiritual advisor, though for him I prefer the Eastern Church term *spiritual father*, was a professor at the University of Notre Dame, Father Charles Weiher. It just killed me that I could only speak with him by phone. I needed to be close to such a highly spiritual, as well as highly intelligent, friend during this brutal time in my life. Like my biological father, Father Weiher really "got" me. He always had advice that amazed me because of his incredible wisdom. My own Father died of cancer at age fifty-eight—when I was twenty-two years old. I sincerely believe that God sent Father Weiher years later to fill the void left by my Dad's dying. Once that summer, while I was speaking to Father Weiher by phone, he said to me, "You're using medicine—probably a tranquilizer. That will get you into serious trouble. It may calm you, but it will take away your mental sharpness. This isn't the time for that." It was too late. I was severely dependent on Xanax. I told him that I would be OK. I was wrong. I now had three different doctors, each one giving me ninety tablets every month. One day, I awoke from a long stupor. I had no idea how long I had been in bed. On the table next to me was a bottle of ninety Xanax tablets from a doctor I didn't even know. I asked my mom if she knew where they had come from. She told me that I had become violently ill, vomiting uncontrollably. She had taken me to the hospital, and the doctor said I was suffering from Xanax withdrawal symptoms. That's why he had given me another bottle of ninety—with three refills.

I have absolutely no memory of the month of July 1996. What's worse is that I'm told I drove around visiting many friends. I could have gotten some poor person killed. I could have gotten myself killed. I only know a couple of things. One, I borrowed two thousand dollars from my best friend Paul to help pay Jack Kaufman. I can't remember that or traveling seventy miles round trip to do it. Also, I guess I used the bathroom at a local fast-food restaurant. Apparently, in my drug-induced fog, I thought I was trapped in the bathroom stall—so I pretty much broke the door down to "escape." I was discovered by some of the high school kids who worked there. They had all known me for a few years from my Coca-Cola buying habits at that place. Two of them got me back to my car and never told anyone how the door had been damaged. Finally, one day at Blockbuster, I sort of came to and couldn't understand why the two assistant managers were restocking the entire long length of two shelves. What had happened was there were two huge bags of trash that needed to be taken out back to the Dumpster. I had thrown one bag over each shoulder then walked between the two long shelves and wiped out every video on both sides. More than one hundred tapes. Those two extremely kind ladies put all of the tapes back and never told me what had happened. I only found out when one of their eight-year-old sons told me about it when he was hanging out at the store. He thought it was the funniest story he had ever heard. I was too embarrassed to ever bring the subject up myself after that.

Eventually, those incidents would end, but it was way too late. I was in serious trouble, and I was powerless to do anything about it.

* * *

When the December trial date came, I was in fairly good shape despite my drug use. Even Jack Kaufman was thrilled to see how alert and positive I was on that day. Though I cannot recall exactly why, the judge again delayed the trial—this time until February 1997. Even I knew that a great moment had been lost. For some unknown reason, I really was at the top of my game during that December court appearance. My mom was happy that the trial had been delayed until after Christmas, yet for me, I could just feel—deep down inside—

that my best chance for a fair trial and, ultimately, real justice, had now been forever lost.

Two final important events took place. In December, I watched my friend Paul's house and babysat his dog while he and his wife, Staci, were at the hospital for the birth of their first son. Later, in January, I flew to South Bend, Indiana, to visit with Father Weiher. It was an excellent visit, though I would never see him in person again. I also got to see my good friends, Sister Patricia Jean Garver, better known as Sister PJ, and Fr. John Patrick Riley, my good friend and former classmate.

Although there were many times since that cop first knocked on my door that I had actually prayed to die, I found out I really didn't mean it—or at least I wanted a say in how I would go. On the way back from Notre Dame, my plane was violently shaken by turbulence. I found myself praying that we would not crash. I guess I wasn't ready to go after all.

# The Trial

When the date for my trial was about a week away, my pessimism and fears dramatically increased. So did my intake of Xanax. On the morning of the first day, I took three tablets at the same time before my mom drove us both to court. I found the entire experience exceedingly embarrassing. That was stupid; after all, I hadn't actually committed the crime. Jury selection took a few hours. Later, I would read the transcript, and I was totally shocked. The jury included the following people: A man with two sons. One was a jail guard. A woman, a physician, who herself was a rape victim. A man whose niece had been recently sexually abused, and that trial had not as yet taken place. One woman wanted out because, as she put it, "I'm the mother of three young boys, and I live in Lowell." Lowell was the city where the Lakeside School was located.

A young guy tried to get out of jury duty, saying he could not be impartial. He later reversed himself. Later events would convince me that this particular guy was the one who'd "led the charge" to convict me.

Jack Kaufman, in my mind, failed to challenge many jurors who most definitely should have been challenged. ADA Johnson had no such problem. Johnson went to work, immediately challenging every older woman who was near my mom's age. Apparently, he was afraid of their identifying with and having sympathy for my mother. Jack did notice that and raised his concern with the judge. The judge then said something to the effect of taking the juror's "cards," cutting them like a deck of (playing) cards and taking those jurors on one side or the other. Reading that in the transcript a few years later, I was taken aback at how trivial a man's being on trial for what would truly be his life actually meant to these three men, all officers of the court.

As the trial began, Ray was the first to testify. Although Ray and I had only known each other for about four and a half months, I knew his manner of speaking. Since he had not been in a "regular" school for most of his life, Lakeside not being his first residential program, Ray had a somewhat limited vocabulary. Earlier in the spring, Jack Kaufman and I had watched a video tape of Ray making his false accusations against me. Beyond any doubt whatsoever, Ray was reciting a script that in no way reflected either his vocabulary or syntax. Now, months later, he again was reciting word for word what had to have been a script prepared for him by either the prosecutor, the state Victim Witness Office, or by Tyler Cohen. At the end of his "description of events," he finished by saying that I had told him, "If you tell anyone, I'll seek revenge on you somehow." *I'll seek revenge on you somehow!* That's how someone with three degrees, one an advanced professional degree, would speak? That sounded more like the speech that Arnold Schwarzenegger's character in one of the two *Terminator* movies might speak but not someone with nineteen years of formal education.

Ray testified that I had brought him into my bedroom and locked the door before assaulting him. The door could not be locked from the inside at all! There was a lock on the outside, but you could not lock yourself *inside* the room. Earlier, Jack had viewed that door lock. He wanted to know why it was there at all. As I explained to him, I used to own a few firearms, and I didn't want anyone getting in there to steal them. Indeed, once inside the room, those guns were again locked up—in a drawer. You could not be too safe when it came to guns. When Jack asked Ray about meeting my sister Joan on the second floor, Ray claimed that he had never met her—another outright lie. Ray said that we were in my room for thirty to forty-five minutes. Another lie. Before I left the Lakeside School, I heard Gale ask Ray about my room. Knowing that I'm an Eastern Rite (Melkite) Catholic, she asked, "Did Kevin's room look like a shrine?" Ray had told her, "I don't remember. I wasn't there long enough."

When it was Jack's turn to cross-examine Ray, he treated him with such gentleness that he should have been asked if he thought that Ray was, in fact, a defense witness! Jack had said that a tough cross-examination could backfire by garnering jury sympathy for Ray, but that was outright absurd. Then Tyler testified, followed by Leroy. Most of that was a blur. However, I could not help but worry over Jack's outright refusal to call any character witnesses in my defense. I could tell that these three people had all painted a somewhat negative picture of me. I should have been allowed to have those people who knew me, even worked in other programs with me, to have testified on my behalf. When I had originally brought the subject up with Jack months before, he had flatly said, "No." He then added, "Any bum off the street can get ten good people to come in and swear they're a great guy. It wouldn't mean anything." "Bum off the street?" Was that how he was viewing me? My witnesses would have been well-respected ministers, professors, and even a reverend-professor- psychologist.

If I hadn't been so afraid, if I had had more financial resources, I could have demanded that he call those witnesses under the threat of firing him. However I was near broke and very intimidated by the entire situation, and thus Jack got away with it. I sincerely believe that if he had called the people I had wanted, the trial's outcome would have been quite different.

Then Detective Callahan took the stand. I had told Jack how this guy had written Ray's name on his notebook in huge block letters and about his "dancing" around until I saw it and asked if Ray was OK. There were many ways that I would have asked Thompson about that, all of them confrontational, such as "Isn't it true that you wrote Ray Swanson's name in your notebook in huge letters then kept repositioning that notebook until the defendant read and asked you about him?" Not easygoing Jack, though. He asked, "Could the defendant have read Ray Swanson's name off your notebook?" Then to avoid an absolute answer that could be challenged, Callahan replied, "I don't think so." Years ago, a famous Boston appeals attorney and Harvard Law School professor angered the local police by coining the term *police testi-lying*. Cops picketed his office and home. Yet what Thompson had just engaged in was just that, and the proper legal term for it is *perjury*.

After the prosecutor rested his case, it was my mom's turn to take the stand. I reached into my pocket, retrieved three Xanax tablets, and took them with the court-supplied water. I remember my mom being highly composed on the stand. She told the truth about all the events that took place when Ray visited our home. As she spoke, I began to feel myself "slipping away." The medication was starting to basically knock me out. I came in and out. At one point, I saw that the prosecutor was treating my sister, who had followed my mom on the stand, very roughly. I yelled something at him. Jack was shocked! He put his hand over the microphone on the defense table, turned to me, and exclaimed, "My God! Are you medicated?" I calmly looked at him and answered, "Severely."

Despite Jack's "shock" at my outburst and the fact that I had just told him that I was "severely" medicated, he put me on the witness stand. I can't remember a thing about that day's testimony. I did know that when I came back the following day that I was going to be cross-examined by Johnson. That night, I kept remembering the nationally televised O. J. Simpson trial. I recalled how when prosecution witnesses were cross-examined, that the attorneys actually, at times, screamed at them. All I could think was that I was going to endure the same abusive treatment the very next day. I drugged myself to sleep.

I won't pretend that I remember how many Xanax tablets I took the next morning, but it was a lot. I didn't stop there. I took another handful in the courthouse cafeteria as soon as I arrived. From reading the transcript of that day, I was a complete zombie. I even tried to quote the testimony of Ray's personal therapist, Jane. The judge then reminded me that Jane had not been present at the trial. (The prosecution conveniently had stated at the beginning of the trial that Jane was unavailable due to a long-planned vacation. He would not have wanted her there since I had asked and received her written permission to take Ray out to lunch.)

I was extremely confused, to use the judge's term. When instructing the jury, the judge told them that they could also see that confusion as "consciousness of guilt." Later, on appeal, the Massachusetts

Supreme Judicial Court would rule that the judge made an error in giving that instruction but "not a reversible error."

I guess I somehow finished. The closing statements were a disaster. I had given Jack Kaufman many reasons why Ray might have made those false accusations. Pressure from Tyler, Tyler's threat to keep him at the school until he was eighteen, even revenge against me for Tyler's finding out that he had spoken to me in violation of his sex therapy group(s) rules. What did Jack say to the jury? Something to this effect: "Why would someone make these false accusations? There could be many reasons." Had Jack put any significant time into either his trial preparation or his closing argument? It didn't seem so.

ADA Johnson, in my estimation, outright lied to the jury during his closing argument. One of the things he said was this: "How could a fifteen-year-old boy know about such things unless they were done to him?" Well, here's how. Ray was part of two sex therapy groups: a sex offenders' group and a sexual abuse survivors' group. Each group spent hours every week going over and over both what every kid had done to others and what had been done to every kid. He had more knowledge of sexually perverted acts than most police officers and more than many psychologists. Johnson's statement constituted perjury—though technically, he was not testifying. Though if any attorney's closing statements are not, in reality, testimony—and unchallengeable testimony at that—then I don't know what is.

What's interesting to note is that during the appeal process, many things that were said during the original trial were miraculously revised—all to the prosecution's benefit. Johnson was present during my appeals; Jack Kaufman was not. Furthermore, there was a glaring omission in the original trial transcript. Kaufman, during his cross-examination of Tyler Cohen, asked her, "Has Ray Swanson ever lied to you?" To that, Tyler replied, "He has lied about everything and anything since the first day I met him." In subsequent testimony, Jack would refer not to those actual words but to the harshness of what Tyler had said. However, in the written trial transcript, Tyler's answer to Kaufman's question reads simply as her answering "Yes." So did the court transcriber just screw up? Did she miss what was said and try a quick fix? Or was she sympathetic toward Ray and simply decide to change Tyler's harsh (but true) testimony? What has to be remembered is that appeals court judges read those transcripts. Whatever the reason the court's transcriber had for dramatically altering Tyler's answer, it did an injustice to me.

The jury received its instructions, and for me and my mom, the waiting began. The only place to wait was the court's cafeteria, so I sat at a table with my mom and Jack, and I kept drinking Coca-Cola and taking Xanax. The deliberations took all afternoon. At one point, Jack looked at his watch and told me, "Someone in there is fighting for you." Early in the evening, the jury came back. As I looked at the jury, three men and nine women, one thing was strange. Of the men, there were two older guys and one young one. The young guy was the juror who had claimed he could not be impartial then had reversed himself. He was grinning ear to ear like the Cheshire Cat, and he kept nodding his head. The verdict was read "Guilty." At that point, that young guy practically jumped out of his skin with apparent happiness. It was painfully obvious that he was the guy "leading the charge" to convict me. I will remember his Howdy Doody–looking jackass face forever. The bastard had just fought and won to convict an innocent man.

The judge told Jack that he was revoking my bail and that he knew Jack would not like it. Jack remained silent. I turned to Jack and said, "Sorry about your perfect record." He said nothing. (I now seriously doubt the veracity of Jack's earlier statement that he had never lost a sexual abuse case.) An elderly court officer came over and said to me, "Say goodbye." I hugged my mom and my sister Janice. Then the old guy put handcuffs on me—in front, not back—and basically, made it look like I was being dragged away. However, we rounded the courtroom, passed through a door, and as soon as the door was closed and we were out of sight, the handcuffs came right off again. It was all done for show!

At that point, the Xanax kicked in again, and everything seemed to fade away.

# The Cambridge Jail

I know that it was around 6:00 or 7:00 p.m. when I was convicted. However, the next moment of clarity for me came when I was basically "dumped" into the "protective custody block." Everyone was asleep. I would later come to see that guys were usually awake in that cell block until around 11:30 p.m.—after the final night's local news. So where the hell had I been during all that time?

I remember only two things. First, I remember taking a shower with around four of five jail guards watching me. Second, I remember passing through the jail's laundry facility. I remember nothing else.

As I entered the cell block, a small guy, who had great difficulty walking, got out of bed and helped me make up my bunk. I was on the top bunk. So when it was finally made up, I took off my new gray jumpsuit and hoisted myself up. One of the cross bars was, for some strange reason, quite sharp. I cut both of my lower legs getting into bed. It would happen every night until I got a different bed. I would have scars on my legs for close to six months after leaving the jail. A numbness came over me, and I quickly fell asleep. The only interruption would be a "screaming sound."

The Cambridge Jail is a high-rise building. When it was built, the Cambridge City Fire Department expressed their fears about housing people on floors higher than their ladders could reach in the event of a fire. From radio talk show hosts to many state and city politicians came the same response: "Who cares, they're criminals."

Anyway, with the winter winds in the Boston-Cambridge area howling every night, it produced a "screaming" sound. The only way to describe it was that it was exactly the same sound that a crowd on a roller coaster makes as the ride makes a steep drop and everyone screams. It would come, in my now messed-up drug withdrawals state, to completely unnerve me. Only toward the end of my nearly two-week stay would I gradually figure out what that haunting sound was.

Here is how the protective custody block in the Cambridge Jail was set up. First there was a guard's office separated from the unit by both some glass and steel bars. Along a long corridor, there were single-person cells each with bars and a barred door that could be electronically opened or closed from the guard's office. Across from the cells was a high chain-link fence that prevented the inmates from getting near the building's windows. Just in front of the fence were a long line of bunk beds. Those beds were there due to overcrowding. At the far end, opposite the guard's office was a wall with a television mounted high up. At the halfway point, there was a space in the bunks where there was a guard's desk. At night, a guard would be assigned to sit there from 5:00 p.m. to 11:00 p.m. Humorously, nearly all the guards would yell insults at all the inmates from the office, yet when one of those same guards had to sit at the desk—locked in with the inmates—they acted like little boys in Catholic grade school, sitting silently with their hands neatly folded. If you're going to run your mouth, at least have the courage to back it up—I had no respect for these cowardly, moronic bastards.

Why moronic? If you don't understand county government in Massachusetts, here's a little help. Even though on paper county government in Massachusetts no longer exists, all the previous county government structures, institutions, and unfortunately, personnel remain. It's all patronage jobs. You have to be politically connected to work in the sheriff's department, the probation department or in the courts. (Though some probation officers are there due to affirmative action hiring. Contrary to public perception, these are the most intelligent probation employees.) Most of the time, these guys are the dim-minded children of either state politicians, relatives, or friends of state politicians or the children or relatives of those who make significant financial contributions to the political campaigns of state politicians. If you're politically connected, but too stupid to accurately make change as a toll collector on Boston's Tobin Bridge, then a sheriff's department job will probably be just your thing.

I was surprised at the huge selection of products at the jail's inmate store or, as it's known, "canteen." The jail also supplied ice, bread, and peanut butter to each cell block nightly. The reason? Most of the guys in the Cambridge Jail are awaiting trial. They were either unable to raise bail or they were denied bail. In either case, as the old song goes, "innocent until proven guilty." I knew one guy who was in the jail for a year and a half before going to trial and being found not guilty. (There is another old song that's hardly ever heard: "Justice delayed is justice denied.") Of course both inmates and guards would later say, "He beat the system." I call it *the old song* because seemingly no one believes it anyway. The worst part of being in the Cambridge Jail was that 99 percent of both the inmates and the guards smoked. And many of them chain-smoked. From early morning until well after midnight, those of us who were non-smokers were forced to live in a virtual fog of cigarette smoke. It was sickening, and I never got used to it. The only benefit to being outside the cells in one of the bunk beds was that the guys in the cells were locked in at 10:00 p.m. When movies, TV shows or sporting events went past ten, the guys in the cells missed out while the guys on the bunk beds got to see the end. Some guys bought small shaving mirrors and held them outside their cells to watch the TV. It never seemed worth it to me.

My first afternoon in the jail introduced me to a jail guard the inmates named Radar. He was a thin, aging, little weasel of a man who never, ever sat at the desk inside the cell block. It was obvious that he had worked there for countless years and enjoyed all the perks of seniority except for promotion to a supervisory position. He was way too dumb for that. Besides, he was such a clown that no other guard would have taken him seriously anyway. He spent each and every shift just sitting in an office chair facing the block and hurling insults at the inmates.

After lunch, pretty much every inmate fell asleep on his bunk. No one wanted to watch daytime television, and there was nothing else to do. I was lying awake on my bunk, trying not to choke on the cigarette fumes when suddenly I heard, for the first time, Radar's monologue begin: "Oh, all the world's pedophiles are asleep. All the little boys in Boston can now go out to play. The world is safe for a couple of hours. Ah, ah, ah, ah, ah, have a nice day!" As soon as that would end, another similar rant would begin, always ending with that foolish "ah, ah, ah, ah, ah," and be finished with "Have a nice day." On other days guys would toss insults back at him, to which he would again reply, "Ah, ah, ah, ah, ah, have a nice day." I even took to imitating this infamous ending, and since I could come extremely close to reproducing the sound of Radar's voice, it seemed to infuriate him. He could be heard asking other guards, "Who the fuck is that?" He never found out, and no inmate ever ratted me out. I was exceedingly happy to be able to get under that asshole's skin. It also made me quite popular with the other inmates.

The second night after dinner, a guard came into the unit and yelled out, "Roof call!" Guys were lining up like that was something good, so despite my continuing stupor, or perhaps because of it, I joined the line. We followed a guard up a few flights of stairs to the very top floor, and behold! There was a rather large gym! I walked around, looking at all the equipment, while more than just a couple of guys asked me to join their workout. I told everyone that I was just going to look around. One Asian guy, Tsai, was in the process of bench pressing what seemed to be many, many times more than his own weight. I was transfixed. I heard someone behind me say, "He's fucking amazing—and scary." To my disbelief, it was a guard! Talking to me —an inmate! All I managed to say was "Yeah." Tsai lived in one of the cells. A few nights later, as the cells were being locked at ten o'clock, I actually watched Tsai grab his cell door as it was closing and slowly reopen it. And it stayed open! Another inmate would later tell me that Tsai had been caught raping an infant. I refused to believe it. Additionally, I had also adopted a personal policy of not judging another inmate—there were plenty of staff people for that assignment.

It had been two days since my conviction, yet the effects of my Xanax abuse seemed to be intensifying. Every morning, some white-coat-wearing guy would wake me up at around 6:00 a.m. and hand me a bunch of pills. He absolutely infuriated me. He would say

"DeCost—a" very slowly, over and over. My father's side of the family was French. *DeCoste* simply means "of the coast." The final *e* in my name is never pronounced—it's always silent. There are people of Italian and Portuguese ancestry that both spell and pronounce their name *DeCosta*, and in their language, it too means "of the coast," but that's not my name. The problem with the Boston area is this: so many stupid people there seem to believe there are only two ethnic groups—Italian and Irish—and they can't wrap their heads around any other ethnic concept.

Anyway, I was having serious problems with hallucinations. One morning, despite several inmates trying to get me to go to breakfast, I was refusing to get off my top bunk. Guys later told me that I kept saying over and over, "Look out for the train!" I remember thinking that I was on top of a mountain. There were trains running on tracks all over that mountain, and I was thoroughly convinced that if I moved a muscle, I'd fall onto the tracks and get killed.

Another night, the guards were seeming to have an endless discussion of the word *tarmac*. I was aware that there had been some news coverage of an incident at an airport, on the runway, but I didn't make the connection. The guards were basically whining that too many news reporters had said the word *tarmac* way too many times. Unfortunately, when a group of guys have the collective IQ of a single basset hound, such conversations can last for hours. In my chemically altered mind, as I kept hearing them repeat the word *tarmac* over and over, I became convinced that *tarmac* was the codeword of a conspiracy to kill me. At some point, the white-coat-wearing medical guy showed up with my handful of pills—and it came to me! These bastards were slowly poisoning me with these assorted pills! Bastards! I faked swallowing them then threw then into a sink. As soon as I could, I got on one of the block's two phones, called a friend, and had her call the state police detective unit in Boston and tell them that I was being poisoned by these eternally damned guards! A few hours later, some well-dressed guy did show up and point in my direction. He certainly looked like a detective. What actually took place, if anything, I'll probably never know.

One day, I was taken by a guard to the floor where the jail canteen was located. The guard pointed toward an office, and it was a psychiatrist! The doc was a small man with black-rimmed glasses and a comical, though pleasant enough, personality. I don't remember too many details except one recurring question. Every so often, he would seemingly interrupt his own train of thought and ask, "Are you hearing any voices?" Now, while I certainly wasn't in my right mind, I wasn't really hearing any conversations that were not actually coming from people around me, so I sort of laughed and said, "No." Dr. Braun would go on for a while then abruptly stop mid-sentence and ask, "Any voices—any at all?" He did ask about drug use prior to coming to the jail. I believed at the time that if I answered "yes," I might be charged with a narcotics crime, so I always lied and told him "no."

There was a guy at the jail, and both he and his wife were on trial for sexually abusing their four boys. He was a huge man and extremely intimidating. Most of the other inmates avoided him. Some, more pathetic, guys tried to befriend him, as in "If your friend's with the biggest man in the block, no one can hurt you," and they used to follow him around like rock star groupies. A few times, I heard him on the phone begging people to change their testimony—I guess they were witnesses against him. Didn't he know those calls were monitored? While making those calls, he used to weep like a baby. This guy also lived in the cells. One night, while everyone was extremely loud cracking jokes back and forth, I guess the big man was trying to sleep. Over and over again, he furiously screamed, "Shut the fuck up!" It was hysterical! All the guys knew that first, he couldn't identify everyone's voices, and second, the big bully was locked into his cell for the night. So whenever he screamed "Shut the fuck up," the entire cell block erupted into uproarious laughter. That made the guy nearly insane, and he screamed all the louder. The guards either did not care or they too were enjoying the moment. Soon, some guy started sarcastically saying "Shut the fuck up" every time the big guy did. Eventually, the bully realized he was losing the battle and he shut up himself. Later, after I had moved to a state prison, I heard on the news that he was convicted and received several consecutive life sentences. Many years after I got out, the local news reported that he had died of cancer in a prison hospital.

There was also a guy named Chad. He was only eighteen years old, and he had a humorous habit of doing some movements with another inmate that looked somewhat like martial arts movements or, as real martial arts practitioners call them, *forms*. But they were just some bullshit stuff that the two of them had concocted together. Still, it took some degree of physical coordination, and I was still messed up, so I used to watch them with some interest. He seemed like an OK kid. There were a few different accounts of how he ended up in jail. Here is a composite: Chad and his girlfriend were on the roof of a parking garage in a Boston suburb. Somehow she fell off the roof and was seriously injured. Some news accounts said that he had called her and asked her to meet him there, then he threw her off the roof. Other accounts were that they had been at the mall together, then afterward, he threw her off the roof. The final version was that they were on the roof together and they had gotten into an argument but that with no contact from Chad, the girl had simply slipped and fallen off the roof. The state, of course, had charged him with "assault with intent to murder." One day, I'm not sure what he had done, but the guards had locked him in his cell in the late afternoon. Like a lot of guys, I used to pace up and down the long block corridor like a caged animal—just for exercise. For some reason, I stopped at Chad's cell and started talking to him. He was obviously angry at whatever had happened, and at one point, he said, "You know, Kev, anyone who fucks me over, at least in a big way, I will eventually kill them, and I will kill them so slowly and so fucking painfully…" Then he stopped. I wonder if I had had a horrified look on my face because he seemed to lighten up and he said, "Hey, anyone who is cool with me, I am cool with them. You've been cool with me, and I'm cool with you." We never had a really long conversation after that. I liked him somewhat, but I have never really known what to think. As I write this, he's now thirty-five years old. I sincerely hope he's doing well.

One day, a sheriff's department lieutenant, an African American and a highly intelligent man, was yelling at Chad. I guess in his boredom, Chad had written a poem about throwing his girlfriend off the roof and he had shared it with one of the guards. The guard took the paper the poem was written on away from Chad. "Are you out of your fucking mind?" the lieutenant asked him. Chad said something to the effect that he thought of the guard that he had shared the poem with as a friend. "A friend!" the lieutenant screamed. "What, are you two going to drink beers and watch the Super Bowl together?" I never knew what came of the poem incident. The lieutenant had told Chad that the guard could possibly give the poem to the district attorney. In any case, Chad was convicted.

At some point, a much older man entered the unit. His name was Vincent. He was a very thin and frail man. I got the impression that he was suffering from some serious yet unspecified disease. One of the guys from Boston's North End, a predominantly Italian neighborhood, swore up and down that he knew that Vincent was involved with the Mafia. I didn't give it any thought. He had just gotten in and, hence, had had no opportunity to shop the jail's canteen store. It was sad; I saw him drinking water out of a sink. I had moved into a cell earlier that day; I had volunteered as it would afford me more privacy. I grabbed a couple of cans of Coke and offered the guy one. He thanked me, and I noticed he spoke like a cross between Marlon Brando in *The Godfather* and Clint Eastwood from the *Dirty Harry* movies. I thought to myself, *Well, this will enhance the Mafia story that is going around.*

There really wasn't any place to sit. At the one unit table, the bully and his pathetic entourage were playing cards. Undeterred Vincent walked up to the table and asked, "Gentleman, is there any way that a couple of you could make room so that my friend and I could sit and have a talk?" They all looked at each other, then all of them looked at the bully. Vincent went on, "It's a serious discussion that we need to have. It would not be in anyone else's best interest to listen in, if you know what I mean." The bully got up like a missile fired out of a trident submarine! His disciples followed suit. So there were things that could frighten that huge bastard!

We now sat alone at the table that previously had seated eight guys. I couldn't help myself; I started to laugh. Vincent seemed to know what my laughter was based upon. He sort of chuckled then said, "It's not always what you can do to a guy. Sometimes, it's what you can have someone else do to a guy. You know what I mean?" I quickly nodded my head. We made our personal introductions to each other without ever mentioning what either of us were in jail for. We went on with our serious discussion for about two hours. We discussed the Boston Bruins, the Red Sox, pizza, and of course, how incredibly stupid the guards were. Oh yeah, those other guys were very lucky they hadn't heard what we were talking about! We sat together at dinner that night and at every meal for the next couple of days, then sadly—for me—Vincent was released. That first night, at dinner, all the guards who were usually watching everyone eat were pretty much only watching Vincent and me. And they were whispering to each other. One night before he was released, a guard called me to the office. I almost passed out when he said, "Sir, you have visitors downstairs." It was my sister Janice and my friend Dan. After Vincent left, the respect from the guards gradually wore off. Screw it, it was fun while it lasted.

One night, a young inmate named David got into an argument during roof call. I wasn't there, but I was told the argument hadn't lasted long. I guess David had asked if a guy was finished with a piece of equipment, and the other guy had answered, "You'll know when I'm finished!" David thought the guy's answer was unnecessarily disrespectful, so he picked up a small bench and bashed it over the guy's head. Some inmates were talking behind David's back saying that he had hit a handicapped man. In fact, the guy *was* slightly handicapped—he had trouble walking. It was the same nice guy who had helped me make up my bunk my first night. It was also true that when that guy was annoyed, he often said regrettably stupid things. That habit cost him that night. He wasn't badly hurt though. David was locked in his cell.

David was prone to long, loud rants—and they were hysterically funny. Now locked in his cell at 8:00 p.m. and full of residual adrenaline from his "roof" altercation, he now set his sights on, of all people, the bully. And nothing was spared. "Oh shit, you think you're such a big man! It takes a real big guy to fuck his own little kids up the ass!" Believe it or not, that was mild compared to the rest of his speech—which I'll leave to the imagination. The bully was absolutely horrified. He ran down to David's cell with a pack of cigarettes and a six-pack of Coke. The two of them spoke quietly for a few moments, then I watched as the bully handed over the entire six-pack to David. Then the bully offered David a cigarette, which David took and the bully politely lit for him. The big asshole started to walk away, and David said to him, "The cigarettes." The bully looked like he was going to cry, but he handed the entire pack to David.

I was just standing a few feet away, trying not to laugh. David saw me and yelled over, "Kevin, we got Coke! Get some ice and come over!" I went to the block's cooler, filled two cups with ice, and we both sat on the floor—separated by the bars of David's cell. We spoke for hours. The guards somehow forgot to lock the rest of us in; they were too busy writing up reports of the "roof" incident, so David and I sat, talked, and by midnight, we had killed off the bully's six-pack. I was still drugged, but I swear, I had never had a conversation that caused me to laugh harder than that one.

David was an extremely funny kid. And I do mean *kid.* Despite being nineteen years old, he seemed like a fourteen-year-old, and I do not mean that as a criticism. It's just the way he was, but it most likely was part of the reason he was in jail. He lived with his mom, and she had placed a curfew on him—he had to be home by 11:00 p.m. every night. One night, when I guess she wasn't home, David was spotted by his uncle out on the street just after midnight. His uncle made a big deal of it, then in an incredibly stupid move, the uncle started singing, "I'm going to t-e-l-l!" the way a child would. David told him that he had better not tell, but the fool of an uncle only sang louder, "I'm going to t-e-l-l." According to the police, David became enraged, took out a knife, and stabbed his uncle to death. I read that in a newspaper that coincidentally, the guy that he beat up in the roof gym had kept. (He had newspaper "files" on many of the inmates in the block—I'm not sure why he kept them.)

David was like the extremely popular kid in high school who had the absolute worst time with academics, the kid that was so extremely likable and funny that the teachers gave him passing grades out of sympathy. Possibly the class clown but not necessarily. David obviously had the impulse control of a ten-year-old coupled with the strength of a quite strong young man. While I know nothing about his uncle, on his last night on Earth, the guy acted pretty stupid and immature. It cost him his life. Many years after I got out of prison, I was having the absolute worst time sleeping one night. I turned on the television and went through the channels. I stopped on one channel, and it was about keeping order in the nation's prisons. I'm sure you can understand that I hate those kinds of shows, but they said they would be "right back with stories from one of Massachusetts' worst prisons." Curious, I stayed on that station. Toward the end of the segment on the state prison in Walpole, Massachusetts, they began talking about an inmate who had sent a letter to the then Middlesex County District Attorney, Tom Rielly, threatening his life. I detested Rielly, so again I stayed with the show. They had a taped interview with the inmate, and it was David. He admitted sending the letter, though when asked why he was in prison, he stated, "Because I killed my uncle… I mean… I allegedly killed my uncle." After the segment was over, I turned the TV off. I felt so very bad for David. Walpole is an absolutely horrible place. You basically sit in your cell close to twenty-three hours a day. With extremely few exceptions, the guys have one hour of physical activity outside their cell each day, one shower a week, no television, no radio, no books, and no newspapers. They can write and receive letters, though that "privilege" can be limited or even taken away. If you think that's the proper way to treat inmates, I would suggest that you're a complete asshole. No human being should live like that. Most of the inmates are in Walpole for life. I spent considerable time that night praying for my friend David.

(The residents of Walpole, Massachusetts, finally got the state to rename that prison Massachusetts Correctional Institution (MCI) Cedar Junction. However, everyone still called it either Walpole State Prison or simply Walpole. If that ever does change, it will take years—something like one hundred years.)

Then there was Rick. With all due Christian charity, Rick was nuts. He had three very young kids, and he had recently become the "stay-at-home parent." He was also a diesel mechanic in the Massachusetts Army National Guard part-time. Rick ran his home like an Army Basic

Training Unit. He wore either camouflaged or all-black army fatigues all day long. He came to the state's attention after numerous neighbors complained that he was screaming at his kids all day long like the drill instructor from the movie *Full Metal Jacket*. I think he was overwhelmed by his responsibilities and he decided to make certain the kids stayed in line. (They were all kindergarten age or younger.) It was a stupid thing to do, and he was an incredibly stupid guy.

Eventually, the state took his kids away from him and his wife. After continuous "interrogation" by social services, they got one of the kids to claim sexual abuse. There was no way. The guy was nuts—not a pervert. Numerous cases have shown how different social workers go out of their way to "plant" thoughts of sexual abuse into the minds of extremely young children, and I'm certain this was one of those cases.

Rick spent all day writing down practically everything that took place in the block as a letter to his grandmother (like Charlie Sheen in the movie *Platoon*). When he wasn't writing that stuff, unfortunately, he was reading it to everyone. He even came up with ridiculous nicknames for everyone. I was mystified when I found out he called me Giggles DeCoste until I thought it through. Every time I spoke with the guy, everything he was saying was so outrageous that I was continually laughing in his face. (God, that sounds so mean!) So in that way, I guess I had earned the name. He was still awaiting trial when I left, so I have no idea what happened to him.

* * *

The worst night there took place on an incredibly cold February night. We had all watched the late news at 11:00 p.m. and had heard the weather forecast: extremely high winds, temperature to fall to around minus 20. Even the high-rise building was swaying slightly in the wind. Everyone, including me, went to bed as usual after the news. (The guards had started leaving the cell doors open until after the late news.) Some guys were still watching late-night comedy shows when I fell asleep. At around 3:00 a.m., I awoke to a hard-blowing wind and freezing cold. The guards were all wrapped up in heavy winter clothing and, while laughing hysterically, were going around behind the chain-link fence, opening up all the windows. Some inmates were yelling, but I felt that that would only increase the guard's sadistic pleasure, so I pulled my blanket up over my head and shivered uncontrollably. God was kind to me; I quickly fell asleep. (Of course, when people actually freeze to death, that's what takes place at the end—they fall asleep. Permanently.)

* * *

As the second week was nearing its mid-point, I was now emerging from the drug withdrawal state, and the hallucinations gradually ended. I was brought up to see Dr. Braun again, and this time, I told him about my extreme overuse of Xanax. He was absolutely shocked. He said that with Xanax, unless there is a controlled detoxification, many people have fatal seizures. I made a joke saying, "Guess I'm not that lucky." It then took me forty-five minutes to convince the guy that I wasn't suicidal. At the end of our session, as I was almost out the door, Braun called out, "Wait, Kevin! Are you hearing any voices?" I cracked up and answered, "No."

It's hard to describe an approaching court date knowing that no matter what happens, you're on your way to a state prison. The term everyone used was "going upstate." It's not a pleasant thought. However, I had either developed a defense mechanism or had become hardened—probably the former—because I was somewhat numb regarding any feelings of fear. I had developed a "deal with it when it happens" approach to everything.

There was a popular Motel 6 ad on both radio and television where, at the end, the folksy guy talking would say, "Motel 6, we'll leave the light on for you." One night, Rick came over to me looking very curious, and he asked me, "How can you be so calm when you're about to go upstate?" I had a short conversation with him after which he ended by saying, "Well, good luck." I don't know why, but I said, "Don't worry about me, Rick." Then I said, "Oh, and Rick?" Rick looked over at me, and I finished, "We'll leave the light on for you." Rick exploded! Not in anger at me but in a frenzied sense of fear.

"That's not happening to me, I didn't do anything!" I laughed and said, "Doesn't matter, I didn't either. The jury just didn't care." Then Rick went basically nuts making endless speeches about how he would defeat the evil Commonwealth of Massachusetts.

And then it took an absolutely bizarre turn. I was sitting on the floor with three other inmates and Rick began a wild-eyed speech. "Do you think the Army is going to let that happen to me?" He went on, "Do you know I'm essential personnel in my Guard unit?" "As a diesel mechanic?" I asked. "Damn right!" Rick continued. "If I'm convicted, the president of the United States will order my release because I'm essential to national security. And if they don't release me, the president will send Delta Force to get me out." Now the entire block was listening. Rick went on. "There will be helicopters and tanks breaking down the prison walls!" Most guys laughed and went back to what they had been doing. Rick climbed up onto his top bunk. I started playing cards with the other guys—right there on the floor. After about twenty minutes, Rick looked at our little group and screamed, "If my National Guard unit's diesel trucks break down because I'm not there—then this country is fucked!" David was quietly shuffling the deck of cards, and he quietly looked up at Rick, and with a cigarette dangling from his lips said, "Fucking shit, Rick, shut the fuck up. You're giving me a headache." Rick started to say something when Tsai jumped in, adding, "Rick, you're one weird fucking dude." Rick flopped down on his bunk and went silent. After the game was over, Tsai, in a rare comedic moment went over to the two telephones and picked up the receiver. "Rick!" Tsai yelled. Rick sat up and looked over. Tsai went on holding the telephone receiver in his hand like he was trying to hand it to Rick and, with his unique accent said, "It's the president. Wants to talk to you. Fucking National Guard trucks are broke down all over the place." "*Fuck!*" Rick screamed. He was silent the rest of the night.

* * *

The day of sentencing arrived. I was brought to a room, and they put chains on my ankles and one around my waist, to which my hands were handcuffed. Then I went to see a probation officer who was to give a presentencing report to the judge. The officer was an older gentleman with gray hair and glasses. I immediately told him I was innocent. At some point, I told him how, on the stand, Ray had obviously regurgitated a memorized script that had been written for him. The officer seemed doubtful. Then I quoted Ray as having said that I had told him, "If you tell anyone, I'll seek revenge on you somehow." I looked at the guy and asked, "Who the hell talks like that?"

The officer looked at me and answered, "No one." Then seemingly thinking out loud, he said, "maybe a guy would say 'If you say anything, I'll kill you' or something like that." Then he went through a folder and said, "Aw, damn! Your jury was deliberating on the Friday before a three-day weekend. They would have convicted Mother Teresa in order not to come back the following Tuesday. Chances are you got screwed." I didn't know what to say. I went silent.

From there, I went to a holding cell near the courtroom. My sister Janice and my attorney came in. Jack showed me a paper, a victim witness impact statement. Ray had obviously filled the form out—this time without outside help. It pissed me off. Shortly after I had first met Ray at Lakeside, he had told me, in a long rambling speech, why he didn't like or trust male staff members. Now he had written down that same speech, word for word, except now he claimed that all that was due to my "abusing him." Jack said, "He can read this out loud if he wants. We may have to endure that." Then Jack said that he had to go get a copy of the probation officer's presentencing report.

When Jack had left, my sister told me that I had to go out there and emphatically tell the judge that I was innocent. I truly love my sister, and I know she loves me, but she didn't understand how these things work. Even if the judge believed me, he had to abide by the jury's verdict. If he didn't believe me, proclaiming my innocence would have a disastrous impact. Judges view that as "a total lack of remorse" of a defendant "failing to take responsibility for his crime." In both newspapers and on television news, I had read and watched judges give such defendants the maximum sentence. I know she was disappointed, but I told her I couldn't do that. Then she left. A few minutes later, Jack came back with the presentencing report in his hands, and he seemed happy. "This is good," he told me "Finally something good might happen." Then Jack told me, "Your sister is going to ask to address the judge. That's OK, he can't hold anything *she* says against you. I'll see you out there."

The elderly court officer, the same guy that was there during my trial, came out to get me. I was ushered into a side bench area of the courtroom. I looked around. Seated toward the back and to the left was Ray and, right next to him, Tyler. They would not make eye contact with me. My mom and sister were near the front in the center. Ron Callahan was in the center but way behind my family. Then there was a guy who looked like a monkey. He reminded me of someone from high school that the kids used to call Chimbazee behind his back, but I wasn't certain. (What the hell would he be doing there? If it was him, he now looked ten times more like a chimp than he did in high school.) Kevin Johnson was at his desk and Jack Kaufman at his.

Johnson got up and asked, "Is June Swanson here? June Swanson? Is Ray's mother June here?" I have no idea why he asked all that. He had to have known damn well she wasn't there. The only one of Ray's life events that she had ever shown up for was his birth. Perhaps he wanted to remind the judge that Ray did, in fact, have a mother and that hopefully that would influence the judge's sentencing.

As Johnson went on, his little "speech" sickened me. I hadn't done a damn thing to Ray other than take the little prick out to lunch and get him a birthday gift. For some reason, Ray, perhaps heavily pressured by Tyler, was out to destroy me, and for that, his weapon of choice was his lying mouth. I tuned out much of what Johnson had to say, though he infuriated me by praising "Ray's courage" in turning me in. Courage? So it takes courage to be a pathological liar? Johnson wrapped up by saying, "Your Honor, let's send a message to the children of the Commonwealth that we take such crimes very seriously." I'll be perfectly honest. I sincerely believe that Johnson knew that I was innocent. If I'm wrong, God forgive me. Earlier, before the trial, I had told Jack that I believed that Johnson knew Ray was lying. Jack had replied, "Maybe." I then asked, "Yet he'll prosecute me anyway?" Jack said, "He wants to win."

Jack came next. He had a copy of a package from Westfield State University of my academic transcripts and personal recommendations from both college professors and work supervisors. The judge had read them. He also presented letters from my Spiritual Father Charles Weiher and my Notre Dame classmate, Fr. John Patrick Riley. Jack told the judge, "You can see what a kind and sensitive man my client is. Judge, I think Mr. DeCoste would be an extremely good candidate for the bracelet program—with house arrest." Though I knew that was wishful thinking, I was praying the judge would go for it.

Then Jack said, "Judge, Mr. DeCoste's sister Janice would like to address the court. The judge replied, "She can't. She has no standing to address the court." Jack pleaded, "Please, Your Honor." The judge relented. I can hardly remember a thing of what Janice said. However, as I sat there listening to her and saw how absorbed the judge was in what she had to say *and* in how well she spoke, I realized that if she had been my lawyer, I would not have been convicted. I also thought to myself, *God, she speaks a million times better than Jack Kaufman*. And then I began to realize that hiring Jack Kaufman had been a horrific mistake. However, it had been a decision made under severe duress.

Then everyone sat down, and the judge began a long conversation with the two women whom I guess were his assistants. One of the women came over to me and said, "You cannot ever work with children under the age of eighteen. You must complete and pay for a sex offender treatment program. Do you understand all this?" I just answered, "Yes."

Then the judge began his speech. "Count one, you are sentenced to five years at the Massachusetts Correctional Institution at Cedar Junction—sentence suspended. Count two, not less than thirty months, not more than forty months at the Massachusetts Correctional Institution at Cedar Junction. You will complete and pay for a sex offender treatment program. We are adjourned."

(Two counts: Ray falsely claimed that we had each performed oral sex on each other.)

Not exactly a long-winded speech, but in truth, the only words I had heard were "Cedar Junction," better known as Walpole!

As the old court officer escorted me back to a different holding cell, I looked at him and I said, "I can't believe this—I didn't do anything!" To my surprise, the officer seemed a bit choked up, and he replied, "I know you didn't. I was at your trial." So a man who had probably spent his entire adult life in that judge's courtroom could see that I was innocent. I now seriously wondered if what the probation officer had said about my not having a chance on a Friday before a long holiday weekend had been true. Yet at that point, it really didn't matter.

Again, Jack came back. "Now what?" I asked him. Jack told me, "You will go to the prison in Concord. After that, I imagine, since you have no prior record and you're not violent, they will send you to a minimum-security institution—possibly the prison farm in Concord."

As "nice" and positive as all that sounded, it didn't sound true. Jack had been at this game for a long time and much longer as an assistant district attorney than as a defense attorney. He had to know that what he was saying was just not going to happen. Then he left and did not return. I would see him three years later.

* * *

I was in a cell in the center of three. There were two guys that I couldn't see on either side of me. A jail guard came in and gave each of us a container of milk and two Alaska salmon sandwiches. That was just great. I hated milk and fish. I wasn't going to have lunch that day. One of the two guys yelled out, "Hey! You in the middle! What are you in for?" (I would hear those words a thousand times over the next three years.) I ignored the question and asked out loud, "Anyone want these sandwiches?" Both guys said that they did, and through the bars, seeing only the other two guys' arms, I passed them the fish. One of the two also got my milk.

After a few hours, I was brought down to a garage area where there were several sheriff's department "paddy wagons." Then the deputies who did transport—mobile jail guards—started running their mouths. One began talking to the other, making sure I could hear every word: "Thirty to forty months!" to which the other quipped, "Thirty to forty months? What the fuck kind of sentence is that?" I had to tune the idiots out. During my time at the jail, I had learned a great defense mechanism. Somehow, I can't even now explain how, I got to the point where the guards became like inanimate objects to me. They would be there, but I would hardly notice. They would speak, and I would hear the sound yet not make out the words. They were in the room yet were like furniture or lamps; I didn't see them as people being present.

Once in the back of the truck, however, I did start listening. The two jail guards were starting a campaign to try and scare me. "Are you sure you know the way to Walpole?" one asked the other. The van made its way to Route 93 North. "I'm not sure this is the quickest way to Walpole," the clown in the passenger seat said. It was a painful ride because the route up 93 that they were taking was the way to my house from Boston that I had driven a million times, from the first time that I had driven into Boston with my mom as a little boy, to the times I drove myself to school in Boston or work in Boston, all the way up to the end of the second day of my trial a couple of weeks ago. It was a surreal picture. The sun was just starting to set as we passed the exit that could take me home. At that moment, I recalled the words of Saint Augustine, when he had said of God, "We never truly rest until we rest in Thee." In other words, there is no true happiness until we are with God in his Heavenly Kingdom. I continued to reflect on that for a few minutes.

Then we turned onto Route 128 South. "Oh yeah," the driver said. "This is the fastest way to Walpole." That was the truth. Route 128, also known as Route 95, would take us to Walpole. I began to steel myself for whatever I might find when we got to Walpole. The jail guards continued their banter about Walpole, but eventually, I tuned them out.

After about twenty-five minutes, we made the turn onto Route 2 West. That was the way to Concord. Jack had been right about one thing after all. Humorously, the two deputy morons continued their Walpole jokes. However, I knew the way to Concord, and I was somewhat relieved. During 1975 and 1976, I was an auxiliary police officer in the town of Concord. One day, I was riding in the police cruiser with a sergeant and we passed the Concord prison. It had snowed, and there were inmates outside of the wall with a couple of guards. They were shoveling the snow off the sidewalk surrounding the place. The inmates started yelling at us and giving us the finger. The sergeant muttered, "Fuck you bastards." I turned and looked at the sergeant and, with all the enthusiasm of a twenty-year-old, said, "I would love to see what the inside of that place looks like." The sergeant laughed and asked, "Are you out of your fucking mind?" Now, twenty-one years later, I was about to find out.

When I got out of the van, I wanted to do something, anything I could to piss off the jail guards. So when I was free of them, as cheerfully as I could make myself sound, I said, "Thanks for the ride, guys!" They just shook their heads and walked back to their truck.

# MCI Concord

Now the chains were off again. I was in a huge garage-like area that had two cages. Those cages were each big enough for a tiger or a bear, but instead, they were for people. I was placed into one of those cages with another guy. He stuck out his hand and introduced himself as Terry.

Terry's story broke my heart. He had been living in the Midwest with his dog. He was either on probation or parole from Massachusetts. Somehow, and he never told me how exactly, Terry violated his probation/parole. He was arrested in his apartment in the middle of the night. He had no idea what had happened to his dog. (If you love dogs, you know just how horrible that must have been—for both of them.) Then after processing and a court hearing, he was transported back to Massachusetts by deputy US marshals. He wasn't flown back; he was driven back in the rear of the same type of truck that had just brought me there from Cambridge only about twenty minutes away. It took a number of days. At night, the marshals dropped Terry off at a local jail facility while they went to a motel. In the morning, they picked him up and resumed their trip. For three meals every day, it was McDonald's. Terry got a cup of water and one hamburger. The marshals had huge extra-value meals. Each day, Terry had three cups of water and three hamburgers. That was for three or four days in a row. Yet surprisingly, he was in fairly good spirits.

After a couple of hours, we were told to follow a guard. At that point, we were somehow separated. I went to the room and there were two inmates—one black, one white—behind a counter. They gave me my prison uniforms: white T-shirts and boxer shorts, blue jeans, a couple of light-blue button shirts, and a denim jacket. The denim jacket smelled exactly like it had been used as a rug in an animal's barn. The jacket stunk! And I could tell that it was brand-new. As I was getting all these things, one of the two inmates asked what size shirt I wore. I said, "I think a 17." The two of them looked at each other and roared with laughter. Apparently, that was one of their favorite "funny" moments with most new arrivals. As soon as they regained their composure, one of them asked, "Small, medium, large, extra large?" I wanted to be safe since I knew if I got one that didn't fit, they would probably not replace it, so instead of large, I asked for extra-large. They also gave me a set of sheets and two blankets. I am not sure what I looked like during all this, but as I turned to leave, the black inmate called out to me, "Hey, man, don't be worried. You're going to be all right. OK?" "Thanks," I replied. For whatever it was worth, I really did appreciate his saying that.

Next, I followed this enormous bald white guard to a smaller room. There he had an electronic machine that looked like a huge arcade video game. It was for taking fingerprints and photos. After both were done, he asked if I had a driver's license "on the outside." I told him I did, and he typed my license number into the huge machine. (I wish I had told him that I did not have a license. After I got out, if the cops pulled me over and ran my license through their computer, it would say *sex-offender*. Try getting a verbal or written warning as opposed to a "money" citation after that.) When he was done, he handed me a prison photo ID that bore the number W62261. The *W* stood for Walpole. That didn't exactly make my day any better.

My next stop was at a medical room where they asked if I had any medical issues. I told them I took medication for high blood pressure. They wrote down the information. Then the staff handed me a small plastic bag, which contained a toothbrush, a tiny tube of toothpaste, and a bar of soap. Lastly, they gave me two sandwiches wrapped in plastic and told me to wait for yet another guard. I opened up one sandwich. The two pieces of bread were easily the largest single slices of bread that I had ever seen. Between them was the thinnest slice of bologna I had ever seen. One lousy thin slice of bologna! And the same with sandwich number 2. Yet since it was night and since I hadn't been able to eat the fish back at court for lunch, I ate both sandwiches in a matter of seconds. They tasted like crap.

While I was waiting, I opened up my "dental" bag. I looked at the tiny white tube of toothpaste. It read "Toothpaste. Product of China. Guaranteed no animal fat." Where in hell did the state buy that shit from? I was sickened. At last a guard showed up and told me to go to Unit B. I was perplexed and asked him, "Where is that?" He pointed toward a door and said, "Go through that door and keep walking. You'll find it eventually." Such a helpful guy!

I walked out the door and saw a group of newer brick buildings. An inmate was walking by, so I asked, "Do you know where Unit B is?" He said nothing but pointed at one of the buildings. I said "Thanks" and went inside. This was like a prison movie. There was a desk. Across from the desk were three levels of cells. Stairs went up the sides of the cells. There were no guards present. Two inmates, one white and one Hispanic, were standing at the desk. The white guy asked, "Which cell do you want?" I knew he had no say in which cell I would get, so I answered, "Doesn't matter." Then the Spanish guy asked, "The real question is, who do you want to share the cell with—white, black, Asian, Spanish?" I was exhausted and a bit tired of all this bullshit, so I replied, "I really don't give a fuck." The Spanish guy smiled and said, "Well, OK then. You're my kind of guy. What's your name?" When I told him, he picked a piece of paper off the desk and said, "You're in 205." I knew he was right, but I couldn't help but wonder where was the guard who should be telling me this? Just to be safe, I reached for the paper he was holding and there it was: "Kevin DeCoste, 205."

I climbed the stairs and entered cell 205. The cells had solid steel doors with a small window. There were no bars in this modern prison building. Inside was a white guy who looked as though he hadn't shaved—or washed for a month. He was half asleep on the lower bunk. At first I tried not to disturb him as I made up my bunk, then I realized that he seemed to be in a semi-coma anyway, so I finished the bunk without caring how much motion I caused.

Later, I would find out that my cell mate's name was Ralph. He was an idiot who lived in Boston. He had been out on parole. One day, he ran into a guy in town selling VCRs out of his car trunk. He bought one for sixty dollars. About twenty yards from his purchase, two Boston cops pulled up next to him, laughed, and asked, "New purchase?" He was arrested and sent back to prison. How stupid was this guy? At that time, 1997, VCRs were on the way out, being replaced by DVDs, DVD players, and DVDRs. I said to him, "Ralph, they sell new VCRs at Target for thirty to forty bucks." To my surprise, he just shrugged his shoulders! The guy could have bought a non-stolen, brand-new VCR for half of what he had paid—and not got arrested and sent back to prison. It just blew my mind.

That first night, we were eventually told, "Count time." All of us had to stand in front of our cell while a guard, standing at the desk on the ground floor, counted up the inmates. I'm sure he would have had no idea if a guy switched places with another guy from an entirely different unit. I could see every inmate's reflection in the huge pane of glass behind the guard's desk. On the tier below, I could see an inmate that, well, looked like he shouldn't be there. He looked to be about sixteen years old. I guess he must have noticed my concentrating on him because in the glass reflection, he looked up and raised his hand as if in a wave. Impulsively, I did the same. The kid smiled and dropped his hand. We would talk the next day. For now, it was time to try to get some sleep. Strangely, I fell asleep seconds after my head hit the pillow.

The morning brought another "count time." I had noticed that once during the night, a guard had shone his flashlight into the cell for about two seconds. Since there was no way out of the cell, I suppose it was sort of an "Are they still alive?" check. The guard said to go to breakfast, and while leaving the cell block, the young guy from the night before ran up to me and started talking away like we were lifelong friends. After a few minutes, he stopped talking mid-sentence and said, "Oh, I'm Tim." I laughed and introduced myself as well. Tim had gotten to Concord a few days before me. He was there for armed robbery. He told me he was sentenced to eight to ten years. Then he told me he was eighteen years old. I shouldn't have been surprised at all—things happen—but I was actually shocked that an eighteen-year-old had committed armed robbery. It was obvious that Tim was an extremely nice kid, so I really wanted to ask him why he had robbed someone, but I figured that if I questioned him about his "crime," soon after, he would ask me a series of questions as well. I switched the topic of conversation to the food at Concord.

"The food here sucks," Tim began, "and there is no salt or pepper." The dining hall looked like something straight out of a Hollywood prison movie. You entered the hall single file. You passed along a counter, picked up a stainless-steel tray, and inmate workers placed food on your tray. Then you took a seat on one side of a stainless steel table that was about seventy-five yards long. Stainless-steel seats were attached to the table and swung out from under it. (No detached chairs, as they could be used as a weapon in a fight or riot.) While you would sit next to the person that you entered with, you had no control over who you would sit across from. We had powdered eggs and an apple. I know that the majority of people in the world hate powdered eggs, but I found that, when scrambled, I really couldn't tell the difference, and I'm pretty choosy about the food I eat. Eggs without salt, however, are not exactly "tasty." After the other side of the table filled in, the inmate across from Tim and I pulled out a Bic pen. He then took the cover off. There was no ink cartridge in it—it was full of salt! After seasoning his own eggs, he handed the pen over to me. I used a little and made a motion to the guy indicating that I wanted to share some with Tim. "Go ahead," he told me. I probably should have kept quiet, but I asked the shaker's owner where he got the salt. Lowering his voice to a conspiratorial whisper, he replied, "I work in the kitchen in the afternoon." As luck would have it, I never again sat near the "salt man." It would be three more months before I would be able to salt or pepper my prison food a second time.

After breakfast, we returned to the block and found that both Tim and I were scheduled for an orientation class later in the day. On the bulletin board, there was also a notice regarding voluntary AIDS testing. Tim asked if I wanted to go with him and get tested. I told him I didn't, so he took off for the medical building. (There was no point—I hadn't ever had sex with anyone.)

As I headed up the stairs to my cell, I spotted an elderly black inmate sitting on the stairs. He looked painfully lonely, so I sat down next to him and started a conversation. The man's name was Willy. I could tell that he was an extremely gentle guy. As we spoke, an hour and a half passed, yet it was mostly small talk. I noticed that like my own inmate number, Willy's number began with the letter *W*, for "Walpole." I suddenly got depressed and told him, "I'm not looking forward to going there." Willy chuckled and told me, "Just because you got a Walpole sentence doesn't mean you're going to Walpole." I was stunned! I was happy! Willy went on to explain that in the past, guys were given either a Concord sentence or a Walpole sentence. Apparently, at one time, a young first-time offender could get a Concord sentence from a judge. That judge's discretion had, at some point, been eliminated by the state legislature. Guys with a Concord sentence were eligible for parole much earlier than their Walpole counterparts, and often, they ended up in minimum security. I met only a very few inmates whose number began with the letter *C*. However, your inmate number is forever. If, say, you went to prison in the 1960s and got a Concord inmate number, then you got out but decades later committed another crime and came back to prison in the 1990s, they simply gave you your old number back.

Willy had been in prison many years before. Eventually he was released on parole and moved to Georgia with his wife. They had a small pig farm. His brother also lived in the same area. One day, his brother went rabbit hunting and shot quite a few of them. Having more rabbits than he and his family could possibly eat, Willy's brother brought some over to Willy's farm. The two brothers sat around drinking lemonade and just talking for a few hours, then his brother took off. His brother wasn't driving; he had walked over after hunting and before returning to his own place. Willy was still sitting on the front porch drinking his lemonade with his wife when his parole officer stopped by for an "inspection." Willy and the parole officer went into the kitchen. Right next to the freezer, where his brother had put the rabbits he had given Willy was his brother's shotgun. The parole officer arrested Willy on the spot. "Convicted felon in possession of a firearm." You would think that such an "accident" would be confirmed at some type of hearing and Willy would be allowed to return home. It didn't happen. Willy was transported back to Massachusetts and ordered to complete his original sentence. (Years earlier, President Ronald Reagan had called the Soviet Union the Evil Empire. From the moment I heard Willy's story onward, I would always call Massachusetts "the real Evil Empire.")

For the rest of my time in that "orientation" cell block, I would be spending most of my time with either Willy or Tim. They were on opposite ends of the age spectrum, yet they were both really good friends, though after I moved to another unit, I would gradually lose touch with Tim. Eventually, I learned that Willy had spent a considerable number of years in Walpole. As time went on, he told me many stories of the horrific violence he had witnessed there. He would actually physically shake while recounting some of those events, and I could tell that whatever he may have been convicted of, it was a total mistake or miscarriage of justice. The man had absolutely no capacity for violence whatsoever.

One story has always stuck out in my mind. I guess Willy was assigned to work in a wood shop at Walpole. He told me that one day, there had been an inmate working with a portable circular saw. As I would come to learn, if a guard decided he didn't like you for any reason, he would harass you nonstop—mostly verbally, though not always. Anyway, as Willy told me, a guard was endlessly taunting the inmate with the saw. At first, the inmate just asked the guy to leave him alone. As the verbal barrage went on, the inmate became angrier and eventually, with quite a few swears, he told the guy to stop. Yet the guard persisted. Finally, the inmate turned toward the guard and sawed him open from the top of his stomach on down. The guard died right there on the wood shop floor. When Willy finished the story, he just shook his head—and there were tears in his eyes.

One day a young, very big black inmate came up to me and began to speak to me—sort of the way I imagine a Sioux warrior might speak to General Custer. It was as though he didn't really want any interaction with me at all. "Me and the brothers appreciate all the time you've been spending with Pops," he said. (Old guys in prison are often called Pops.) He went on, "So thanks." I sort of wanted to laugh at the guy, but he was way too big and way too serious. I looked at him and replied, "No need to thank me. Willy is my friend." "OK then," he answered. Then he just walked away.

One morning, the block's guard called Willy over. "Pack up your shit. You're moving to Newline," he told him. Ever the gentleman, Willy simply replied, "Yes, sir." The guard handed him some trash bags. Willy packed up his belongings in the bags, and then we had to say goodbye. He told me that Newline was just on the other side of the prison and that we would "still run into each other from time to time." After Willy left, I went and sat on the same steps where I had met him less than a week before, and for the first time in prison, I cried. It wouldn't be the last time.

Tim wanted me to accompany him to the prison gym. I had always worked out—with less than great results —but I was so damn bored I would have tried anything. After an hour or so I was spent. Tim seemed shocked. "Are you hurt?" he asked. "No," I told him, "I'm spent." Tim looked incredulous. "Why?" he inquired. I started to laugh and told him, "Because I'm forty-one and you're eighteen." Tim laughed—that he understood. For another hour, I just "spotted" him on the bench while talking his ear off. My mouth seldom tires out.

Later that same day, I went to the prison library. There I found that Terry, the guy from the "cage" on my first day, had already secured an inmate job working in the library. We spoke for a few seconds, then I whispered to him, "Can you get any pens?" I could see that he instantly understood what I meant, and though he could only get me a pencil, I was extremely happy to get it. I was learning a brutal lesson about personal "property" in prison. At the Cambridge Jail, I had purchased quite a few necessities: soap, shampoo, toothpaste, toothbrush, deodorant, pens, writing paper, and stamps. When I went to court and was sent to Concord, that all remained behind. I guess my former companions got whatever was left behind. The jail guards at Cambridge had already confiscated my watch and a religious medal.

Those at least were returned to my family. (Some jails in other counties allowed guys to keep their watches, but not Middlesex.)

I needed a pencil to fill out the order form for the prison canteen—not to mention write letters. It would be two weeks before I could submit the order and then an additional week before I could actually pick up my stuff. In the meantime, I had to shower with a tiny piece of soap that the prison had given me. The lack of an antiperspirant, however, drove me nearly insane. Thank God it was still winter! If that wasn't bad enough, eventually my tiny tube of "no animal fat" Chinese toothpaste ran out. I couldn't stand having a foul-tasting mouth! I made my way back to the medical building one day and asked a dentist there if I could get another tube of toothpaste. The miserable prick looked at me and said, "No, those are only for new guys." I asked, "What should I brush my teeth with?" Sarcastically, the dentist replied, "Use water." At the end of time, I hope God makes that guy wait one hundred years before letting him brush his teeth! A few days later I noticed that Ralph never brushed his teeth. He never, at least while we shared a cell, ever took a shower either. All he ever seemed to do was sleep. One day, I was thinking about asking him if I could use his toothpaste. I had a strange feeling that he would probably say no. So much to my discredit, one day, I simply stole his unused tube of Chinese, "no animal fat" toothpaste.

My mom sent me a card, and she enclosed some postage stamps. I was summoned to see an IPS officer. IPS stands for "Internal Perimeter Security Team." They act as detectives in inmate cases and as "internal affairs" in the case of the guards misbehaving. The regular guards wore blue pants and light-blue shirts. IPS officers wore black pants and black shirts. They looked like a SWAT team. This particular IPS was OK. He told me that I couldn't have the stamps because some inmates had stamps sent to them with "micro-dots." "What's a micro-dot?" I asked. He seemed surprised that I didn't know. Apparently a very small sized dot of LSD can be attached to the back of the type of stamp that used to require licking to make it stick on the envelope. One such lick and the licker would be off on quite a drug trip. If an inmate needed stamps, he had to buy them through the prison canteen.

The next morning, a guard called me down to his desk in the cell block immediately after the count. He unceremoniously handed me two trash bags and said, "Go pack your shit and after breakfast, go to unit A-3. (The newer building units in Concord all had letter-number designations. However, I actually cannot recall the exact unit numbers, and so I'm just giving them any letter-number designation.) I packed up my stuff while Ralph slept. He had set a new record—he had gotten out of bed for the "count," and five minutes later, he was fast asleep again. I wouldn't miss him.

After breakfast, I went to the medical building to stand in the medication line. I took Atenolol for high blood pressure. While standing in line, the guy behind me came up way too close to me. I stood frozen. Did this guy perhaps have some type of blade weapon?" (In the prisons I was in, any bladed, cutting weapon was called a *shank*. To be stabbed or cut by one of those is to be *shanked*. It's a common prison term, though once, a guy that had been in another state's prison system said there it was called a *shiv*.)

He whispered in my ear, "My name is Mario. Mario," then he stepped back. A minute later, he moved up against me again and said, "My name is Mario. Please don't forget me. Please! Do not, not forget me." All I could think of was some movie I had watched about political prisoners in South America disappearing after arrest. It was an exceedingly strange encounter. I have no idea at all what it was about. I have to laugh now because I never did forget him. When it was my turn a nurse handed me a month's supply of Atenolol. I guess if it's not a narcotic they would rather you take care of them as opposed to your taking up a space in their line every day. I returned to the block, grabbed my stuff and headed over to A-3.

Before going on, I need to discuss ethnicity. My Father was half French and half Irish. My mother, on the other hand, was entirely Irish. Having said that, in the three years that I was confined in the Massachusetts prison system, nearly 100 percent of the "troublemakers" were young guys of Irish descent, generally in their early twenties. (Irish guys in their late thirties and older were usually very nice guys.) These guys most often lived either in South Boston, Charlestown, or Somerville. I have no idea why this is. There seems to be a public impression on the part of white people that all the trouble in prison stems from black inmates. I found that except in very rare cases, that was simply not true. If anything, the black inmates seemed more intelligent. Again, I have no idea why. (Though once, while talking about drug dealers with a black inmate, he told me, "The difference between black drug dealers and white drug dealers is that black dealers are not stupid enough to start using the 'products' they sell.")

Once I got to A-3, I was assigned to a cell with a twenty-year-old named Doherty, an Irish guy from Dedham, a town bordering Boston. This guy was hostile from the very beginning. "What the fuck are you in for?" he asked. The question and the forcefulness with which it was asked temporarily shocked me, and unfortunately, I said nothing. "Oh fucking shit!" he exclaimed. "I can't share a cell with a skinner (a sex offender)!" At that moment, an inmate that was moping the tier's floor while everyone else was locked in their cell, came up to the door and asked, "What are you yelling about, Dotty?" Doherty seemed hysterical, "I don't know—I got a guy in here who doesn't want to talk about his crime, and you know what that means! Something will have to be done about this!" "OK," the guy outside said, "we all know what to do."

This was definitely not going well. I could almost "feel" an assault or a knife attack coming. I made a decision. If I was going to die in prison, then I would take myself out rather than let some self-righteous, low-brow punk(s) do it. I could fight—the Army had trained me well—but how many would come at me? Would there be weapons? I quietly wrote a letter home and explained what I was going to do. After that, I placed the thirty-day supply of Atenolol in my pocket. If things went badly, I would take all of them at once—hopefully stopping my heart with a minimum of pain. I also spoke silently with God. I told Him, "If I have to do this, please don't send me to hell. I sincerely believe Lord that the guilt of this sin should be given to this animal, Doherty."

Every hour, the cell doors are open for twelve to fifteen minutes. It's called *movement*. You use that time to go to a class, medical appointments, the yard, gym, etc. When the door opened, I was careful to walk out with as much "slow dignity" as I could muster. I walked out of the block and ran into a guard who looked surprisingly like former unsuccessful presidential candidate Pat Buchannan(?). I told him I thought I was being set up for a violent attack. His thoughts took off in a strange direction. "You look like a cop," he said. "Shit, is that it? Did someone find out you used to be a cop?" That, of course, wasn't the case, though I did work for Emerson Campus Police. I thought this might be my best chance to survive. I looked at him and said, "Yeah, I was a cop." The guard wrote down my name, unit, and cell number. Then surprisingly, he told me to go back to my cell.

Once locked into the cell with Doherty again, I got a small cup that I had been given by Tim out of my "trash bag," filled it with water, and kept my hands on the container of pills. I also kept studying Doherty, trying to figure out the best way to attack him, should that become an option. Doherty was pacing back and forth in the tiny cell like some type of caged animal. I felt a certain calm come over me, and I said to him, "You should relax before you have a heart attack." "Don't talk to me!" he screamed. For some reason, I no longer cared how upset he was.

After about thirty minutes, the cell door opened. The guard I had spoken with was standing there, and he said, "DeCoste, you're wanted at IPS. Take your stuff with you." Again, as slowly as I could, I picked up my belongings, poured my cup of water into the sink, and walked out. The cell door closed behind me. (This is a solid steel door, not one with bars.) Once outside, A-3 "Pat" told me where IPS was located and told me to go there. When I tried to say thanks, he just turned and walked away. Most likely, he had gone to IPS and they had looked me up on the computer and now he knew what I had been convicted of.

When I got to the IPS office, I entered and stood there while an officer basically ignored me for ten minutes. Finally, the guy looked over and said, "Take a seat," then he left the office. My mind must have been a mess because I made a huge mistake—I sat behind the desk in the officer's chair! The next thing I knew, the IP was back, screaming like a drill sergeant, "Get the fuck out of my fucking chair! What the fuck is wrong with you?" "Just a mistake," I muttered. "Shit, you do look like a cop! Where did you work?" "Emerson

College Police," I replied. "Oh fuck!" he started again. "That's not being a full cop, that's like being half a cop!" Strangely, I thought to myself, *More of a cop than you are!* but I kept silent. "So who the fuck did you rape?" he continued. "No one," I answered. "Who accused you then?" he went on. "Some kid," I told him. "How old?" he persisted. "Fifteen," I replied. "Oh shit! My son is fifteen!" I had had enough. Without standing, I screamed back at him, "The little prick lied! I didn't do a fucking thing to him!"

"Oh my god! the officer yelled. "I'm trying to fucking help you and you're yelling at me!" I was now beside myself. "What would you do if someone was accusing *you* of doing something *you* didn't do?" I hollered. And for some reason, that seemed to calm him down.

"OK, OK. I'll get you out of there. There is a unit called Newline. Downstairs it's all guys with parole violations. Upstairs it's sex offenders. Fuck, at least you'll be safe up there," he said. Then he picked up the phone and called Newline. He gave them my name and asked if they had a bed upstairs. He looked at me and nodded his head in the affirmative. He got off the phone, gave me directions to Newline, and sent me on my way. No "goodbye" or "good luck"—we just silently parted ways.

There were two things that the IP had said that at first failed to register in my mind. First, "Newline." That was where Willy had been sent to. I remembered that the next morning. However, my greatest memory failure was in forgetting until months later that he had said that the upstairs of Newline was all sex offenders. I should have remembered that.

* * *

The Newline building was old—really old. It was a long wooden structure painted white. I entered through a door that opened up to a guard's desk on the first floor. The guard sitting there was an older guy with white hair. He looked at me and said, "Stairs to the right—through that door. Go upstairs."

I climbed the stairs, and at the top was the ugliest inmate I had ever seen. He looked like a poster boy for alcoholism. Then again, he looked like the poster boy for drug abuse, poor mental health, poor personal hygiene, poor dental hygiene, bad haircuts… He stared at me—obviously trying to intimidate me. Even though he was quite big, it didn't work. I had already been through enough. I would later learn his name was Steve Hogg, and though I never said it out loud, in my mind he was and always will be Steve the Hog.

A guard with longish hair and a mustache came out of the office and said, "Follow me." I followed him down to a cell where he raised his hand and someone in the office behind us opened the door. (No electric doors here, there was a hand crank in the guard's office.) I stepped inside, and the door closed behind me. There was a small, heavy-set guy on the lower bunk who seemed to be sleeping. Since I had to make the bed, I turned on the cell's overhead light. For some reason, I was extremely angry over the day's events, and without considering the poor guy on the bottom bunk, I started making up my top bunk kind of roughly. When I was finished, the guy on the bottom looked up at me sheepishly and asked, "Excuse me, sir, if you're done, could you turn off the light?" I felt bad for him, but I reached over without saying a word and turned off the light. "Thank you, sir," my new cell mate said.

I have always been amused whenever they show jail or prison cells on television shows. My favorite was on one TV cop show when one of the cops himself was locked up after being framed for something. His police partner came in and asked how he was. The cop in the cell replied, "How do you think I am? I haven't been out of this damn cell for five days already!" *Really?* I thought. *Where have you been going to the bathroom?*

With few exceptions, all jail/prison cells have one distinct feature: a stainless-steel combination sink and toilet. If the cell has a door made up of bars, then basically everyone walking by can watch you crap. A solid steel door and you're lucky—only your cell mate will see you defecate. Either way, it takes some getting used to. That first night at Newline, I awoke in the middle of the night and I definitely had to crap. I got down from my bunk as quietly as possible, pulled down my shorts, and sat on the cold, steel toilet. But something was different about this. The seat was tingling furiously like… like it had a strong electrical current passing through it. I had no choice; I flicked the light on. "Shit!" I screamed out. The entire toilet/sink combination was crawling with cockroaches! Tanner, my new cell mate, looked over, and with a pronounced Southern drawl said, "Oh yeah. It's best not to shit at night." I was sickened. After checking my ass for roaches, I climbed back up onto my bunk and "held it" until morning. Interestingly, no night guard came down the block to see what the yelling had been about. I guess if someone had gotten killed, they would have found out in the morning.

When morning came and the roaches were gone, I got back on the toilet. Just as things "got going" for me, I looked up and a female guard was walking by my cell. I was just frozen still. I don't think it was anything for her. For me, it was severely embarrassing. When count time was about to take place, a guard would yell out, "Count time! Stand for the count!" This, however, was the first time that I had heard a woman yell that out. Somewhere on that second floor, some inmate, seconds after the female guard had announced count time, yelled out, "Cunt time! Stand for the cunt!" The guard ignored that while seemingly the entire building—both the first and second floor—roared with laughter. And of course, one inmate spoke up saying, "That's not funny, man. What are you people laughing at?" That was followed by three or four guys yelling, "Kill yourself!" I cracked up laughing both times.

When breakfast was announced, the doors suddenly opened, and everyone poured out into the hallway and down the stairs. I recalled that in a few prison movies I had watched, that was when someone got stabbed. I was watching everyone around me intently. At the bottom of the stairs, just returning from breakfast, was Willy. He saw me and smiled hugely. I was extremely happy to see him, but I knew stopping at that moment would get me in trouble. Willy yelled out, "Meet me at first movement—we'll walk the yard!" "OK!" I hollered back.

At first movement, Willy and I met up and walked to the snow-covered yard. Walking the running track was out of the question—the snow was simply too deep. We found a picnic table, brushed the snow off, and sat down. As we were talking, I looked up and saw a passenger plane crossing the cloudless sky, leaving a long vapor trail. Willy saw me looking up, and he too started watching the plane trek across the sky. I said, "I wish I were on that plane, no matter where it was going." With a lot of thought and feeling, Willy shook his head slowly and repeated, "No matter where it was going." I think that plane—and what I had said—brought both of our moods down. After an hour of talking, the cold was starting to get to both of us, and we decided to go back to Newline. Willy told me that during both lunch and dinner that the entire building, first and second floor, went at the same time. We agreed to meet at lunchtime.

Once I was back in my cell and "movement" ended, the cell doors were closed. A young, somewhat distinguished-looking black inmate was coming down the hallway, mopping the floor. He stopped at my cell and asked, "So what are you in for?" I told him I had stolen money from my company. He laughed and said, "Aw, c'mon, that's not true." Just then, Steve the Hog started up, "You know how we know that's not true? Because the fucking guards showed us your entire record on their computer." That was disturbing. Was it true, or did they know something from another source? I became determined not to answer the Hog. The black inmate was still mopping near my door, so I asked, "What did you do?" He looked at me and answered, "I stole trade secrets from a computer company and sold them. I should have known better. But I'm young. I can start over again." And with that, he continued mopping down the hallway. The guy seemed a lot more intelligent than the average inmate—I believed him.

Then the Hog started up again. "So, DeCoste, what was it like when you were sucking on that fifteen-year-old boy's dick?" "It didn't happen," I replied. "The computer says it did," he shot back. I let it drop. When the Hog was talking, a number of inmates—I couldn't see who—were yelling, "None of your business, Hogg." I wondered who those inmates were. Then the Hog changed targets. "Hey, Rivera," he shouted, then talking as if he were a cop with a bullhorn, "Mr. Rivera, drop the Skittles and step away from the sandbox." Then he continued, "Hey, Rivera, how many toddlers did you actually fuck up the ass?" Rivera, whoever he was, said nothing.

The Hog and his cell mate were both from the city of Worcester. His cell mate hardly ever spoke, but I could tell he was a complete animal. One day, when an inmate worker was passing me a cup full of ice, Hogg's cell mate grabbed my wrist and tried to break it. I got my arm free by some unknown stroke of luck. What's funny is that a month later, that guy's brother also was assigned to our block, and he was one of the nicest guys I had ever met. It just didn't make sense.

The Hog's cell was to the left of mine. The cell to the right had a guy named Jeremy. According to Jeremy, he was a restaurant owner and the son of a cardiologist. He claimed to be from a very wealthy suburb of Boston. In the prison canteen, you can purchase what looks like a plastic electric coffee pot. Of course its primary use is, in fact, to heat up water, but some talented inmates actually cooked complete meals in those pots—something I was never able to do. Because of the "meals" that Jeremy produced in his pot, I did, in fact, believe that he owned a restaurant on the outside. (For safety reasons, boiling water can be used as a weapon—the pots heated up the water, but not to the boiling point. Usually you had to pay an inmate with mechanical/electrical skills to "fix" the pot so it would boil. When used as a weapon, inmates would often boil baby oil and add sugar—I guess those two "ingredients" increased the target's burn injuries.)

Jeremy was a genuinely likeable guy. He was gregarious and friendly. However, whenever he got into an argument with another inmate who was a sex offender, Jeremy would call the guy a *skinner*. It's just a word, but Jeremy could say *skinner* with the same distaste that President George W. Bush used to say the word *terrorist*.

Jeremy seemingly was always cooking food or just making peanut butter sandwiches and passing them around. At first, I got none of that food. One day, Tanner received a big bowl of spaghetti with tomato sauce from Jeremy. I was lying on the top bunk reading a book while Tanner ate sitting on the edge of the lower bunk. The man was making sounds that were driving me insane. Every couple of seconds, he would start, "Mmmm," followed by the sound of a guy slurping the pasta into his mouth—lips mostly closed—like a four-year-old. After about fifteen minutes of that, I had to look. I wish I hadn't. I sat up and looked down. There was Tanner sitting on the side of his bed, clad only in his boxer shorts. His entire body was splattered with tomato sauce—from his feet to his face. Worse yet, his dick was sticking out of the opening in the front of his shorts, and it too was covered in sauce. "God almighty!" I exclaimed. Tanner looked up—even the lenses of his thick glasses were splattered with sauce. Tanner said, "I'm sorry. I'm making a lot of noise, ain't I? It's just that this is so fucking good." "It's OK," I answered. I then went back to reading, and finally, it hit me just how funny it all was. I nearly died laughing. Tanner got up and asked, "What you laughing about?" I held up my book and told him, "It's a funny book." "Oh," Tanner said, laughing himself. "I don't read much, but I do like a funny story." The book was a biography of Joseph Stalin.

I started to notice something about Steve the Hog. He was friends with, and constantly "praising," inmates that, I knew were raging sex offenders and, well, total wimps. It just didn't sit with his tough "convict" persona. Eventually, from conversations I heard between Tanner and the Hog, I realized that they had both met in the Plymouth County Jail. Tanner had been convicted of raping his thirteen-year-old daughter, so he most definitely would have been in a "protective custody" unit of the jail. So how did he meet the Hog? I began to suspect that the Hog was also a sex offender. Yet to say anything would have certainly led to a fight with the Hog, and from what I could see, there wasn't a single inmate who wanted to do that. I decided it was too risky to bring my suspicions up with anyone. One day, guys were yelling stuff at Tanner—joking, really—about his being from West Virginia. After silly things like a guy saying, "You people get up in the morning and have corn flakes and beer," Tanner would yell out, "Yup, that's hill law." Tanner seemed to be getting "intoxicated" by all the attention he was getting, and at one point, he yelled out, "Back in the hills, when a girl turns thirteen, she had better be able to outrun her daddy! It's hill law!" The entire block howled laughing—except Steve Hogg. He screamed, "Tanner! Are you out of your mind? Shut the fuck up!" I looked at Tanner. It was like he had just been hit in the face with a sledgehammer. "Shit, I'm sorry," he said. Hogg replied, "It's OK. But fuck! Watch what you say!"

On my side of the cell block, in the very first cell, were two inmates. Jules was probably in his early fifties. Jules's cell mate, Fred, was in his sixties. They were an odd couple—not in that they were very different from each other—they were just plain odd. One day, while filing out my canteen order sheet, my pen suddenly stopped writing. I walked down the row of cells looking for a pen to borrow. Some guys were out of the unit—others I wanted nothing to do with. Finally, I was able to borrow a pen from Jules. After I had filled out my sheet, I went back to return the pen, but neither Jules nor Fred were in. About two hours later, I spotted Jules standing outside of his cell. I called out, "Hey, Jules! Here's your pen!" It was as though Jules and I had been having a conversation with the president of Russia and I had said that Jules was a CIA officer! Jules ran up to me, and with incredible fear in his voice said, "Holy fucking shit! Don't ever say my name out loud!" I was amazed! "Why?" I asked. "Everyone here knows your name." Jules looked like he was having a heart attack. He barely got out a whisper. "You never know who might hear you."

A few minutes later, someone called out my name. I looked over, and it was a really huge-ass guard sergeant. I walked over. He pulled me aside, and very much to my surprise, asked me, "You want to know why he doesn't want anyone to know his name?" I answered, "Yeah, but what I really want to know is why he nearly went insane over his own name—I mean, everyone knows his name." The sergeant went on to tell me an incredibly sordid story. Both Jules and this sergeant lived in the same neighborhood in a north of Boston city. Jules had started dating a recently divorced woman. They never really had sex until after two years when Jules made his move—on the woman's three sons, whose ages ran from eleven down to four. He had never had any interest in the woman whatsoever! He had waited out two years in the quest to molest her sons! As shocking as it was, could I really believe this guy?

A while later, when the two evening shift guards suddenly decided that they sort of "liked" me, I asked one of them about the story. All he said to me was, "Later." The next day, he brought in a newspaper article that confirmed what the sergeant had told me. A younger guard who also worked on that shift looked at me and shook his head saying, "You should have believed him. The sarge is Polish. He's too fucking dumb to lie." I was blown away. It was the sickest story I had ever heard.

I knew that Jules cell mate, Fred, was also out there. The thing was, Fred once told me quietly that he knew he (Fred) was a "sick bastard." "I need help," he told me. "I'm just not sure if there is anyone who can actually help me." I don't know where Fred ended up, but hopefully there was some kind of help available to him. Jules, on the other hand, would never have to worry about hurting anyone again—he got several consecutive life sentences. While it's usually hard for me to hear people say, "Lock them up and throw away the key," in Jules's case, I'd toss the key into the deepest part of the ocean myself.

I have never liked my first name. When I was in school, regardless of which grade I was in, there wasn't ever anyone named Kevin in any grade behind or ahead of me. It really bothered me. In today's world, many parents strive to give their kids an unusual or rare name. Yet growing up in the 1960s and early 70s, most people—especially me—just wanted to "fit in." So it totally sucked that the first other Kevin that I met was a young little pervert in Newline. This Kevin apparently never had enough money in his inmate account for anything more than the basics, i.e., he couldn't really afford soda and snacks. Jules and Fred, on the other hand, seemed to have plenty of cash. One day, after everyone had visited the canteen store, Kevin went to his cell, took off all his clothing—except his boxer shorts—and walked over to Fred and Jules's cell and begged for some snack food. And he left with quite an assortment. On his way back to his own cell, the Hog chewed him out.

"You know you're just turning on those two child molesters, and you know that you're the closest thing— in looks anyway—to the kids that they're attracted to," Hogg told him. Kevin just looked down and walked on. Of course he did it the following week too. He just made sure that he didn't walk by the Hog's cell.

A few times, I ended up behind Jules in the medication line. (I had received sleeping medication from the prison psychiatrist.) Whenever Kevin would be at the back of the line and spot Jules closer to the front, he would just walk up, and Jules would let him cut the line in front of him. Twice, I was a few guys behind Jules. It infuriated me! The third time he did it, I made up a little melody and kept singing, "Sugar daddy, sugar daddy, let me in…" Jules gave me a pleading look, so I sang my little tune all the louder. That was the last time Jules let Kevin cut the line—at least when I was there.

* * *

One day, I received an envelope from "inmate accounts." They had taken $60 out, and the receipt said, "Victim witness fee." I saw Jeremy in the hallway and asked him what it was all about. Jeremy said, "Remember that lying punk—what was his name, Ray?—who said you had sex with him?" "Yeah," I answered. "Well, you just sent him a sixty-dollar check for lying and sending your ass to jail." I couldn't fucking believe it! That piece of shit committed perjury, fucked up my entire life, and I had to give him $60 for doing it!" My hatred for Massachusetts grew exponentially that day!

My day couldn't get any worse—or so I thought. Before lunch, a guard handed me a note saying I had legal mail (mail from an attorney). Regular mail, mail from anyone other than an attorney, was frequently screened/read by prison staff. Worse yet, the unit guards gave out this already opened mail and reread it for anything that they could use to make fun of you. Legal mail was different. Legal mail was given out by an IPS officer who, according to procedure, just "shook it out" to make sure there were no drugs inside.

After eating lunch with Willy, I went to the place where IPS gave out the legal mail and handed the black-uniformed guy my slip. He went through the envelopes, found mine, then stood there reading it while I watched. I was shocked! Then the IP handed me the letter and envelope and gave me a dirty look. I walked away, bewildered and angry. I read the letter while walking. It was from Jack Kaufman. It was like some kind of summary. It read, "On February 15, 1997, you were convicted of the following..." That total moron! Did Kaufman really believe that I didn't know what I had been convicted of? Was that the kind of document I would want in my possession while in prison—not knowing who might get hold of it? Asshole!

The very next day, as I was sitting down to lunch, an enormous inmate got up, walked over to me, and said, "I heard you're a fucking child molester." I looked at him and said, "That's bullshit." Without another word, he sat down. After lunch, I wrote Kaufman a blistering letter and told him how the IPS officer had read the entire letter then, in all likelihood, sent a goon after me. I accused Jack of trying to get me killed. Jack never responded to my letter; however, a week later, the job of handing out legal mail was taken away from IPS and given to one particular regular guard.

I will never know if Jack had anything to do with that.

Two days later, as I was walking back to Newline from the library, I ran into Tim. He was on his way to a visit. He asked me, "Did you really rape some kid?" I was deeply saddened. I answered, "Tim, look, a kid did say that I did that, but I swear to you, I didn't." Tim pushed his hair, which hadn't been cut in a couple of months out of his face, and said, "Do I have wild hair or what?" Those were the only words we said to each other. We never had the opportunity to speak with each other again.

* * *

Visits at the Cambridge Jail were tough—you were separated from your visiting family and friends by a thick pane of glass. The sound of your voice traveled through a small hole at the bottom of the glass. Concord was different. There was an absolutely huge room with rows of metal folding chairs. You sat next to your visitors—not across from them. There were signs that said "No physical contact permitted," but everyone got away with a hug at the beginning and end of the visit.

My mother was a very modest woman, so it was very hard for her to be "patted down" by a female guard. What particularly bothered her was that the female guard would run her gloved hand between her bra and breast. For a woman born in 1924, that was tantamount to her being sexually assaulted! My sister and brother in law took it better—at least they never said anything to me. As inmates, as soon as the visit was over, we had to wait to be called two at a time to a room where we had to completely undress. Then the guard would say, "Lift up your balls," and he would look under there for pills or anything else that might fit there. Next you would turn and face away from the guard as he said, "Spread your cheeks." And you pulled apart your butt cheeks so he could look in there. It sounds bad, but I gradually got used to it. Besides, it was more than worth it to see my family and friends!

* * *

Catholic Mass was held every Sunday night. One of those nights, a guard refused to open the cell doors until after "movement" was over. It was done by this blond-haired guard on purpose. I was furious! You can screw with me as you wish, but not on matters of faith. Once the doors opened, I walked up to the guard. I had never seen him in Newline before. He looked like he had been sent from "central casting" to play a Nazi officer in some war movie. I just sort of snapped. "You total prick!" I began. "You kept the doors closed until after movement to make sure the Catholic guys would miss Mass." "So what?" he replied. "At the end of time, you'll burn in hell with the rest of the nasty pricks from here who abuse their authority on a daily basis!" I yelled. I could tell he was violently angry. He stood there without saying a word. He could have had me sent to "the hole" for chewing him out. The fact that he didn't pretty much proves his guilt. He didn't want a hearing on this matter.

I sent a letter to the chaplain complaining about the incident. The following Tuesday afternoon, the priest came up to my cell. He looked at me and just turned around and left. I was dumbfounded! One of the day guards—who was a real asshole—walked up to my cell and started laughing. Finally he said, "He didn't want to talk to you, did he?" I ignored his sarcasm and asked, "What the hell just happened?" He answered, "It's not your fault. You're just not the holy man's type. If you were younger and cuter, he would stayed all day talking to you." And with that, the guard walked away. Later, after I was out of prison, I told a priest that story. He asked what the chaplain's name was. When I told him, he said, "Oh, that makes sense. You know, he himself has been accused." I guess I wasn't the guy's "type."

* * *

One morning, the "nice" day guard walked up to my cell door and said, "Tanner, pack up your shit! You're going to SECC." Tanner jumped into the air like a nine-year-old and exclaimed, "Yee ha!" He was thrilled. South East Correctional Center was in Bridgewater, not far from where he had been living. But Tanner was most happy because he was getting out of Concord. At a permanent facility, you had more freedom and privileges—possibly a single cell, a television if you could afford it, better food… salt and pepper. Myself—I was happy he was leaving. I've had more stimulating conversations with insects; still, I wondered who would replace him.

I didn't have to wonder long. My next cell mate was a nineteen-year-old Spanish kid who probably weighed all of eighty-five pounds. He was OK, though—he was gone at one activity or another almost all day every day. The only problem was that he too had been prescribed sleeping pills. Every night, he got his pills before count time and went into a near coma—no doubt because of his incredibly light body weight. At count time, he couldn't stand on his feet. The first time that happened, the counting guard screamed that if he didn't "stand for the count," he was going to the hole. I had to hold him up until the guard passed then basically "throw" him onto his bed. I ended up doing that for two weeks. One day, I came back from the library and he was gone. No one knew where he went, and the guards said nothing. It was really strange.

Next, I got a cell mate who had lived on the opposite side of the cell block. His name was Jim. He was half black, half white. He didn't like his own "psycho" black cell mate, so he complained, "I'm half white. Let me move in with DeCoste." He got his wish. (When Jim wanted an inmate job he told the guards, I'm half black, there are no black workers here—he got the job.) He was hysterically funny. One day, he was explaining to me that he had a great "handy man" business on the outside. He told me, "Damn, man, I had it made. I had a good pick-up truck, bought some tools, stole me a couple of ladders…" I nearly died laughing! He told me his girlfriend had broken up with him, so he went to where she was working to "get her back." He said her boss called the cops, so with a pistol, he took everyone hostage.

One day, a social worker came up to our cell and said, "Jim, you weren't at my anger management class today. Why not?" With a completely straight face, Jim replied, "I can't take that class anymore—being there makes me mad."

As luck would have it, Jim and I got along great, and Jim was friends with Jeremy. So suddenly, I started getting a "cut" of everything Jeremy cooked, and his cooking was excellent! At some point, Jeremy decided that we were friends too. Sadly, Jim was transferred not long after, and on the same day, Jeremy's cell mate left as well. Jeremy, who had an extremely good relationship with the guards, had me transferred into his cell. On the first day we were cell mates, I told Jeremy that every time our side of the tier was told we could use the phones, everyone ran so incredibly fast that I never got to make a call. Jeremy said nothing—he just left the cell. After a few minutes, he called out my name. He was standing there with the mustached guard from my first day in Newline. The guard looked at Jeremy then at me and said, "Well, you have never given me any shit, so when it's phone time, I'll open your door first. Then go make your call." I couldn't believe it! I was beyond happy! I started to thank the guy, but Jeremy cut me off, "And he needs a job. Let him have Jim's old job." The guard shrugged his shoulders and said, "OK, fine with me." That was unbelievable! OK, a prison job usually pays a dollar a day, half going into your inmate account and half into a savings account for when you're released, but the big deal is what's called "good time." For every month you work an inmate job, you get a day taken off your sentence. I couldn't believe my luck. At that point, the much younger guard came up to me with a roll of toilet paper that was at least 98 percent depleted. "Your first job—bring this to the guy in cell 12." That was weird! Why? "Tell him it's from Mike," he added. (Mike was the guard's first name.)

I went to cell 12, and there was a dark, Middle Eastern–looking inmate in there, all alone. I handed the paper through the bars. With a heavy accent he asked, "What is this?" I answered, "Mike said to give it to you." As I walked away, both guards burst out laughing. "That foreign fuck!" Mike howled. I found out later that I had unwittingly been used in an abusive joke. The guy needed toilet paper, and Mike was sending him a roll that was just about all finished. Later that night, I was told to take a bucket of ice on a cart and fill up the cups of any inmate who wanted some. I quietly grabbed a new roll of toilet paper and passed it to the guy who had just been "cheated" by Mike. While he said nothing, his look was one of gratitude. He told someone later that he knew I had been used.

* * *

One afternoon, a sergeant came up to my cell after lunch and told me I was "wanted" at the Property Department." I had an idea what it was about. I was short one pair of pants and one shirt—they must have come in. When I got to the place, I was surprised—it was like a big warehouse. A guard asked my name. He then took out a brown paper bag that contained my clothing. And then he got nasty. He threw the bag on the floor then handed me a pen and a clipboard and yelled, "Sign to the right of wherever you see your fucking asshole name!" I was shocked! But that was just the beginning. He then took out a box that had been sent to me by my mother. He opened it and showed me that she had mailed my watch to me. He said, "Look closely at it—because you can't have it. We're sending it back to whatever shithole you call home at *your* fucking expense. Sign this slip for the fucking postage." I numbly signed the paper, picked up my new clothes, and then turned and left.

It sucked. I had had that watch in court. Then the Cambridge Jail had taken it from me and sent it to my home. Other county jails let the inmates keep their watches. So if you came to Concord with a watch from a jail that allowed inmates to keep their watches, you got to keep it. If not, your only option was to buy the cheapest Casio digital watch available from the canteen store, though you couldn't buy one at Concord. I had used Casio digital watches ever since basic training at Fort Polk, Louisiana, in 1975. Eventually, I got one in prison. After getting out, however, I never again could bring myself to use any digital watch. I'm now an analog guy forever.

What was up with the prick guard at property I'll never know. He had really got all worked up over dealing with me. Too bad he hadn't given himself a fatal heart attack in the process. I would have enjoyed watching that!

* * *

One morning, after Jeremy had cleaned out the guard's office, he returned to our cell with a paper plate with some utterly disgusting substance on it. He wedged the plate onto the grate of the heating vent in the cell. "Sick!" I exclaimed. "What is that?" Jeremy gave me a sly look and answered, "Money."

The inmates at Concord who smoked cigarettes were out of luck. They simply did not sell them in the canteen. There was a day shift guard, a huge black guy who used to sit and draw pictures all day long. He was a veteran of the Vietnam war, and for some reason, he just sat in the office drawing pictures of the M-60 tank (the American tank in use during that war). His pictures were beyond perfect—but they were all the same. When he finished drawing one, he threw it into the trash can and began another, identical, drawing. He also chewed tobacco all day long as well, and every morning, as Jeremy cleaned the guard's office, he would take the can of spit-out tobacco, pour it onto a paper plate, and bring it back to our cell for "drying." When it was dry, Jeremy rolled the dried combination of spit and tobacco in toilet paper and then "sold" them to other inmates. I asked Jeremy, "Do the guys know the source of those cigarettes?" Jeremy laughed and replied, "Oh fuck, no—and don't you tell them either!"

Of course, prison inmates never had actual cash in their possession, so deals were made. The number one form of inmate "currency" was soup. In Concord, cups of soup, in all other facilities, packages of ramen noodle soup. There were exceptions. For big ticket items—e.g., if you wanted to buy a guy's watch or some other clothing—he might tell you what he wanted for it off the canteen order sheet. You would then purchase the item, and when it came in, you made the exchange. (Though prior to the Department of Corrections banning the sale of all tobacco products in prison, the primary form of "currency" was, in fact, cigarettes. However, like salt and pepper, you could not obtain cigarettes in Concord.)

Jeremy didn't stop at cigarettes however; he also picked up the day-old newspapers that the guards had tossed out and those he "rented" to news-hungry inmates. The cost to have the newspaper for one hour was three soups, or 75 cents, for an hour with yesterday's newspaper. He also got nearly all his "cooking ingredients" the same way—through cigarette sales. There was one guy who made sure that the payments were made. He was more than happy to enforce the deals for a plate of whatever Jeremy might cook on a particular day. He also had an older guy named O'Reilly, who was basically his "gopher."

According to Jeremy, O'Reilly was from the City of Lynn, Massachusetts, and he was a compulsive arsonist. O'Reilly even admitted as much. One day, we could hear the sounds of what had to be many fire trucks passing the prison with their sirens on. For some reason, I shouted out, "Holy shit, there's a fire! Does anyone know where O'Reilly is?" The entire upper floor erupted into laughter. O'Reilly, as he so often did, yelled out, "What the fuck!" in his rapid, high-pitched voice. That, in turn, only increased the laughter. One day, O'Reilly was told that he was to pack up. It was announced in the morning as always by the big tank-drawing guard. "O'Reilly, pack your shit. SECC," was all he said. He was a man of few words.

Unlike many guys, O'Reilly did not look happy to be moving. Jeremy shouted, "Oh, just fucking great! Now I have to break in a new nitwit!" O'Reilly had always done whatever Jeremy asked him to do—for absolutely no compensation at all.

That afternoon, I learned quite a lesson. Steve the Hog had always been messing with people he knew were charged with sex offenses. Often, Jeremy would get into an argument with another Newline inmate, and with the ultimate tone of disgust, he would call the guy *skinner*. In fact, all of Jeremy and Hogg's friends were always calling guys *skinner*. That very day that O'Reilly left was "canteen day." I was beyond excited since I had ordered twelve cans of (generic) Cola. Since I technically worked for the evening shift guards, I was hesitant about walking into the office with a cup to get some ice from the huge ice-making machine.

I kept walking up and down in front of the office with my plastic cup. In the office was the tank-drawing guard and a much older guard lieutenant. The lieutenant was always pleasant though not friendly. (I guess that probably means *professional*.) Finally, the tank drawing guard looked up and yelled, "Fucking shit, DeCoste, if you want some fucking ice, just come in and get it!" I was ecstatic! As I was getting my ice, I decided that maybe I should make some small talk with them. I watched as the guard began drawing yet another tank, then I said, "I guess the fire danger here has been cut in half now that O'Reilly is gone, huh?" The lieutenant looked up from the paper he was reading and asked, "What are you talking about?" "You know," I began, "he's a serial arsonist—he set a ton of fires in Lynn. That's why he was in here."

The lieutenant and the guard broke into fits of laughter. Without knowing why, I suddenly felt very dumb. When they started to regain their composure, the lieutenant began, "You know, I've been watching you since the day you first got here." I didn't like how this was sounding. "And I can tell you something," the lieutenant continued. "If someone showed up with a gun and told me to pick the one guy in here that didn't actually commit any crime, and that if I chose wrong he'd blow my brains out, I'd tell him *you* were the innocent man. And I *wouldn't* be getting shot either." I was blown away! "I've been at this a long time," he concluded. Then he began again, "But O'Reilly? He's a child molester from way back." I was pretty surprised, and I started, "But Jeremy told me…" The lieutenant cut me off, "He's in here with a sex charge too. Everyone in this building on the second floor was convicted of a sex offense. Everyone." I just said, "Oh," and went back to my cell. It's hard to explain, but I wasn't angry at anyone except the Hog. He was the only guy who had said anything negative to me. I figured the other guys, including Jeremy, were just trying to survive as best they knew how. I never said anything to anyone until I met that inmate named Rivera at SECC about three months later. When I told him that Steve Hogg was a sex offender, he just smiled. It's not that he already knew; I just think he was happy to get the information.

* * *

I would always tell people that I had been a Republican since the age of twelve. During the summer of 1968, I volunteered at the local Nixon campaign office. With only two exceptions, every public school in my city of Melrose was named after a Republican president. I was going into Calvin Coolidge Junior High, and along with two brothers from Abraham Lincoln Junior High, I and they delivered Nixon campaign pamphlets to nearly every home in the city. We were directed by the state legislature's House Minority Whip, William Robinson. He was a great guy to work with. When Richard Nixon won that November, I finally felt like I was part of the political process that I was always so interested in. I was incredibly proud. (No, I never stopped liking President Nixon, and I still honor all of his achievements to this very day.) Later, when I turned eighteen, I actually waited outside city hall until it opened so that I could both register for the draft—and register to vote as a Republican. Strangely, however, I have only voted for a Republican candidate for Massachusetts governor once—Mitt Romney—and I now realize that because of his lieutenant governor, that was a mistake.

Anyway, I'm not sure if things went terribly wrong with Governor William Weld or with Paul Cellucci, but one of them came up with a horrific plan. Any inmate sex offender who did not agree to be assigned to the Massachusetts Treatment Center for the Sexually Dangerous, was grabbed in the middle of the night by mask-wearing guards, chained up, bussed to a local airport, and flown to a county jail in Dallas, Texas. As time went on, Cellucci decided that the airplane was too expensive, so they bussed the inmates to Texas in non-air-conditioned buses. The trip took days. They did stop at night—at local jails. The *Boston Herald*, a hardcore Republican paper, even ran a front page photo of the buses with the headline "INHUMANE!"

One day in Concord, I met a new "resident" of Newline and I was shocked! His ID photo and his actual face were seemingly not of the same person! When I questioned him about it, he explained that the picture had been taken before he was shipped to Texas. He had recently returned home, and because he had attempted suicide *with a firearm,* he was now back in prison on a gun charge and for violating his probation. He told me a horrible story. After being grabbed in the night by the masked guards, he claimed they had seriously roughed him—and others—up. He was lucky; he traveled to Texas by plane. However, he was somewhat afraid of air travel, and being seat-belted into the seat while also being waist-chained and ankle-cuffed, drove him nearly insane. He said the Massachusetts guards on the plane would not allow anyone to use the bathroom, so he was forced to crap his pants.

At the Texas jail, the Massachusetts inmates were forced to lie still chained on the floor while police dogs were all over them. He said that if you moved a muscle, you got bitten. (The dog part of the story was later confirmed in a Boston newspaper article.) Once in a cell, he told me, there was a light that was never turned off, making sleep exceedingly difficult. However, it was the food situation that caused the man's incredible physical transformation. This inmate told me that for all three meals, every single day that he was there, he got a bean burrito and a tiny portion of rice. He told me you could buy soup there, but that was it. I met this kid about six months after his return from the jail in Dallas, and he still looked like he had just been liberated from a Nazi death camp.

Shortly before the end of my time in Concord, the guards—which ones, I never found out—warned Jeremy that a night raid was coming and that "many" guys were going to be sent to Dallas. Somehow—and I know it wasn't Jeremy that told—but the entire Concord prison became aware that the raid was happening that very night.

In the cell next to Jules and Fred, there was a huge man, Dennis, both huge in stature as well as severely overweight. Every week, he bought an enormous amount of junk food—cakes, donuts, soda, candy bars, and chips. His weekly supply would literally last me more than a month. During the evening before the post-midnight raid, he announced his "plan" to his cell mate. He said he knew that if they grabbed him for the trip to Texas, he wouldn't be able to take his food with him. He also said that there was no way he'd leave it behind because the guards would "scoop it up" and either throw it out, or worse, enjoy it themselves. So at around 8:00 p.m., he began his personal "mission" to eat and drink every last food item in his footlocker.

After the evening shift guards left, the entire Newline second floor became eerily quiet. The midnight shift guards usually had the office lights on for an hour or so after they came on shift—not that night. At the time, among the inmates anyway, it was not known that only sex offenders who refused to go to the Treatment Center were the ones "deported" to Texas. There was complete silence among the inmates. The usual bedtime banter was entirely absent. For the first time since I had been in Newline, even Steve the Hog was entirely silent. Neither I nor Jeremy had a watch, so we had no idea what time it was.

Jeremy and I sat on our bunks quietly talking. Just as I had at the Cambridge Jail, when I believed that I was going to Walpole, I began the process of numbing my feelings. If I got taken that night, I was going out without giving anyone the satisfaction of seeing me fearful. Jeremy and my cell faced the huge wall of the front of the prison. The guys on the other side had a view of the walkway leading up to Newline and the interior of the prison. After what seemed like a couple of hours, a few of the guys on the other side—without shouting and without emotion—said, "They're coming." Another inmate was heard to say, "A whole shitload of them." I once heard on the news the final radio call of a pilot and co-pilot who could not get their plane high enough during takeoff to avoid hitting a building. The co-pilot said calmly, “Pull it up.” Even more calmly the pilot replied, “It’s too late. It’s too late.” That’s how calmly the guys on the other side of the block spoke when the saw the masked guards coming.

I was blown away by the sounds of the guard’s boots on the ground. It reminded me of the sound my entire training company at Fort Polk made when we were all running in formation. Somewhere in the building, I could hear a guy sobbing. Then there came the sounds of men running up the stairs. On the opposite side of the floor, a cell door was opened. There was a divider between the two sides, so all we could see was the heads of five guards with black helmets and black shields. Then we heard the cell door close. After that, it became quiet again. No one knew if the guards would be back for more guys. I lay down on my top bunk and eventually fell asleep. The rising of the sun woke me up in the morning just before count time. Only one man from Newline had been taken. Many, many others were taken from other buildings—there were “hidden” sex offenders all over the prison.

Later, I told a guard that I thought it was unfair that they had “grabbed” a very sick inmate—he had AIDS. The guard laughed and told me, “He didn’t have AIDS. He only said that so no one would dare give him a beating.” I looked at the guard and said, “I don’t get it. Who would say they had AIDS if they didn’t?” The guard answered, “Think about it. A guy pisses you off so bad that you want to kick his ass. Do you really want to punch out a guy with AIDS and take the risk that if you both get cut in the fight, you’ll get AIDS too?” Another lesson learned.

Dennis did, in fact, eat every last food item in his possession—including a six-pack of Cola. The entire next day, he looked like a man with a severe case of the flu. I had to give him credit, though—he never threw up.

* * *

The weather started to warm up around late April, and Willy and I spent most afternoons after lunch just walking the running track in the prison yard. Being out there with Willy was like hanging out with a celebrity. His easy way and Southern gentleman charm had made him immensely popular—particularly with the younger black inmates. As we walked around, Willy would stop guys that he had come to know and introduce me. "This is Kevin. He's good people." I had never heard that term before, but I liked it.

One afternoon after quite a few laps around the track, Willy and I sat down at the picnic table and began watching an inmate softball game. I found it hysterically funny. A couple of inmates were the umpires, even though there was really no organization to the game. Whenever there was a close-call "out" at the plate, a near riot would erupt. Willy and I just sat there and laughed at the spectacle. As we were watching the game, another black inmate, Ritchie joined us. Ritchie was well known; he was trying to become a woman. He even had had some hormone therapy, and his "breasts" were beginning to grow. I don't think Willy ever fully understood what was going on with Ritchie.

As the three of us were watching the game, Willy let out a really long yawn. He seemed thoroughly exhausted. "Have you been sleeping OK?" I asked him. The saddest expression crossed Willy's face, and he told me, "I've been sleeping in bed with my wife for so long I just can't seem to get used to sleeping without her." At that very moment, with great emotion, Ritchie cried out, "Ohhh, do I miss my man!" Willy gave me a look of total bewilderment. His look was so—well—*lost* that I cracked up laughing. Though not knowing why, Willy started to laugh too. Ritchie wasn't finished. "Oh, how good I used to feel in bed when me and my man's thighs were across each other!" Again, poor Willy gave me a "What's he talking about?" look. Again, I had to laugh, and again, Willy joined in.

Then we were interrupted by Ritchie exclaiming, "Oh Lord, look at that beautiful specimen!" I looked in the direction he was facing, and there was Tim walking the track with another guy, both of them wearing just gym shorts and sneakers. I was shocked. It almost looked like he had been doing steroids! He was always a "solid" kid, though, never skinny. Now he looked as though his body fat index was around 3 to 5 percent. And he seemed to have added at least 50 pounds of pure muscle. He must have been spending hours every single day working out. Tim looked over in my direction and waved. I waved back, and Ritchie gushed, "Oh my goodness! Are you telling me you know him?" Again I just cracked up. I couldn't stop laughing. Ritchie grabbed my arm and asked, "Any chance of you introducing me to him?" Still laughing, I said, "No." Ritchie put on an indignant expression and asked, "Why not?" Now Willy was laughing along with me, and I just barely got out the words: "Because I don't think I could survive the embarrassment of getting my ass kicked by a kid who's twenty-three years younger than me." At that, all three of us broke into peals of uncontrollable laughter.

* * *

Sadly, a few mornings later, as the tank-drawing guard passed my cell, he said, "DeCoste," as he handed me two trash bags. "Treatment Center." Jeremy patted me on the back and said, "Be happy you're out of here!" Concord sucked. The food, the cells, the lack of a radio, and only thirty minutes a day in a TV room. Yet I had made some really good friends. I didn't feel all that threatened by violence, even though it was constantly going on around me. (Fights in Newline, fights in medicine lines, fights during "movement.") Worse yet, I was probably about to become the only person among both the inmates and staff at the Treatment Center who had actually never had sex with anyone!

After breakfast, for the second time since coming to know Willy, I had to say goodbye to him. Despite the complexion of his skin, Willy, in some ways, had always reminded me—just a little—of my own dad. Willy had me write down his address in Georgia. He was certain that he would be released before me. He told me to write to him if I needed to buy anything while I was "in." "I'll send you the money," he told me. Then it was time to go.

After I got out three years later, I sent Willy a Christmas card at his Georgia address for three years in a row. I never heard anything back. Using the Internet, I tried to locate him both in Georgia and in the Massachusetts Department of Corrections. I should have called the Corrections Department, but understandably, I wanted no contact with them. Eventually, I gave up. In June of 2014, as my family home was being sold—and I knew I had nowhere to move to—I again typed Willy's name into Google before my Internet service was disconnected for the final time. This time, an obituary from Georgia came up. There were pictures of a man who was much, much younger than I had remembered Willy being. I guess they were taken before his "parole violation" sent him back to the Evil Empire. But the photos were definitely of Willy. While I can't prove this, I firmly believe that Willy died of old age in some Massachusetts prison.

One day in Concord, at dinner, I had looked into Willy's eyes and told him, "I have no idea what you were ever charged with, but I am certain of one thing: whatever it was, you didn't do it." Willy's eyes filled with tears, and he told me, "The Boston Police were looking for a black man, and I was handy." Willy was one of the kindest and most gentle persons I have ever met. In the Bible, Jesus tells us that we must forgive those who harm us, otherwise the Father will not forgive us. Well, I have one wish. Whomever it was who framed Willy for a crime he didn't commit, I hope God never forgives them.

# Massachusetts Treatment Center for The Sexually Dangerous

Along with about fifty other inmates, I was once again chained up, both hands and feet, and put on a Department of Corrections bus. You should have seen the looks we got from people driving by us on the highway. Fortunately, the bus windows were darkly tinted. That kid Kevin from Newline was on the bus, as was Ritchie, who sat next to me. As we pulled out of Concord, Ritchie exclaimed, "Concord, I spit on your grave!" I'm not sure what that meant or how a huge prison ends up in a "grave," but what the hell—it was funny.

Once we approached what could only be called a prison complex in Bridgewater, Massachusetts, I was utterly blown away at the vast amount of land that the Department of Corrections occupied. On that land were three prisons and the state hospital—for the insane. There was the Treatment Center, South East Correctional Center (SECC), Bridgewater State Hospital, and Old Colony Correctional Center. If the land was occupied by private businesses, the Town of Bridgewater would be collecting an unbelievable amount of property taxes! I was surprised when the bus first stopped at SECC. That's where Ritchie was getting off. He wished me luck and got out. I was somewhat surprised since at times he could really embarrass me, but I knew I was going to miss him.

Next, we drove up to the Treatment Center. When the gate opened, an extremely powerful set of motion-activated spotlights went on between two extremely high fences. The area between the two fences is called "no man's land." If an inmate, most likely trying to escape, is caught between the two fences, he can legally be shot by the guards in the tower. Those powerful spotlights are to make target acquisition much easier for the guards—especially at night. It sort of made me feel sick to see those damn lights, I'm not sure why.

Once in the Treatment Center, we were brought to a large room where we were unchained and told to strip entirely naked. Since the strip searches after visits in Concord, it was something that no longer bothered me. We had to stand there while two guys at a time were "examined" by IPS officers. They were writing down on our records the locations of any scars or other identifying marks. Suddenly, an inmate said, "Everyone standing around naked. This is exactly what the Nazis did just before they gassed people." An IPS officer yelled, "Shut the fuck up, you moron!" No one spoke after that. When they got to me, they started in, "Surgical scar, lower right abdomen." Another IP quickly wrote that down. Then the guy said, "Deformed little finger right hand." I was livid! I spoke up, "When I was fourteen, the tip of that finger was cut off in a tractor accident! It's not deformed!" The IP writing looked up at his partner. "Deformed!" the bastard yelled out. I decided it wasn't worth getting into serious trouble over, so I just stopped talking. My only satisfaction was that the jackass failed to see two surgical scars on my lower back. I guess he was too busy looking at my fucking little finger.

At some point, one guy, Charlie, who had also come from Newline, looked at the wall clock and said, "It's 3:15 (p.m.), are we going to have lunch?" The IPS looked at each other, then one asked, "You people haven't had lunch today?" We all answered "no." The IPS talked it over quietly with each other, then one said, "We might be able to feed you. I don't know." Charlie started to laugh, but I turned and just said, "Charlie, shut up!" He stopped laughing. As I told him later, "Hungry people shouldn't piss off the guys who control access to the food." The IPS left, and we all got dressed again.

After about twenty minutes, the officers came back, and one said, "OK, you guys can eat, follow me." We were led into an extremely nice dining area, and we got into a line. Inmate workers gave each of us two fried chicken sandwiches. It was the best food I had eaten in months. There were even salt and pepper shakers on each table! Charlie looked over at me and said, "This food is awesome! I'm going to like it here!" As it turned out, there was no available food in the inmate kitchen. We were actually in the staff dining room, eating food that staff members had to pay for. It would be years before I'd have food that tasty again.

* * *

After we had finished eating, the IPS officers read out our building assignments. Each of the buildings that we were assigned to were brand-new two-floor, prefabricated buildings recently erected to house the huge numbers of inmates who were now being sent for psychosexual treatment, as opposed to straight prison time. Somehow, despite being premade, they had connected all of the new "modular" buildings with the old, dungeon-like Treatment Center Building. Before getting to the new buildings, however, we had to walk through the old. It was a shock to my system! Years before, I had gone with a very curious friend to look at the closed-down Danvers (Mass.) State Mental Hospital. There were single person cells that had solid steel doors. It was bleak. It was like all the cells in old Alcatraz movies—except for those huge steel doors. I remember telling my friend that the state didn't "treat people like that anymore." Yet here it was 1997 and these "inmates" were living in these cells of a design straight out of the 1800s.

I say "inmates" because their status was ambiguous. These men had finished their prison sentences for sexual crimes, then the state had dragged them back into court in a "civil process" and had them declared a "sexually dangerous person." Once civilly committed, the chances of these guys ever being released was virtually nil. These guys were different from any inmates that I had encountered up to this point. Some of these guys actually seemed mildly mentally retarded. I have often wondered if they came to the Treatment Center that way or if years of confinement, coupled with not knowing if they would ever get out, had actually beaten their minds into this strange state. Originally, the Treatment Center was part of the Department of Mental Health, and these guys were treated reasonably well. Later, however, the facility came under the control of the Department of

Corrections, and with DOC guards came far rougher treatment—if only just verbally and psychologically.

(I once got a quick glimpse inside my court file while at the Cambridge Jail. Kevin Johnson had placed a form inside with my name on it. It said, "Motion for Sexually Dangerous Person." I still remain convinced that he knew I was innocent.)

When we got to our building, a guard told us who was going to the first floor and who would be on the second. I got the second floor. On the second floor, we awaited a corrections officer who was busy with some inmates who were arguing with each other. (In my mind, the DOC has two types of employees: corrections officers and guards. The corrections officers try to treat inmates in the manner in which I'm sure *they* would want to be treated. Some of them even offer constructive advice to the guys. The other bastards are nothing more than security guards in a human warehouse.)

Coming into the second floor was a surprise. We were in a huge room. Next to the door was the guard's desk. Beyond that there were tables and chairs. Some of the tables were occupied by some guys playing cards, some reading books, while still others were writing in notebooks. To the left, against the wall, was a large television with a couch and some rather comfortable-looking chairs. Further back were a set of chairs that were arranged—I knew from working in residential programs—for "group therapy" meetings. I wondered if I would ever have to sit there.

Eventually, Officer Steve got free. He gave us our room assignments, and we were shown to a very long hallway with six-man rooms on each side. Upon entering my assigned room, I saw that there were three bunk beds all against the same wall. On the opposite wall were three desks. I guess you could write letters there, but everyone seemed to both read and write in bed. (That had been my practice my entire life.) An inmate named Ken came in. Ken was a strange-looking guy. He looked like the guy you always see stumbling out of a bar drunk in the early afternoon. He walked up, stuck out his hand, and said, "Hi, I'm Ken. Whatever you do, don't use the overhead neon lights—they burn the retinas of my eyes." "OK," I slowly replied.

Then I heard my worst nightmare come true. "Dominick!" yelled out a guy coming through the door. It was an idiot from Concord's Newline, Marc Savoy, who had left Concord long before I had. He had had a childhood friend named Dominick, and I guess I looked like him. I was annoyed. "You do know my real name, don't you?" I asked. "Yeah, Kev," he answered. "I just like calling you Dom." God, the poor man was an ass.

As a "sex group" ended, three more guys came in, all named Tom. At first I thought it was a joke, but no, the DOC had assigned three guys—all with the same first name—to one room. "This has to be a conspiracy," I mumbled. One of the Toms heard me and quietly cracked up laughing. That was Tom Ahern, who would turn out to be the only normal Tom in the group. One of the other Toms was a tall, lanky guy from Western Massachusetts who claimed that he had turned himself in for molesting his daughter. He also eventually told everyone in the room that he was a trained commando. When I asked him what branch of the military he was with, he backtracked and told me that he was trained by his uncle who had been with the Army's Delta Force. "He trained you how?" I inquired. Without hesitation of any kind, this Tom said, "From the time I was twelve until I was sixteen, I went on every Delta Force training mission with my uncle." "They let you do that?" Marc Savoy asked with a heavy dose of sarcasm. "That's what I fucking told you, isn't it!" Commando Tom screamed. Tom Ahern looked aggravated and said, "Shit, will you guys argue somewhere else? I've got a fucking headache!" Then Ahern looked at me and started laughing—the quietest laugh I had ever heard. I tried not to crack up lest I anger the commando. Ahern's quiet laugh would turn out to be the best entertainment I would have in that place.

The last Tom was the strangest of all. Despite Commando Tom's somewhat bizarre story about turning himself into the local police, at least that story was probably untrue and I'm sure the "commando" knew it. The final Tom, however, described how he had molested his sister's three sons in disgusting detail without— I'm sure of it—changing a single fact. It was strange for me because he was seemingly the most sorrowful, repentant pervert that I had ever met, yet while in Christian charity I should have tried to applaud his repentance, I found that the guy made me want to vomit. This Tom had also appointed himself the protector of, well, the more stupid of the inmates—guys that were easily borderline retarded. Whenever he defended one of them, he'd call them "the less-fortunate." Every time I heard him say that, I wanted to say, "Your sister's kids were the less fortunate," but I held back. I wasn't afraid of the guy, but a fight in prison can send you to the hole—and it all ends up in your permanent record. And at the time, I thought I might someday want parole.

An hour later, we went to dinner. There I learned two things. First, the food was somewhat better than Concord's. Second, the dining room was a hundred times nicer. There were round tables with four chairs each. Real chairs. And there were salt and pepper shakers on each table. I was sitting at a table with two black guys and Tom Ahern. I looked at Tom at one point and said, "I can't believe there are three Toms in our room." At that, one of the other guys spoke up and said, "Three, that's cool! Me and my bro here, we're both named Kevin." Before I could say a word, Ahern cracked up laughing with that totally quiet laugh. "I'm Kevin too." I added. "No way! All three of us!" the other Kevin said. He looked at his friend Kevin, and the other guy said, "Oh shut the fuck up!" The first Kevin continued, "Oh, he's the unfriendly Kevin." Then all of us, minus unfriendly Kevin, laughed. Tom Ahern then asked, "Then that makes you friendly Kevin?" Before I could answer, "friendly" Kevin said, "That makes two friendlies and one unfriendly!" Then his friend repeated, "Oh, man! Will you all shut the fuck up!" I thought it was a serious moment, then Ahern began that incredibly quiet laugh again. Friendly Kevin and I looked at each other, and we started laughing too. Unfriendly Kevin didn't utter another word for the rest of the meal.

* * *

The weather had turned miserably hot and humid, and once again, I was at a new facility without soap or deodorant. By day two,

I felt like a pig. I remember sitting at a table in the big room and saying to no one in particular, "God, I can actually smell myself!" Someone tapped me on the shoulder. I turned and saw a man, probably in his late sixties to early seventies, bald on top with just a little white hair on the sides. He put up his finger as if to say, *Wait here.* I wondered what it could possibly be about—I had never once met the guy. In a couple of minutes, he returned and handed me a bar of soap and a roll-on deodorant. The bar of soap was new; the deodorant, well, it wouldn't have mattered—I'd have used a dead guy's deodorant at that point. As I thanked the man profusely, he put a finger to his mouth in a "shhh." I wondered if he were unable to talk. Then he disappeared back down the long hallway, I guess back to his room. I quickly made my way back to my room, grabbed a towel and washcloth, and ran for the showers.

I couldn't have felt better! Finally I was clean, but I quickly realized that at least for me, my hair was way too long. I asked the CO (corrections officer), Steve, about getting a haircut. He told me that the barbershop was located in the old building and that the inmate barber might be able to take me without an appointment. Steve said to try at the next movement.

Being an inmate barber was one of those jobs that paid a dollar a day, but the barbers at every prison had their way of "charging" their clients. I had gotten a haircut in Concord, and the barber told me his name was Jimmy 5 Snickers. Unfortunately for Jimmy, I never bought him those candy bars. They had to be careful. The guards couldn't care less, but if any of the prison administrators ever found out that the barbers were charging, they would lose their job.

When I got to the barber shop, the inmate barber told me he could get me in right after the guy he was working on. Since this was all being done after "movement" was over, the guy in the chair and I would both have to stay in the shop until the next hour's movement. When he got through, he brushed off the chair and motioned for me to sit. "What can I do for you?" he asked. Without a second's thought, I replied, "It's so damn hot—skin me." The barber and his previous customer both let out an audible groan. *Oh God!* I thought to myself. Sex offenders were insulted by being called *skinners*, and the act of sexual rape was called *skinning*. I had just asked this civilly committed sex offender to—skin me!

"Bad choice of words," I mumbled. "It's OK," said the barber. "You're new here." The man proceeded to give me a pretty good haircut.

* * *

One night, a guy was out in the hallway while most of the room doors were open. He was having a loud argument with some other guy. Then at some point, the other guy said, "Why are you even here? You should be in the state hospital, you fucking crack baby!" It seemed that every inmate in the entire place cracked up laughing at the same time. Off and on, there were shouts of "Crack baby!" Then someone else yelled out, "So that's what's wrong with Dave! His mom was a crack whore and he's a crack baby! His fucking brain is fried!" At that point, Tom, defender of "the less fortunate," jumped out of bed, went into the hallway, and started screaming at, well, everyone. He must have said *less fortunate* a hundred times. For his effort, he was bombarded by endless calls of "faggot" and "pussy." Once in a while, his tirade was interrupted by someone yelling that prison favorite phrase: "Kill yourself!"

When Tom got back into our room, Marc asked him, "So which is it? Are you a faggot or a pussy?" I looked at Ahern, and we both died laughing. This time, though, Ahern was laughing at full volume. Defending Tom went insane, and we started getting a lecture about the less fortunate. Eventually "the defender" calmed down, got his toothbrush and paste, and headed for the bathroom. When he was about five feet past our door, Marc made the sounds that junior high kids make when they are making fun of the mentally challenged. (If you don't know what that sounds like, ask any twelve-year-old boy.) Defending Tom came rushing back into the room in a total rage. He walked up to Ahern's bed and actually punched the metal bed frame. "Ahern, you have no respect for the less fortunate!" I couldn't stand the Defender and I really liked Ahern, so while laughing my ass off, I said, "Don't yell at him, I made the noise." The Defender looked at me, and then Ken said, "No he didn't, I did!" Marc spoke up and said, "You fucking liars—I'm the one who did it!"

Defending Tom stomped out of the room and flicked on the overhead neon lights as he passed the switch. Ken let out a scream and started rolling around on the floor screaming, "My fucking retinas are burning—kill the lights!" Marc, Ahern, and I couldn't stop laughing. Commando Tom jumped into action! He jumped off his top bunk, raced over to the light switch, and turned them off. "Fucking guys!" Commando yelled. "Can't you see his retinas are burning?" It was way too much! Marc, Ahern, and I were absolutely hysterically laughing. Even my ribs hurt; I was laughing so hard. The commando helped Ken to his feet and got him to his bunk. Ken slumped down on his bunk like he had just run a marathon with a twisted ankle while also dehydrated. The Commando ran out and returned with a wet washcloth and placed it over Ken's eyes. Everyone else was watching with complete amusement. Ahern asked the Commando, "Oh fuck, Tom, did you steal someone's washcloth out of the laundry room?" The Commando replied, "No thanks to you guys, I may have saved Ken's sight!" Ahern looked at me and whispered, "Oh, brother!" With that, we both started howling, laughing all over again. (Ahern and I had lower bunks about two feet apart. Our pillows were at the same end, so we could talk while we either wrote—or just hung out.)

After more than an hour, Defending Tom returned, grabbed his soap and shampoo, and went to the showers. Once he had been gone about five minutes, Marc said, "Watch this." Marc went down the hall, and Ahern and I stood in the doorway to our room. Marc stood outside the bathroom/showers and, masterfully disguising his voice, yelled into the bathroom, "Hey, Tommy, your three nephews are here! They want to know if you're free to skin them tonight!" Then Marc followed that with that junior high noise I mentioned before. Defending Tom started screaming like a madman—no actual words, just screaming. The night guard came running, and we all jumped into our bunks. It was three hours—around 2:30 a.m.—when the Defender came quietly back into our room. As he got into bed, I could hear Ahern very quietly laughing away. I bit down on my tongue trying not to laugh, but it didn't work. I burst out laughing, as did Ahern and Marc. The Defender didn't make a single sound. Loud enough for everyone to hear, Ahern said, "Oh shit! They must have medicated him!" Again, the three of us cracked up laughing. After a few minutes of silence, I was actually starting to drift back to sleep when Marc spoke up. "Seriously, Tom, what did they give you, because I need some of that shit." Ahern and I died laughing all over again.

When the morning count was called at 7:00 a.m., Ahern, Marc, and I were thoroughly exhausted. Ken said that he was convinced that some permanent damage had in fact been done to his eyes. When breakfast was called, the Defender didn't go. When we returned from the dining hall, Defending Tom had been moved out of our room. Marc, Ken, and the Commando had a group therapy session to attend. Ahern and I both lay on our bunks and tried to catch a much-needed nap. As we lay there waiting for the gift of sleep, Ahern suddenly spoke up. "Shit, I'm going to miss him." We both died laughing, and eventually, we both fell asleep.

* * *

No good thing lasts forever. Later that afternoon, the Defender's bunk was assigned to a guy named Jonathan, or "Jon" for short. This guy was as smooth-talking as any James Bond character and twice as creepy as Defending Tom. Jon was a good-looking guy. With someone else's brain in his head, he would probably be a film star. As it was, no one in our room was in his therapy group, so we had no direct knowledge of what had got him sent into prison, but before long, other inmates were calling him the Exhibitionist.

Jon had an inmate friend named Tony from one of the other rooms, and Tony was constantly in our room visiting and whispering with Jon. On one of those many occasions while the two of them were talking very quietly, I was on my bed writing my journal and Tom Ahern was reading a paperback book. Suddenly Jon and Tony started giggling like little first-grade girls, and Ahern quietly said, "For God's sake, get a room." I nearly died laughing! Jon got wicked pissed off and demanded to know what we were laughing about. I couldn't think of anything to tell him, but Ahern confidently said,

"It's something you wouldn't understand." Jon replied, "Try me." After a couple of seconds, knowing he wasn't going to have his question answered, Jon and Tony resumed their whispering.

At one point, I heard Tony say, "I've got to find a way to be friends with him. Alan is so beautiful." That I didn't like. There was only one Alan in the Treatment Center that I knew of, and he was a nice, very polite kid—probably twenty-three to twenty-five years old. Alan was sort of a bodybuilder type, and he had helped me set up a gym routine that would at least prevent me from losing what muscle strength I had. I wasn't in any way in "Alan's League." Alan and I had both lived in Westfield, Massachusetts—he had grown up there and I went to Westfield State University. When I graduated from WSU, Alan was probably seven or eight years old, but we had visited a lot of the same restaurants and parks. He once laughed his ass off when I told him that the one thing I couldn't understand about Western Massachusetts was why they insisted on cutting a round pizza into square slices. Alan told me, "It's just the way it is."

Obviously, Alan didn't need any help from me in defending himself against Tony—not physically—but Tony was in his early thirties and had definitely "been around the block" more times than Alan. I was genuinely afraid that Alan might find a way to take advantage of the kid. So very delicately, I approached Alan at the gym and warned him that Tony had the hots for him. Alan took it well. I told him that my only reason for informing him of the situation was that I didn't want him to be surprised by any smooth moves that Tony might make. "Besides," I told him, "Tony has a mustache—never trust *anyone* with a mustache!" Alan laughed and told me, "That makes sense. My father has a mustache and he's a prick."

About a week later, Jon came back to our room and I was alone writing. "You fucked up what could have been a nice experience for Tony and Alan!" he shouted at me. "There's just one problem," I countered calmly. "Alan's not gay—it wouldn't have gone anywhere anyway." Jon was beside himself. "This is prison! Anything can happen!" I had had enough. "Look, Tony is a sleaze ball grease bag with an equally greasy mustache, and Alan's a nice, clean-cut, normal kid. Leave him the fuck alone." Jon walked out of the room just as Ahern was returning from group with Marc. Jon came back and slammed the door like a ten-year-old having a tantrum. "Fuck's up with that?" Ahern asked with a somewhat mischievous grin. After I had explained the whole affair, both Marc and Ahern cracked up laughing.

Marc reopened the room door, and we could hear Jon and Tony talking out in the hallway. Ahern walked calmly over to the doorway and said, "Hey, Tony, look, I'm older and not all that cute, but fuck it, I'll go out with you." Jon walked over and again slammed the door, prompting Ahern to raise his hands up in mock disbelief and to say again, "Fuck's up with that?" Things between Jonathan and I were pretty frosty after that. One night, as I was heading for the showers, Jon apparently had just finished his own shower, and when he saw me, he yelled, "Hey, Kevin, look at this!" At that point, he opened up his robe like a movie exhibitionist opens up his trench coat. He was totally naked. He then kept doing some motion with his tongue that is indescribable and something I don't think most people are capable of doing. As deadpan as I could, I said, "Good one, Jon." The disappointment hit his face like a sledgehammer. I seriously think I had ruined his night. I guess he was used to getting a different reaction on the outside.

Later that night, Jon made a point of telling me that on the outside, his father owned many apartment buildings. He said, "If you hadn't screwed things up for Tony, I would have gotten you an apartment when you got out. Good luck finding a place to live as a convicted sex offender when you leave here." "Really?" I asked him. "And would you be doing your flasher act there too?" That was the last real conversation that I would ever have with the guy. A week or so later, a bed opened up in the room that Tony lived in. Jon asked to be moved there and he was.

The day officer, Steve, asked me that afternoon, "What are you guys doing to make all these guys ask to get out of that room?" I looked at him and replied, "God, Steve, they were both total freaks." With a very thoughtful look, Steve said, "That's true. That's very true."

* * *

One Tuesday morning, I got a real shock. The guy who had confronted me in the Concord dining hall after the IPS officer had read

Jack Kaufman's letter—well, I saw him walking across the Treatment Center's yard. I was sitting on the grass talking to Alan and some of his friends. Not to anyone in particular, I said, "You've got to be shitting me!" Alan laughed and asked, "What's with you?" I then told Alan and his friends the whole story. They were shocked! Alan and his two friends had come over from the Norfolk Prison, and they actually knew the guy *and* they knew that he was convicted of a sexual crime. The big moose from Concord had also been in Norfolk.

"Kev," Alan said, "Ahern is walking the track. Go hang out with him." I looked at him and said, "Shit, Alan, don't get in trouble." Alan had a faraway look in his eyes, and he said, "Just go." I walked over to the track and started walking with Ahern, all the while watching Alan and his two friends walking up to the guy from Concord. Nothing bad took place. It seemed that they were just asking the big guy a lot of questions. Later at dinner, Alan told me that back in Concord, the IPS officer that had read my legal mail had approached the guy and told him to either mess with me or that the officer would tell the whole camp what he was in for. Alan said the guy had felt trapped. The guy had told Alan, "I might be big, but that won't stop a shank (knife) from behind."

While I sympathized with the guy, I was burning up with hatred for him. One Sunday morning, after enduring yet another "You guys are sick" sermon at Mass, the "sign of peace" moment came. I shook hands with the inmates on my left and right. Then I turned around. I was shocked to see the big guy from Concord standing behind me. Almost timidly, he held out his hand. I shook his hand and sort of nodded an "I understand" look at the guy. He did the same. At that moment, I let the entire matter go. As Jesus said, "If you don't forgive your brother from your heart, your Heavenly Father will not forgive you." It was over.

* * *

What wasn't over was my growing frustration with the priest who was the Treatment Center chaplain. No matter how a Sunday sermon started out, somewhere in the middle, it would become a long, drawn-out harangue about what "incredibly sick people" we all were. For me, I knew that not only was I *not guilty* of the charge that brought me to prison but that I had also practiced lifelong celibacy as I was studying for Catholic priesthood. In the poor man's defense, he was probably saying we were all "sick" as a way of mitigating the inmates' responsibility for their crimes, but as a falsely convicted person, it didn't sit well with me. How could it?

There came a Sunday Mass when I knew it had to be my last time—at least at the Treatment Center. I called my mom in the afternoon and asked her to mail me my Melkite Catholic service book, *Byzantine Worship*, as well as a small Eastern Orthodox prayer book. I wasn't certain if the property officer would allow me to have the books, but it was worth a try. The deal with inmates having books in prison is that you're allowed to have ten. If you receive an eleventh book, you have to either mail one of your other books home at your expense or allow the property officer to dispose of it. The problem was, you could only receive books from a publisher or a catalog book outlet.

A week later, Officer Steve gave me a slip to see the property officer. I hadn't met the guy before, and all I could think of was that foul-mouthed prick in the property department in Concord. When I got there, the guy was actually pleasant! He smiled, had me sign for the two books, and that was all. From that time on, I prayed one of the Hours each day, and I prayed twice on Sunday. I would not attend regular church services in that facility again, though that chaplain and I would meet each other again months later.

* * *

One morning at around 10:00 a.m., while I was thoroughly enjoying a morning nap, all the other guys suddenly came rushing back into the room. I looked up, still half asleep. Marc looked at me and said, "Lock down." During a lock down at most prisons, the inmates are either locked into their cells, their dormitories, or their cell blocks. We were told to remain in our rooms. They didn't even want us in that large room with the television.

All of a sudden, an earsplitting siren started going off outside. It would get exceedingly loud, then very low, then back to loud. I looked out the window and saw the source. A thing that looked like a huge metal stereo speaker was turning in circles—to broadcast the siren in all directions. I later learned that it was normally used to alert the residents of Bridgewater to a prison escape. Eventually, the siren stopped, and we all just sat around talking about what it could all be about.

Marc was, well, I'd say a "jerk," but that's way too nice a description. Marc was an asshole. In fact, at times, he was a flaming asshole. In the middle of our discussion, he suddenly said, "I'll bet it's Debra. I hope right now that someone is raping the shit out of her." Everyone was stunned. Even Ahern, who loved to say incredibly tasteless things just to see the reaction, looked disgusted. "Marc," Ahern yelled, "can't you ever keep your fucking mouth from saying stupid things?" "I don't care," Marc replied. "I hope someone is fucking her right now." Ahern looked away from Marc, shook his head, and said, "Sick bastard." Debra was one of the sex therapists. She was young, blond, and quite beautiful.

Around 1:00 p.m., a guard captain entered our room with a cooler. Another guard also brought in a cooler. They handed out turkey sandwiches and orange juice. The captain was one of the most unpleasant-looking guys I had ever seen. I had been raised to be polite, so when I took the sandwich from the captain, I quietly said, "Thank you." I think that actually pissed him off! He just gave me a dirty look and went on with his task.

Around 4:30 p.m., the entire floor was called to the big room. There were chairs already set up and the therapists were sitting in the front facing all the inmates. Though they were doing their best to remain composed, they were noticeably tense. The oldest and most senior of the group, a woman with white hair, began to speak. "This morning, our colleague Debra was sexually assaulted by a man she was counseling." She went on to name the inmate, but the name meant nothing to me. After she had finished, that kid Kevin from Newline in Concord raised his hand and began to speak. "I want to say that I am very sorry that something like this has happened to anyone, but particularly to someone as nice as Debra." The older woman replied, "Thank you." And then Kevin ruined the entire moment. "I hope this is not going to affect my 'good time [time off your sentence for work or school].'" At that, a loud groan arose from the assembled inmates. One guy in back shouted, "You already had your good time, now you're paying for it!" All I could think was, *What a stupid, self-centered moron.* An hour later, the meeting was over and the various buildings began sending guys to dinner.

Later that evening, I was sitting watching television with Tom Ahern in the big room. We were watching a gymnastics event. A few more guys joined us. Finally, an inmate came walking over, sat down, and said, "Excuse me. Please change the channel." I looked at the guy and said, "We've been watching this for twenty-five minutes." "I have a right," he replied. "The gymnasts are adolescent girls and I'm attracted to them. The rules say I can force a channel change." I leaned over and whispered to Ahern, "Seriously?" Ahern, just as annoyed as I was, just nodded. A guy switched the TV to a rerun of ABC's *Home Improvement.* Then another guy spoke up. "Oh, excuse me, I can't watch this. There are little boys in the show and I can't be watching them." Under my breath, I said, "Oh, fuck me." Ahern started his quiet laugh. Again the channel was changed. A commercial was on, and there was a Golden Retriever running through a field. Then someone in all seriousness said, "Excuse me…" I jumped out of my seat and exploded, "Everyone just say fucking nothing until I completely leave the room!" Ahern started laughing louder than I had ever heard him laugh. The last thing I heard as I opened the double doors that led to all the six-man rooms was an inmate asking, "Wow, what's wrong with him?"

Writing this years later, I'm shocked. None of us ever made any connection with what had happened to Debra and what Marc had said when the lockdown began. It honestly never entered my mind back then. Marc was always saying horrible things. He went on an anti-Princess Diana rant the day she was killed in a car accident. Marc had an evil streak. No one in the room ever mentioned it again, at least not while I was there. Did the inmate attacker have a conversation with Marc Savoy and tell him he was planning to attack the therapist? True, it's dangerous, even deadly, to be a rat in prison, but in the Treatment Center? Ratting people out was practically a way of life. If

Marc had advanced warning of a threat against Debra and failed to inform IPS, then he carries on his soul the guilt of an unspeakable sin.

* * *

With one exception, all the therapists at the Treatment Center were women. There was, however, one guy—a very unmanly sort of guy. Even from a distance, I didn't like him. One day, as I was passing through the big room, that therapist looked at me and said, "Oh! There's a face I haven't seen before!" I just sort of waved and kept walking. Each time I encountered him after that, I was aware that he was looking at me with suspicion. Time was running out.

You go to the Treatment Center to receive, well, "treatment" for whatever sexual deviancy had landed you in prison. When an inmate enters the therapy group, he has to tell the entire story, and that story must coincide *exactly* with everything the person who accused the inmate had reported. If the victim said that the inmate raped him/her while singing "The Star-Spangled Banner" in Chinese, then the inmate had to agree—and quite possibly would have to sing the national anthem in Chinese for the entire group!

Myself, I couldn't enter a group. The therapist would never accept a plea of innocence. I spoke with the corrections officer who often worked in the infirmary. He said, "God, Kevin. If you don't get into a group, they'll send you to another facility—into the general population. Your life could be in danger." After that conversation, I spent less than five minutes deciding what to do. God's Ninth Commandment states, "Thou shall not bear false witness." Ray Swanson had violated that Commandment and got me sent to prison. How could I now bear false witness against myself? I couldn't. I decided to evade the therapy staff for as long as possible to extend my stay in the land of very strange inmates, because that land was nearly 100 percent safe.

* * *

Stupid decisions will almost always come back to haunt you. After earning my degree from Westfield State in 1981, instead of searching for that perfect postgraduate job, I went right back to working for my father and his brother's landscape business. (Though my dad had died in 1978, both the garden center which he ran, as well as the landscape side of the business, lasted for quite some time.) One day, at a customer's house, I was beginning to pack the tools onto the high dump truck. When I got to the two lawnmowers, I looked around for one of my crew members to help me, but they were both around the back of the house. Instead of waiting, I picked each mower up and heaved it onto the back of the truck. The first time was just fine. The second one? I instantly felt an unbelievably severe pain in my lower back. I ruptured a disc and was unable to work for more than a year. In fact, it would be ten years before I finally found a surgeon who would fix my spine.

Despite two disc surgeries, my back would still act up every now and then, and the only relief that I could get was by putting ice on my lower back for thirty minutes at a time. (In fact, it still acts up from time to time.) Anyway, I had gotten one of the Treatment Center's doctors to write me a "prescription" for a bag of ice pretty much whenever I needed it. Of course, after thirty minutes, the ice cubes were still quite solid, and not wanting to waste that, I would share it with my friends. We bought Pepsi in plastic bottles and saved the empties. We then cut the top portion of the bottle off about five inches down from the bottle cap, and presto—a plastic cup that would hold ice for a new Pepsi!

There came a night when Ahern and I were watching television and drinking our ice-cold Pepsis out of our unique plastic cups. We heard a voice say, "Wow, you two really know how to live." It was that damn fruitcake of a male therapist standing behind us. "I'm Don," he began, obviously waiting for me to introduce myself. Tom Ahern and I sat there silently. It didn't work. Don came around and read my name off my ID card, which always had to be worn on your shirt. "Whose group are you in, Kevin?" I was trapped. "No one's." I replied. Then Don turned and walked over to the guard's desk and spoke with Steve. After a few moments, Steve came over and asked me why I wasn't assigned to a group. I had to simply tell him, "I didn't commit the crime, so I can't be in any group." Steve looked seriously concerned and said, "You know, there is a waiting list to get into this place." I knew that was probably true, but it sounded so damned funny that I actually laughed. Ahern looked at Steve and sarcastically asked, "Do you mean like a really good restaurant or like some exclusive country club?" Steve laughed, but it was all over. He would have to tell whomever was in charge of such things that I needed to be transferred out.

Later, back in our room, we told Marc what had taken place. Marc looked at me and started in. "Are you insane? This place is heaven compared to a real prison! Just fake it. Tell them what they want to hear." "I can't do that," I answered. Then Ken spoke up. "I can coach you on all the right things to say. It will be easy." Commando Tom then asked, "But how can you fake the plethometer?"

Ah yes, the "penile plethysmograph." I wasn't certain if that device, so well known in the Treatment Center, actually existed, or if it did, if they actually used it. It was a measuring device attached to a person's penis, and it measured whatever it was that got the inmate sexually aroused. If an inmate was accused of rape by a woman, then while the plethometer was attached and recording, he would hear some woman talking dirty to him through a set of headphones. It was said to be used, for example, if an inmate denied being attracted to children. With the device attached and a little kid's voice saying sexually suggestive things in the headphones, if the inmate started to get an erection—well, he couldn't very well go on claiming not to be aroused by kids.

"It doesn't matter," I told the Commando "I'm not saying I did something that I didn't do. That's lying."

I actually lasted at the Treatment Center for two and a half more weeks. I requested that I be sent to the prison in Norfolk, Massachusetts. However, one morning, Steve told me that some time during that afternoon, I would be moving to the Southeast Correctional Center (SECC) just down the road.

I'll give the guys in my room a lot of credit. They were hoarding Pepsi and snacks for a going-away party for that day we all knew would come. We sat around talking, eating, and drinking right up until the last moment. A black inmate named Jerome that I had often seen but never really interacted with stopped by and asked to see me in the hallway. It was said that he was with a Boston street gang before coming to prison. It was strange; the guys that were supposedly gang members were probably the friendliest and most intelligent of all the inmates that I encountered. Jerome handed me a small sealed envelope. On the outside of the envelope, in block letters, it read "Jamaica." I put the envelope into my pocket and jokingly asked, "Tickets to Jamaica, I hope?" The guy laughed and said, "Good one, Kev. No, when you get to SECC, go to the kitchen and ask for a guy named Jamaica. He's one of the cooks. He will have dreadlocked hair. Give him the envelope." I'm sure I wasn't supposed to deliver messages, but what the hell, as I heard so many guys in prison say, "What are they going to do, put me in jail?" "OK," I told him. Then he shook my hand and wished me luck.

A few minutes later, I was sent downstairs, chained up and told to wait for a truck. With me was a huge Korean inmate named Kang who was also going to SECC. I tried to make conversation with the man to no avail. He either didn't want to talk to me, or perhaps he was scared. I could understand; I was a bit scared myself. When the truck arrived, we were brought to the back of it. The transport guard opened the back door. Damn it all! There was a young red-haired inmate in back. His ID card read, "Sean O'Rourke." Could my luck possibly get any worse? O'Rourke looked at Kang and me like we were the scum of the earth. As the van took off, he was trying his best to simply look away from the two of us. This was not a good beginning to a new prison.

# Southeast Correctional Center (SECC)

After being processed into SECC, Kang, O'Rourke, and I were sent to a large one-floor prefabricated blue building that was simply called *Orientation*. This was the hugest "dormitory" that I had ever seen. Once again, I was in a new place without soap, toothbrush, toothpaste, deodorant—you get the idea. As soon as I made up my bunk, I approached the guard's station, all behind glass, to ask for at least the standard kit of soap, a toothbrush, and some Chinese "guaranteed no animal fat" toothpaste. I had to laugh; the guard sergeant behind the glass had red hair and a thick mustache, and he looked shockingly like one of my bosses from years back. As I was waiting for one of the sergeant's guard gophers to fetch my hygiene kit, an absolute idiot of an inmate stood behind me, apparently not realizing that I was observing his reflection in the glass wall in front of us. He was tall and stupid-looking, and he got the sergeant's attention by waving his arms. When the mustache looked up, the inmate pointed at me and made the hip motion of someone having sex. He was asking the sergeant if I was in prison on a sex charge. The sergeant very slowly nodded, and the inmate drew his finger across his throat. At that point, I quickly turned and faced him. He scurried away like a suddenly illuminated cockroach. Damn coward.

I went to take a shower. There is some asinine belief among inmates that a naked man is somehow at a huge disadvantage in a fight. Certainly, it's far better to be able to *kick* someone with a pair of boots on, but otherwise, a general lack of clothing should pose no disadvantage in a physical battle. At least there is no clothing for your opponent to grab onto, and being wet from a shower can make a punch basically slide off. I heard a guy walking up, and just as I turned, he tried to punch me in the midsection. I kicked him in the groin and threw several punches into his face. He looked stunned! He turned and ran. When I had finished my shower, I walked back to my bunk. I could see my former attacker far off in a corner of the building. Though he was watching me, he was working extremely hard to avoid eye contact. I kept watching him until I knew he was looking directly at me—then I deliberately laughed. I wanted him to know just how feeble his "attack" actually was. He turned away. I suppose I should have slept that night, as they say, "with one eye open," but I didn't. I slept like a log that first night, though I severely missed the end of night jokes that Tom Ahern had always provided.

The next morning at breakfast, as we walked through the kitchen's serving area, I quietly asked an inmate food server if he knew where I could find Jamaica. He turned and called over a black inmate who had dreadlocks in his hair. The man was about my height, which is to say, short, but he was about two feet wider and heavily muscled. Without saying anything, I handed him the envelope. Jamaica quickly put it into his pants pocket. "From Jerome," I told him, and then I went to eat. Five hours later, while sitting in the dining hall eating lunch, I saw Jamaica walking along the ridiculously long stainless-steel table with a pitcher. Every so often, there was a pitcher of juice on the table. Starting two pitchers away, Jamaica started adding a little ice to each pitcher. When he got to the one nearest me, he said, "Tonight in the rec building, they are showing a movie. Be there at 7:10 after movement." And then he went to the next juice pitcher and poured in the rest of the ice. The whole thing was starting to remind me of a spy novel.

Within the Orientation Dormitory, there was a small clique of young Irish guys who all seemed to be friends with Sean O'Rourke. Even in the late 1990s, there was still quite a bit of racism in Boston, and O'Rourke and his friends always seemed to avoid *any* contact with black inmates whatsoever. So I had to laugh as I entered the rec room. A movie had already begun playing on a small TV screen, and the only two people in the room when I arrived were one of O'Rourke's pals and, of course, Jamaica. Out of the corner of my eye, I could see the absolute shock on O'Rourke's friend's face as I casually walked in and took the seat right next to Jamaica.

"You're late," Jamaica said as I sat down. I didn't know what to say, and I actually started stuttering. Jamaica just cracked up, laughing. It's hard to explain, but his laugh had a certain warmth to it. I knew instantly that he was a good guy. "How is Jerome doing over there?" he asked. "He seems OK," I answered. I didn't want to tell him that Jerome had really bought into the therapeutic bullshit and that it didn't seem quite natural for him. "He has to get out of there," Jamaica added. All I could think to say was, "I know." Jamaica went on, "Jerome says you're a good friend and that I should look out for you." I started to speak, but he held up his hand to stop me. Then he continued, "If someone fucks with you, I need to know. It will get taken care of. Don't get into any fights—you don't want a trip to the hole. The right words from the right person are better than a hundred punches."

Then he switched up. "You and Jerome, you didn't eat the soup over there, did you?" I was scared and said, "Oh shit! I ate the soup all the time—so did Jerome." Jamaica shook his head. "They don't cook *anything* over there," he said. "It's all cooked here. The food is OK, but when some of these assholes know the soup is going over to the Treatment Center… they sometimes do fucked-up things to it. Shit, I got to get a letter over to Jerome!" I probably should have felt sick, but I didn't. For a while, we both sat there silently watching the film, then finally, our conversation turned to the movie itself. When the movie ended, we walked as far back to our respective living units as we could, then we each had to go our separate ways. Before we split up, Jamaica told me, "Tomorrow, sign up for the four o'clock computer class. There's a waiting list, but I'll get you in."

Back in Orientation, I could tell that word of my liaison with Jamaica had already reached O'Rourke and company. It was hysterically funny! I could see they were trying to figure out which one of them should ask me about the matter. Eventually, they sent a guy who was always very quiet and respectful—you couldn't help but like him. "Good movie tonight?" he asked. "It was OK," I replied. Then he went right for it. "You actually know that guy you were with tonight?" he asked. "He's an old friend," I lied. His final question almost caused me to screw up and start laughing. "Business friend or personal friend?" he inquired. "Both," I lied again. "Oh," was all he could say, and then he was gone.

The next morning, I wrote my name on the computer class's sign-up sheet. After a visit to the library for a book to read, I went back to the dorm and read Victor Sheymov's *Tower of Secrets* right up until lunchtime. Again, I ran into Jamaica, who told me, "Come to the yard at two." After lunch, I continued my reading, then at the two o'clock movement, I went to the yard and met up with him. We spent two hours just walking and talking. I realized that he was highly intelligent and he had an awesome personality, not to mention a keen sense of humor. He told me that the next day at 3:00 p.m., I would have to start the computer orientation class. I looked at him in disbelief and asked, "How? I just signed up this morning!" Jamaica laughed and said, "Just be there—you're on the list. Now"—he changed subjects—"you need to get into a private cell. These dorms are no good." "There's supposedly a long waiting list," I told him. He quietly laughed and said, "Put in a sick slip about not being able to sleep. You'll see the shrink, tell him you're afraid, and that you know the other inmates are watching you while you sleep." I looked at Jamaica and said, "What if he asks me *which* inmates are watching me sleep?" "Even better," he laughed "Then you tell him *all of them are!* You'll get your cell, trust me." After dinner that night, I put in my sick slip then spent the rest of the night reading.

The following afternoon, I had an appointment with the psychiatrist. This guy was "out there." He was a thin man, average height, with black plastic-rimmed glasses. He wanted to know how I ended up in prison, so I told him the entire story. "You should have had that bastard killed and tossed him in a river long before the trial!" he told me. I know I should have been shocked, but I also could tell that he was joking—sort of. OK, I wasn't entirely sure.

As I looked over his desk, my eyes were drawn to two catalogs of helicopters. He saw me look and picked one up, saying, "I'm thinking of buying one, I'm just not sure which make and model." It was the first time I had ever met anyone thinking of such a huge purchase.

"So you can't sleep?" he asked. "Everyone is watching me sleep—it freaks me out," I replied. "How could it not!" he exclaimed. *Oh great*, I thought to myself, *he thinks I'm nuts*. He grabbed a form from his desk and said, "OK, what you need is your own cell—and some sleep medication." That was almost too easy. "Thank you!" I told him. Then he said, "I'll see you in a week to check on how you're doing." I left his office amazed. Hopefully my time in Orientation Building would soon come to an end.

At the three o'clock movement, I walked to the school building and on to the computer room. A teacher named Herve told me to go to another room for computer orientation. A few minutes later, at that new room, Herve began going over the very basics of computers. I knew absolutely nothing about computers, and I was very grateful for the chance to learn things from the very beginning. Herve was a small guy with gray hair and wire-rimmed glasses. He was definitely firm with the students, but I could tell he was a really nice guy. I could have sworn that I once saw Herve and a old friend named David from Westfield State at a McDonald's in Natick, Massachusetts, way back in the early 1980s. I figured I had to be wrong until at one point, he mentioned that he had worked for Prime Computer of Natick "a while back." I never mentioned anything since I wouldn't have wanted Dave to know I was in prison.

Herve covered so much in one hour, but he made it understandable, even for someone as technically challenged as I was. There had been a computer class at the Treatment Center, but there was simply no instruction provided at all. There I had approached the "instructor" and asked, "What should I do?" He was a really young guy and, looking up from his newspaper as though I had just interrupted a church service, he simply said, "Do whatever you want." I played with the keyboard for a while, then I just sat there and waited for movement. I never returned. Hopefully, the state was paying Herve more than that loser, but I doubt it. Herve said that we would start out learning the proper way to type. (I did learn that, but after a couple of months, I went back to the two-finger method. I have no idea why.) There would also be one more "orientation hour" before we actually hit the computer lab. This guy was seriously just as committed to teaching the inmates as was any teacher or professor that I had had on the outside.

After class, I stopped at the Catholic Chapel to pray. There was a man in the office all dressed in black and wearing the Roman Collar. I asked him if I could go to Confession. He motioned to a chair, and I launched into the Confession ritual that I knew so well. When I finished, he made the sign of the Cross over me without saying any words. He told me that there was a service every morning at 9:00 a.m. and that I should stop by. I told him I would, even though I left the chapel at movement an hour later still baffled over the lack of words of absolution. That had happened only one other time during my entire life. Once, at St. Anthony's Shrine in downtown Boston, I finished saying my confession and the priest started saying the Confeitor entirely in Latin. I had studied Latin in high school, and I knew this was not the prayer of absolution. At that time I simply got out of that Confessional, went into another, and repeated the Confession. I couldn't do that here. The next morning, I returned to the chapel only to see the chaplain wearing the stole of a deacon. He was not authorized nor empowered to hear Confessions! Normally I would have been worried sick, but this was not a normal place nor a normal time in my life. I just let it go. (I mentioned it again years later during two separate Confessions. One of the priests said, "Then this absolution will have to cover that too." Hopefully, he was right!) Anyway, I kind of liked the chaplain, and months later, I would get the inmate job of chaplain's assistant.

* * *

The first night that I received my sleeping medication was a near disaster. I got back to my Orientation Building bed and started to read. The next thing I knew, a guard was yelling in my ear. It was count time and I was out like a light. (I was now like that Spanish kid from Newline that I had to hold up during the count.) The moron guard stood there until I was in the correct position, standing in front of my bunk, as if it really mattered. The red-haired sergeant looked over at Sean O'Rourke, whose bunk was across from mine, and said, "Nice going, O'Rourke. You see a guy asleep and don't help him out at count time?" O'Rourke looked surprised by the criticism, though he wasn't angry. The next morning, I was told that I was moving to an older dormitory. I wasn't unhappy, but I had been expecting a private cell. When I got to the dorm, it was a complete dump. Although the inmate janitors kept it clean, it was ancient, dark, and the floorboards creaked like something out of a cheap horror film. There was one huge room full of bunk beds and a smaller one also filled with beds. The shower room was like many health clubs—one big open room with six showers. It had a heavy wooden door that would muffle any sounds if someone were getting their ass kicked in there. It took a while before I showered without keeping myself on "high alert."

I had the top bunk with a very old man sleeping on the bottom. He seemed OK, albeit incredibly dumb, and he was constantly picking on a big, bald Spanish guy with a mustache. "Hey, Maurice!" he always started. "They gonna deport your ass back to Cuba" (which the old guy pronounced the Spanish way, *koo-ba*). Maurice would just shake his head and say, "I'm from Puerto Rico. I'm just as American as you!" To which the old grouch would respond, "Bullshit! You floated to Florida on an inner tube from Koo Ba." What was surprising to me was that Maurice seemed truly worried that *I* would believe the old guy. Maurice was a quiet guy who bothered no one. I really didn't care where he was from originally.

Back at the computer class, I was learning everything, from Word to Excel to Power Point. During the last ten minutes of class, Herve allowed the students to play the pin ball game that was installed on the computer. God help you if Herve caught you screwing around before the final ten minutes! He would threaten to kick out the "offenders" from his class—permanently. I don't know if he actually would have, but no one ever tested him. Those final minutes I devoted to trying to beat Jamaica at the game. I never beat him, not even once. As we talked during those games, I learned a lot. Jamaica was born, well, in Jamaica. His parents brought him to the United States when he was four years old. Under American law, after he finished his prison sentence, he would be automatically deported back to Jamaica, where he had no family and no friends. All arguments aside, it just wasn't right. The first time I heard it, I said, "Oh God, Ian, that's wicked unfair." It was the first time that I had ever used his real name. It didn't seem to bother him in the least, so from that time on, I stopped calling him Jamaica.

Eventually, another new guy joined our computer class, a black inmate from Boston called "4-5" (pronounced *four five*, not *forty-five*). This guy was beyond huge. If he had told me that he once played professional football—I would have had no doubts. Ian and 4-5 were polite to each other but not friendly. I assumed that *if* they had been gang members on the outside, then they were probably from different gangs, though I doubted they were from rival gangs. Again, I have no idea what either of them did on the outside or, as they would say, "on the street." At a later date, 4-5 would become a vitally important friend.

* * *

I had a lot of visits. My former Westfield State roommate and best friend, Paul, visited; Sgt. Steve Day from the Emerson College

Police; my sister Janice, brothers-in-law Jeff and Tom; and most importantly, my mom dropped by. It was a very long ride for all of them. Both the Treatment Center and SECC had good visiting rooms, each with food and beverage vending machines. (Concord had nothing in the way of snacks. Your visitors had to purchase white "money cards" for use in those machines as the prison in no way wanted any type of cash falling into the hands of the inmates. If you had a "balance" on the card after release from prison, all the better for the canteen company. It was rumored that the canteen company was run by a group of former guards. I never found out if that was true.)

On one such visit, Steve Day told me that a former Emerson deputy chief had asked him, "Did you hear about Kevin?" I was blown away! "How could he possibly know?" I asked. "He lives in Virginia!" Quite stoically, Steve replied, "Bad news travels fast." I was pissed off. The former deputy was, in my opinion, a little weasel. He used to stand and bullshit me to my face, and I know he thought I was an idiot for believing him. I *never* believed him—I was protecting my job.

One of Paul's visits was amusing. He hadn't known about the money card system, and we both desperately —well, I desperately, wanted a cold Pepsi. I got up and approached an inmate "friend" and basically negotiated a beverage deal. He used his girlfriend's card to buy me two drinks, and I had to pay him back three bottles of Pepsi from my next canteen order. The whole thing cracked Paul up.

My brother-in-law Jeff's first prison visit was to Concord. He was wearing some "prohibited" clothing—clothes too close to what an inmate might wear—and he had to go into the Town of Concord and buy different clothes. He's an awesome guy; most people would have just gone home. All during his visit, there was a loud thunderstorm going on. Being there that particular night was harder for him than me. I realize how hard it must be to leave someone you care about behind in that dump. At SECC though, Jeff admitted to thoroughly enjoying the vending machine hamburgers. (They were good.)

One night in Concord's Newline, I was called for a visit with my sister Janice. On the first floor, there was an old guard. He stopped me and asked, "Was it a boy?" I looked at him perplexed and muttered, "What?" He was smiling like an eight-year-old looking at a hot fudge sundae and he asked, "Did you have sex with a boy?" His smile was absolutely fiendish. I said nothing. Then the old prick said, "You know, North Andover, that's a very long drive for your sister to make. I would hate to make her leave without seeing you. Now tell me, was it a boy?" I looked at the fool and replied, "I was falsely accused by a fifteen-year-old kid." That seemed to physically excite him. Rising slightly from his chair, he leaned forward, his demented smile wider than ever, and he asked, "A fifteen-year-old boy?" I replied, "Yeah." "Oh good!" he exclaimed. "Now run along, don't keep your sister waiting!" What a sick bastard.

On another occasion, Tom visited with my mom. He sat down in the chair next to me and started, "My life sucks." From that point on, there was no stopping him. He went on and on about how bad things were going for him. Eventually he stopped whining, and I had a great conversation with my mom. When they left, I had to take my seat next to another inmate while we waited to be called in for our post-visit strip-search. The guy was black, and clearly he seemed like something was *deeply* troubling him. At exactly the same moment, we turned and faced each other, and he went off. "Who was that ignorant motherfucker sitting with you telling *you*—of all fucking people—how bad *his* fucking life is on the outside where he's a fucking free man?" I just laughed and said, "Yeah, I know. He's like that sometimes." "Seriously?" my newfound friend asked. "Yup, what can I say?" I replied. "Where the fuck does he live?" he asked, still obviously quite angry. "Wakefield," I told him. "That's not that far from Boston," he went on. "You want me to send up some niggers to straighten his ass out?" At that, I just collapsed into a full laughing fit. That seemed to calm the guy down completely; he started laughing himself. After we were searched and started to go our separate ways, he shouted over to me, "You let me know, Wakefield's not that far away!"

By far, I imagine my mom had the hardest time of all. I cry when I leave my dog for a grooming appointment, so I doubt I'll ever know how tough it was for her to see me in those places. Mom grew up in Boston, and she liked to think of herself as a tough city girl, but really, that doesn't mean anything. Yet she never, ever had anything but a smile on whenever she visited me. As I have said, she absolutely hated it when a female guard would "frisk" her. She was from a very different, more modest time. She wrote me letters constantly. Mom, Janice, and Jeff spent all three of my imprisoned Christmas holidays with me. No turkey dinner, just a vending machine hamburger. I never asked her what it felt like when she left from a visit. Fourteen years later, after visiting her in a nursing home at the very end of her life, I sat in my car, hugged my dog Yuri, and cried my heart out. It's just possible that I finally now know just a little better how hard it was for her when she left from one of her many prison visits.

* * *

After my first Christmas prison visit, I returned to the old dirty dormitory. I took out my Bible and read the Christmas story. Maurice came over to my bed and asked, "Are you ready for Christmas dinner?" "What dinner?" I asked. Maurice smiled and said, "The one I cooked for us. Come on!" He was serious. I told him I'd be right over. I opened up my footlocker and retrieved two bottles of Pepsi and a box of Little Debbie cupcakes. On his footlocker, Maurice had two bowls of spaghetti with sauce and pepperoni. We toasted each other with the Pepsi and had a great Christmas meal. A few bunks over, a very young inmate sarcastically yelled out, "This is the best Christmas I've *ever* had." Maurice and I looked at each other, laughed, and went back to our feast.

* * *

One afternoon, I came back from my computer class and an inmate was being hauled out of the dormitory by three IPS officers. The dorm guard looked at me and said, "His job was to clean the big (bed)room, you want the job?" I was a bit worried and asked, "Won't he be back?" The guard laughed and said, "Trust me, he's never coming back. Good time plus a buck a day," while holding out a pushbroom. Of course all I heard was "good time." "OK," I replied, and I started sweeping the floor.

Each inmate was given a roll of toilet paper every so often for his personal use. What was disgusting was that they also used it to blow their noses. I used to walk my used tissue over to the trash can and toss it in after blowing *my* nose. No one else did that. They would simply "blow and throw," depositing the paper now filled with nasal debris onto the floor. Now part of my job was to sweep that up. After sweeping the floor, I had to mop it as well. It wasn't that bad; other guys had either the toilets or shower room to clean. One night, while finishing up the mopping, my back "went out." I walked over to the guard and asked if I could have two trash bags. "What for?" he asked. "My back is messed up. I want to fill it with snow and ice myself." I replied. The guard handed over two bags and said, "Cool. Knock yourself out." Fortunately, the snow did the trick.

On a Monday night, the guard called all the inmate workers together for a meeting. "I'm going to start rotating the jobs on a weekly basis so no one guy gets stuck doing the shit house and shower room all the time." I was exceedingly unhappy with that idea and I started to wonder just how you go about "quitting" an inmate job. After his announcement, the night guard began looking at a Ford Truck brochure. I asked him if he was about to get a new truck. He said that he was, and we spent an hour talking about the different trucks on the market. I was going to try and sneak in an "I quit" into our discussion, but I chickened out.

The following morning the day guard told me to pack up my stuff, as I was moving to cell block A-3. I was elated! The shrink had finally gotten me out of the dormitory. The only downside was leaving Maurice behind, but what could I do? Just as I was finishing packing up, the old grouch on the bottom bunk decided it was time to give me some (unwanted) advice. "You have to be careful in a cell block. After movement and all night long, the doors to the block are locked. The 'screws' (guards) only walk through once an hour, so don't make any enemies. And stick to your own kind—stop hanging around with blacks and Spanish guys. I don't know why you want to associate with those people in the first place, but you do it all the time." I laughed and simply answered, "OK." He shook his head and said, "You'll never learn."

At A-3, I quickly found my assigned cell and made up my bed. The three cell buildings, A, B, and C, are the oldest part of SECC. More than one of the guards had told me that these old cell buildings dated back to the American Civil War. One guard told me that Confederate POW's had been held there, but I have no way of knowing if that was true. Each floor, or "block," was a long narrow corridor holding about twenty cells. Opposite the cells were large barred windows. Unlike more modern prisons, these cells did not have their own toilet/sink combination. Attached to the building was a very modern bathroom building. It was apparently added on like an addition to an already existing house. There were toilet stalls and individual shower stalls that actually had shower curtains! The individual cells were about seven feet wide and ten feet deep. There was a shelf/table thing at the front of the cell near the end of the bed. On the back wall there was a window with bars that looked out over a courtyard. The door to the cell was part metal, part wood and about eight inches thick. There was also a small window to the left of the door so that the guards could look in during count time. In two and a half years, I only knew one inmate stupid enough to sleep with his head down by the door and directly under the window. If an inmate wanted to hurt you and most likely never get caught, all he'd have to do was throw boiling water through that window onto your face.

What surprised me was that only one inmate on that block ever spoke to me at all. I've found that, generally speaking, in any given prison living situation, at least eight out of every ten inmates are friendly. Not on A-3. The guy who did speak was a short, bald, and quite rugged older white guy. He was friendly though he never smiled, and he seemed to be perpetually angry. Apparently he was there on a sex conviction and his case was well-known by both guards and inmates alike. He explained the fact that everyone hated him. As he told me, whatever he did or was charged with, it took place in the Bridgewater area, so when he came to prison, every guard already knew every detail of the man's "story" from the local newspapers, and the guards in turn went out of their way to make sure *every* inmate knew the story as well. As he was telling me about his plight, I remembered that Tanner, my first cell mate from Concord's Newline, had also lived in the Bridgewater area. Tanner had been ecstatic the morning when he was told that he was moving to SECC. So where was Tanner now? After a couple of years, one thing became clear: Tanner *was not* at SECC. My guess is that he ran into some serious persecution and was most likely returned to the Plymouth County Jail where the most notorious child molesters were kept in protective custody. I went to dinner with the guy just once. Many eyes were upon me during that meal. It was quite uncomfortable.

I slept extremely well that first night in A-3. It was nice to be alone in my own "room." So far, the only thing I didn't like was the extreme unfriendliness of the guys on the block. Early the next morning, I heard a lot of noise emanating from the far end of the cell block. I got up, still extremely groggy, and stepped out into the hall. In front of the last cell on the block, there was a huge puddle of blood. There were two IPS officers, one of whom was taking photographs of the cell and the blood. They both looked at me, and one of them said, "Either go to the bathroom or stay in your cell." I went to the bathroom then returned to my cell. I would love to say what took place down there, but no one ever told me and I never found out.

From the old cell buildings, you had to cross into what was called the cement yard. There were two sections of that yard. The first was surrounded by the school building, the property department, and a dormitory building. That dormitory was then attached to the dining hall. You then passed through a narrow opening into another section of the cement yard. Straight ahead was a high wall separating the cement yard from the other half of the prison. That section also housed three chapels: Catholic, Protestant, and Muslim. The yard then took a left turn to where, once a week, the canteen store distributed the purchased goods to the inmates. It was a very long walk to the infirmary when you had to go and receive your medicine. Oftentimes, the length of movement was at the whim of the individual guards manning the many gates and doors. At times, you could go and receive your medication and actually make it back to the cell block. Most of the time, however, you got stranded in the cement yard and had to wait forty-five to fifty minutes for the next movement time. If a blinding blizzard or a raging thunderstorm were taking place, that was *your* bad luck. Only once during a particularly violent thunderstorm did one of the guard's supervisors force them to keep the gates open after movement had ended.

So on my second night in A-3, right after taking my sleeping medication, I ended up "trapped" in the cement yard after movement ended. I remember standing near the basketball court in the cement yard when it became clear to me that I was losing consciousness. I fought as hard as I could to stay awake, but I just knew I wouldn't be standing for much longer. Then everything got fuzzy, then it all went black.

# Shattuck Hospital

As I slowly became more and more alert, I realized that I was in an ambulance and handcuffed to the stretcher. Eventually I was wheeled into an emergency room of some local hospital. I had either received the wrong medication or too much of the right medication—that's something I'll never know. One really bad thing about being transported by the Department of Corrections anywhere—to the hospital, court, or even just to another prison—is that the accompanying guards have to carry legal documentation proving that they have custody of the inmate being transported. Those documents list what the person was convicted of. Guards who heretofore had no idea what a person was incarcerated for soon did.

In the emergency ward there was a municipal policeman. He was talking to the guards and looking at my papers. I heard the cop say, "You know the 'fleeing felon law'—you un-handcuff him and tell him to go to the bathroom, then I'll yell 'Stop!' and shoot the bastard. It will all be legal." I wouldn't have been worried, except that none of them—neither the cop nor the two prison guards—even cracked a smile. I sincerely believe that the cop was making a deadly serious threat against me. I eventually had some x-rays and blood tests. Then it was back to another ambulance for a trip to the Shattuck Prison Hospital. It was absurd; all I really needed was to go back to my cell and sleep it off.

I arrived at the Shattuck emergency room and was shocked to see that it was a little after midnight. For some reason, they opened up the Intensive Care Unit just for me. A kindly older doctor was there, along with two nurses. That doctor asked the guard to un-handcuff me. At first he refused, then the doctor said, "Look, I don't go into your prison and tell you how to do things, so please don't tell me how to run the ICU." Reluctantly the guard did as he was asked. And once again, I was tapped for a series of blood tests. I could see the guard wince as the nurse later brought me a large cup of ginger ale.

Around 4:00 a.m., the doctor decided that I could be transferred to a hospital prison ward. He wished me well. I really liked the guy. The guards re-handcuffed my right hand to the stretcher and wheeled me to an elevator. When the door opened, I was in a hallway with a guard's station straight ahead, the elevator and a flight of stairs right behind me. The desk guard, a sergeant, looked like a nasty old bastard who probably should have retired several years before. He scrutinized my documents then said, "Accidents happen. Push the fucking stretcher down the flight of stairs and let's see what happens." Again there were no smiles, no laughter. He repeated his request again. If I was worried before, I was ten times more worried as the guards from SECC began arguing with the guy, telling him that they wanted no part of pushing me down the stairs—and the paperwork that would follow. Eventually the old prick relented, and I was wheeled through a set of doors and into a rundown hospital ward.

The two SECC guards then left, and a DOC hospital officer showed me to a room with four beds. I got the only empty bed nearest the window. Then the officer surprised me saying, "I'll see if I can find you a television." I fell asleep, and in the morning, that same corrections officer entered the room and set a small television on the table next to my bed. I couldn't believe my good fortune! I immediately tuned the set to the local morning news. Eventually, a woman delivered trays with scrambled eggs and cereal.

To my left was an inmate patient who looked like a death camp survivor. I was shocked. If the guy weighed eighty pounds, I would have been amazed. He looked over at me and raised his hand in a wave, but he could only hold it up for a second or two. The guy directly across from me was highly talkative; I enjoyed his company immensely. He was also the only person I ever met who actually had suffered a "sucking chest wound." He told me in great detail how they had to deflate one of his lungs. It sounded extremely painful.

Next to him was a man who simply slept all the damn time like he was drugged or something.

Later in the afternoon, I took a walk down the hallway. Although there was a barrier between wards, there was a women's ward attached, and I ended up having an hour-long conversation with a female inmate through the bars. It was somewhat refreshing! You sort of get tired of being surrounded by other men all the damn time.

Around 9:00 p.m., a middle-aged Spanish-speaking woman stopped outside our room with a metal push cart. She entered the room and came over to me and said, "Jell-O, pudding?" The guy across from me said, "Tell her which one you want." I wasn't expecting a snack delivery, and I answered, "Jell-O." The woman repeated "Jell-O!" Then she brought me three containers! She brought each patient three containers each. It was like heaven on earth! After finishing off all the Jell-Os, I started to settle in to sleep. Then the very thin man next to me stretched out his hand with two full pudding containers. "Oh no," I told him. "You really should eat them—even if you save them until tomorrow." Then he spoke very quietly. "I'm dying of AIDS. I can't stand to eat more than a couple of times a week. I want you to have them." I started to object, but he went on, "If I die tonight, do you want my last moment to be you refusing my gift?" What could I do? I took the pudding and ate one right away. The poor guy smiled and fell asleep. I spent some time praying for him before I too fell asleep.

The next morning, my "mini vacation" was over. I was chained up and brought to a DOC sedan and driven back to SECC. What I was about to find out was that my cell had already been given away to another inmate and all my belongings were in plastic trash bags at the property department. So where would I end up now?

# SECC "The Hole"

Now the hole is well known as a place where inmates who cause trouble are sent. However, I was told by a guard sergeant that I was going to the hole because of "lack of housing." The hole was in the same building as the infirmary. There was a windowless corridor with high doors on one side. Everything was painted white. A guard opened up one of the cells for me. It was a room somewhat larger than the cell in A-3. Each wall was made of concrete cinder blocks. The ceiling, for some reason, was quite high. There was the combination toilet/sink and a mattress lying on a bare floor. There were no sheets. The guard handed me a blanket then told me to wait there a second. He returned and handed me a pillow saying, "Since you're not here for being an asshole, you can have a pillow." Once he shut the door, there was only the very slightest of light coming through the door's small window. When the evening shift came in at 4:00 p.m., they turned off the hall lights and there was total darkness. I wondered if it was done on purpose to screw with the inmates.

At dinnertime, a small trap door on the bottom of the large door opened and a guard slid a tray of food into my cell. The lights had been turned back on for a few minutes so I could at least tell what I was eating. Later, around 8:00 p.m., a guard banged on my door and told me to put my hands through yet another trap door in the center of the larger door. I extended my hands out, and they were handcuffed. The guard then opened the door and placed leg irons on each of my ankles. All of this was done in order to walk thirty yards to where the nurse was giving out the evening medication.

The nurses in charge of medication lines were easily *the* nicest people in the entire prison. There were two nurses, and the one at the hole tonight was as close to looking like my grandmother's "missing" twin sister as she could possibly be. I always enjoyed seeing her in the regular medication line. "Did you get in trouble?" she whispered to me. "No," I told her. "Lack of housing." She gave me my sleeping medicine, and she had to hold the cup to my mouth since my hands were now chained to my waist chain. She asked, "More water?" I gratefully nodded. As she was giving me yet a third cup, the guard got impatient and said, "That's enough water." The nurse snapped back, saying, "Mind your own business!" The guard, quite shocked at being yelled at by this little woman, looked like a grade school kid who'd just been scolded by his teacher.

Then I returned to my cell. My hands, though still cuffed, were released from the waist chain, which was removed. Then the leg irons were removed. I entered the cell, and the door was closed. Then I had to extend my hands through the trap door to get the damn handcuffs off. It was a lot of work for a pill, but since I was in a pitch-black cell with nothing to do, I might as well sleep as much as possible. And sleep I did. I only woke up for meals and medication.

Unfortunately, I snore. And I snore like a hibernating bear. It must have started to really bother one of the day guards since every so often he would pound his hands on my big cell door. Although I was aware of the noise he was making, it hardly disturbed my sleep at all. On the third day that I was there, that day guard slid my lunch tray through the bottom trap door. It was a hot dog with beans. I looked at the hot dog roll, and for the first time ever in prison, it looked like it had been buttered. I placed the hot dog in the roll and squeezed a pack of mustard onto it. Then I realized that I could smell something foul. It was urine! My roll wasn't yellow from butter—someone had pissed on it! It had to have been the day guard who was so disturbed by my snoring. What a damn animal. I imagine he was disappointed when he later saw that I had not eaten either the hot dog or the roll. (Since Ian worked in the kitchen, he would later tell me that no one in the kitchen would ever have done that.)

That night, I again was chained up for my thirty-yard walk to the medication line. As we were approaching the nurse, a lieutenant with a Spanish surname approached from the opposite direction. He looked at me puzzled and said, "Wait, I've seen you around. You're not a troublemaker—what are you doing in the hole?" Before I could answer, the nurse said, "He's never been trouble. He's here for lack of housing." The lieutenant's face turned red. "Take those damn chains off this man." The guard looked shocked and replied, "But it's procedure. I'll get in trouble." The lieutenant's voice turned cold as he said, "I'll take responsibility for him, and I'll escort him back to the cell. Now get those goddamned chains off him!" I almost cried. Someone in uniform was actually sticking up for me. I got my medication, and the lieutenant brought me back to my cell. I thanked the guy with more sincerity than I had probably ever experienced. He said, "One size doesn't fit all. Get some rest. We'll find a way to get you out of here." I knew he meant every word. What an awesome guy. The next morning, I was sent to cell building B, 4th floor.

# SECC B-4

I had just settled into my new cell on B-4 when a tall bald guy named Williams called my name. I walked down to his cell. He held up a new package of razor blades and asked if I wanted to buy them. I knew this guy. He worked in the property department. After I went to the hospital, they had packed up my belongings and sent them over to property—and this asshole had stolen my new razor blades. Now he wanted to make a deal to sell them back to me. I simply replied, "No thanks, I'm all set." As I walked away, he called after me, "Are you sure?" I answered "Yup" and kept walking. I would now have to wait at least a week before getting the blades that I needed.

I got the biggest kick out of guys like Williams. They walked around acting like they were the "ultimate cons," like guys in some Hollywood prison movie, yet they were rats and thieves and spent all day kissing the guard's asses for whatever they could get out of it. If they pulled that crap in Walpole, they'd have been killed. Yet in Concord or SECC, they were looked upon as "super cons." It was a sad joke. Williams should have known better—he was in for life.

That first night, I was just sitting in my new cell reading a book. At least none of those dumb bastards would steal my books. Suddenly, through my door came 4-5, carrying a bowl of soup. He set it down on my table and said, "I know you probably didn't get any food from the canteen this week, so I made you some chicken soup." It was an incredible act of kindness. I was also thrilled to have a friend in my new cell block. While I ate, we talked—mostly about our computer class. It was one of the most relaxing nights I had ever had in any prison. At one point, 4-5 asked, "So before you got 'behind the wall,' were you warned to look out for the black dudes?" I laughed and said, "Well, television and movies always show black guys in prison as kicking everyone's ass, but from my experience so far, it's the asshole white guys that cause all the problems." 4-5 roared laughing and said, "And when you finally get out and tell people that, no one is going to believe you!"

The next day, I got another slip to go to the property department. This was big. It said "TV" on the slip. My sister Janice had given me the $75 to buy one of the canteen store televisions while I was in the Treatment Center. Somehow there was a huge mix-up, and it took weeks to get the TV sent over to SECC. My sister had kept up pressure on the superintendent (warden) of SECC to get to the bottom of the problem, and I guess that pressure had finally paid off.

The property department was staffed by two guards: a man who was the property officer and a woman who assisted him. A lot of guys in their late forties to early fifties were already there when I arrived. Most of them were trading in old prison clothes for new ones. It's funny how awesome it feels to get new socks when only the state can provide them. The canteen sold T-shirts and underwear, but I don't remember being able to purchase socks. When my turn came up, I got the female guard. She took my slip then launched into a speech that she hoped would get me hurt or even killed. "Here is your TV from the"—and then at the top of her lungs, she shouted, "*Treatment Center*. Sign here saying that you have received your property from the *Treatment Center*!" Humorously, only four or five older Hispanic inmates heard her—and they completely ignored every thing she said. I later told Ian about the whole incident, and he just laughed. "She's always been a wicked bitch," he told me. "But old Spanish guys—they just want to do their time then get out. They don't mess with anyone."

Once I got my new television back to my room, I began to set it up. It was built in South Korea specifically for prison use—in other words, it didn't have a speaker. The only way to listen to the sound was through a set of cheap headphones that were included. I was having some trouble getting reception, and I started to swear. Then a voice behind me said, "Let me help, I know these junk TVs." It was Sean O'Rourke. He was just passing through while visiting a friend, which of course is not allowed. I was somewhat surprised that Sean would even consider helping me. I don't think he liked me, and I wondered what his "angle" was. Sean got the channels all programmed for me, and I thanked him. A week later, he asked if I would buy some batteries for his radio, and out of gratitude, I did. I don't think Sean had much in the way of spending money.

A guy from the cell next door named Pedro asked if I had a Pringle's potato chip container. He said that he could make a speaker for me. I thought he was nuts, but I did have a nearly empty chip can in my footlocker. We ate the chips, and he left with the container. Half an hour later, he returned. The chip can was now riddled with little holes. The plastic cover had a small square hole cut into it. Pedro took the headphones and placed one earpiece over the square hole in the can's plastic lid. It worked! I even had to be careful to lower the volume. The "speaker" was, of course, not allowed, so Pedro warned me never to keep it on during count time as the guards would take it away. I can't begin to describe just how greatly having this television improved my life at SECC. Just like books, it was something that I could immerse myself into, thus "escaping" the prison for a while, if only in my imagination.

You're not allowed to be in another inmate's cell. Even for casual conversation, you either have to talk in the hallway, in the bathroom, or from the inside of your cell, you can speak to someone standing at your door. However, every once in a while, another inmate would stop by and watch a TV show with me while sitting on my footlocker. I enjoyed the company.

* * *

4-5 was a major league weightlifter, and he spent as many hours as he was allowed in the prison's weight room. One Saturday afternoon, he came into my cell with a huge Ace Bandage on his right arm. "What happened?" I asked. 4-5 shook his head sadly and said, "Hurt myself at the gym. Now I can't write to my girlfriend. If I tell you what to write, can you do it for me?" I felt bad for him and he was a very good friend, so of course I agreed to write the letter for him.

As we went along, it seemed that I had to suggest most of the words for the feelings that he was expressing. After thirty minutes or so, we were finally finished. I handed him the written letter and began putting away my pen and legal pad. 4-5 interrupted me saying, “That’s just the letter for one girlfriend. We have to write two more.” I cracked up laughing, then we began the second letter. I have to give the man a lot of credit. If I were in his position, I would have sent basically the same letter to all three girls. 4-5 had a totally different letter for each one. What I didn’t know that first day was that this would become our Saturday afternoon “thing.” Every Saturday, 4-5 would show up with a new “injury” that would incapacitate his “writing arm.” I almost thought of telling him that the Ace Bandage thing each weekend wasn’t really necessary, but I didn’t want to embarrass him. It’s not that he couldn’t write; it’s just that he felt that I would do a better job. I was glad that I could be of help to my friend.

* * *

B-4 also had a very strange guy named Roland. Roland had long gray hair that he kept tied in a ponytail. Just to look at him, you would quickly realize that he was both meek and physically weak. No one ever seemed to bother the guy. On occasion, I used to borrow his *TV Guide* magazine. I had a subscription to the same magazine, but the evening shift guard started giving it to an inmate who was one of his “informants.” I only got my copy a couple of times. I spent a lot of my time in prison reading. Once in a while, Roland would see what book I was working on and he’d ask if he could read it after me. I always let him.

One night, Roland stopped by my cell with what looked like a comic book. He handed it to me saying, “Just in case you’re interested.” I hadn’t ever read a comic book in my entire life—it just isn’t my thing. However, I thought he was probably offering me the book to pay me back for the books that he had borrowed from me. So not wanting to hurt his feelings, I took the book and told him I’d read it before bedtime. After the eleven o’clock news ended, I lay back in bed and began reading the comic book. It seemed incredibly childish. It was about a group of junior high boys who were starting a rock band. Eventually they were interviewing a kid who wanted to try out as their new drummer. Again, it seemed incredibly boring. And then the book took a nasty turn—it became highly sexualized with graphic illustrations. It was comic book "kiddie porn!"

I was horrified! I quickly got up and walked down to Roland's cell. He was still watching something on television. I put the book on his table and told him, "This is disgusting." Roland shrugged his shoulders and simply said, "To each his own." All I could think of was, where the hell did he get something like that? It was obviously professionally printed somewhere. Even more to the point, how did something like that end up inside the prison? It's the job of the property department to check everything that an inmate receives from the outside. The SECC property guards were real bastards; they would have absolutely loved catching Roland receiving something like that. How it got in will always be a mystery. Roland was doing ten years for having sex with male minors. He always used to argue that it was 100 percent consensual, ignoring the law that says that a minor cannot consent to sex with an adult. One of Roland's more absurd "sayings" was, "The entire universe is gay—even the sun goes down." Roland was a sick guy. And his linking his kind of "activities" to "being gay" would most likely severely anger the gay community.

Roland used to tell me that after he got out, he was going to change his name then disappear. About five years after I got out of prison, I did an Internet search on Roland. He was listed as a Level 3 sex offender. That didn't surprise me. What did surprise me was that he was listed as being seventy years old. I never would have guessed that he was that old. I guess the opportunity to "disappear" never came around.

* * *

There was an inmate named Dennis who, for some reason, decided that we were friends. Dennis was a really big white guy, though despite his size, he was not physically strong. I spoke with him at times, and once in a while, he would watch a TV show with me. I never knew what he was in prison for until one day when we were walking through the gate separating the old part of the prison from the new. As we passed the guard manning the gate, he said, "Hey, Dennis, rape any children lately?" Dennis gave off a forced chuckle. For me, that was the strangest thing about the guy. He never laughed spontaneously. I had known a kid in college that was the same way. It was as though something in both these guys' minds said, "This might be funny—you should probably laugh," and then they *forced* the laughing sound to come out. I suppose a shrink might be able to explain the phenomena, but I can't.

Dennis was always writing to someone in the Worcester County area. I only briefly saw one of his envelopes that had a woman's address on it. Whenever anyone got close to seeing one of his letters that he was bringing to the mailbox, he freaked out and quickly covered the letter with his hands. I have a feeling that he didn't want anyone to know what town he came from. He too was listed on the Massachusetts Offender Registry's website as a Level 3 offender. What was so surprising to me was that he was listed on the site while he was still incarcerated. Apparently, Dennis went to prison for a sex offense then got out. When I knew him, he was back again on new charges. I tried to look him up again in the spring of 2014. Dennis was no longer listed. I have a strange feeling that he must have died in prison.

* * *

I have no idea what my next-door neighbor Pedro had been charged with. Pedro at first came off as being a very affable guy. He was only in his early twenties. After he came back from dinner one night, he asked me if I could help him with his boot. He said that he had injured his back and couldn't get it off. "Just pull it off for me," he said. When I pulled on the boot, half his leg came with it. He howled laughing. He had half a prosthetic leg. Pedro told me that a gang member had blown his lower leg off with a shotgun.

Pedro "fixed" my hot pot so that it would boil water rather than just heat it. Usually guys that did that for anyone wanted to be paid for the service. Pedro wanted a different arrangement. He said that he would fix my pot if he could borrow it whenever he wanted to cook something. I told him that he had a deal so long as fish was never cooked in my pot. He agreed. Sadly, one weekend, Pedro returned my pot and there was a distinct odor of fish. From that day on, I refused to let him use it. I also turned Pedro into an enemy. I had to boil soapy water in that pot at least six times before the smell of fish was gone.

At some point, Pedro and Dennis also got into an argument. I was never certain what it was about. Pedro went back to his cell and got a homemade blade weapon. He went into Dennis's cell where Dennis was lying in bed reading. He held the knife up to Dennis's throat and said, "If you want to fuck with me, you'll die." Dennis was scared out of his mind. What Pedro had done was take two blades out of a shaving cartridge. Then he took a toothbrush handle and melted it with a lighter. When the handle was soft, he inserted the blades into the handle. You couldn't stab anyone with it, but it made a vicious slashing weapon. Strangely enough, there was a block "shake-down" by IPS that very afternoon. Those guys were experts at uncovering any hiding place that an inmate might use to conceal contraband. Supposedly they found nothing in Pedro's cell. Either Pedro had disposed of the knife after threatening Dennis or he was an IPS informant and he was "protected." I guess we'll never know.

I came back from the chapel one Sunday only to find that my light windbreaker jacket, along with a sweatshirt, was missing. Rumor had it that one of Pedro's friends from B-5 had stolen and sold my jacket. He still had my sweatshirt. (Both of those items were purchased through the canteen—they were not "prison issue.") I went up to B-5 where some of Pedro's friends lived. Whether by coincidence or design, B-5 was predominantly a Spanish cell block. An inmate that I knew from chapel told me who had taken my stuff, but he wouldn't say too much. As he put it, "I have to live up here with these guys."

4-5 and Ian both "put the word out" to their friends that my jacket was stolen, that it had my name written on the inside tag, and that anyone who saw it should take it and hold it. In two days' time one of Ian's friends had caught the guy who bought my jacket and had taken it away from him. Both the guys who had bought the jacket and my friend from B-5 named a young kid named Julio as the thief.

Wearing my newfound jacket, I went to Pedro's cell. I told him, "Tomorrow, whenever there is movement, I'm going to wait for Julio, and when I see him, we are going to do combat with each other. Julio can avoid that by returning my sweatshirt." Pedro was both surprised and angry. "Every Spanish guy will hate you if you do that," he told me. "Maybe," I replied, "but that's not going to save Julio from getting fucked up." An hour later, at the next movement, Julio, along with two other guys, came down to my cell—and returned my sweatshirt. Not a single word was spoken. After that, Roland came to see me. He asked, "You're not going to hurt that Julio kid, are you?" I seriously wondered why he cared. "No," I told him. "I've got all my stuff back. "Oh, good!" Roland exclaimed. "He's way too cute to get beat up!" I looked at Roland and just laughed.

* * *

I had begun to attend the Catholic chaplain's Communion service nearly six days a week. (The chapel was closed on Saturday.) The Deacon, Reverend Jim, had a chaplain's assistant named Doug. One day when I was at chapel, Father Jim asked if I would like to preach a sermon every Tuesday morning. He had had a former Protestant minister who was in prison doing just that but he was recently released. I jumped at the chance. After my first preaching Tuesday, Doug came and told me that I had pronounced the name of a biblical city incorrectly. I told him that how I had pronounced the name was correct. Doug went to the chaplain's office and came back with a book of biblical pronunciations. As I explained to him, the book itself was incorrect. Now Doug was beside himself. He couldn't believe that anything written in a book could possibly ever be wrong. Getting nowhere with me, Doug ran complaining to Father Jim. The deacon told him that, indeed, the book was wrong and I was right. I actually believe that broke Doug's heart. However, the incident gave

Father Jim an idea. He came and asked me if I would be willing to teach a class for those inmates who would like to be either baptized, confirmed, given First Holy Communion, or all three. (On the outside, that would be called an RCIA, or Rite of Christian Initiation for Adults, class.) I was absolutely thrilled by the prospect! I immediately agreed and got my sister to order two Catholic catechism books for me.

I began teaching just two inmate students in the chaplain's office. Later, we moved into the larger chapel building itself. Eventually, I had eight students. Just as I had when I taught Sunday school (CCD) on the outside, I found that it took me around five or six hours of research and preparation for every hour of actual teaching. The midnight shift guards used to pass by my cell in the early hours of the morning and ask, "Still at it?"

On my way one afternoon a supposedly religious guard walked alongside me. "Why are you wasting your time teaching religion to these animals?" he asked. "Because they have asked to learn," I answered. He seemed unmoved. "You are 'casting your pearls before swine,' and trust me, these guys are pigs." I laughed and replied, "Think how much worse they would be if I didn't teach them." The guard shook his head and walked away.

At the end of six months, an auxiliary bishop from the Archdiocese of Boston came and administered the Sacrament of Confirmation to the class. The week before, the deacon had baptized two men and had given First Holy Communion to some of the others. I was extremely proud of the work those guys had put into the class. No corners were cut; we had covered everything a new member of the Catholic Church should know. In a sense, it was the only accomplishment that I had during my three years in prison. I also knew that unless my cases were overturned on appeal, I would never be allowed to either preach or teach the Faith ever again. It was a bittersweet moment.

Eventually, Doug was transferred to another prison, and the chaplain hired me as his new assistant. I had to play recorded hymns during the Communion services, which the guys tried to sing along to. I typed all of the deacon's letters. When it came to requesting

Bibles as well as Christmas cards from outside groups, I simply wrote the letters myself and the deacon signed them. The chapel had a typewriter, but for serious requests addressed to outside religious groups, I typed the letters in the computer lab. Herve was very strict about the use of the printers. He only was allowed so much paper, and if he allowed every inmate to print as he pleased, he'd quickly run out of printer ink. "But, Herve," I used to tell him, "this isn't for me—it's for the chapel, which means it's for God. You wouldn't tell God he can't print something, would you?" Herve would grumble, then as always, he would let me do the printing.

We got bibles from a group in Boston. They even provided us with bibles in Spanish and Vietnamese. We received tons of Christmas cards from a Catholic religious order of priests. It was well-known that we were giving out the cards, and even guys who never attended our services came to get a box. Humorously, the Protestant chaplain, a former guard himself, used to tell his "flock" never to enter the Catholic chapel. His guys used to stand just outside our chapel door and ask me to pass them a box of cards. I often wondered exactly what they thought would happen to them if they came inside. It made me recall that in first or second grade in my Catholic elementary school, the nuns had told us that if we ever entered a non-Catholic Church, we very likely would be struck dead and then go to hell. If we were not struck dead, then we would still be going to hell when we did finally die. Yet that was during the early 1960s. I guess now it was someone else's turn to say foolish things. Just before Thanksgiving, the deacon had scheduled an "Ecumenical service to give thanks." Although the Protestant chaplain always said that he would come, neither he nor any member of his congregation ever did. Only the Islamic imam and his assistant ever showed up. I liked the imam; he was an honorable and decent man.

Just before my last Christmas on the inside, the choir of St. Michael's Episcopal Church from Holliston, Massachusetts, came and performed a concert in our chapel. It was one of the best performances I had ever heard. I marveled at their courage—particularly that of the women. It was a truly missionary activity on their part.

I'm sure God will reward each of them for their kindness toward those of us who were spending Christmas locked up.

* * *

You know it really doesn't matter how strong you are, how big you are, or even how well-trained you are in fighting skills. The day will come when someone bigger, stronger, or perhaps even better trained will come along and defeat you.

There was a guy on B-4 named Bill. At one time, Bill had worked with Williams in the property department. No matter whenever or wherever Bill thought he might get into a confrontation, he made certain that Williams was close by to back him up. It was strange that he always felt compelled to have Williams at his side since Bill was a very big man. Like Williams, he also thought of himself as some type of "super con." Somehow Bill got the idea into his head that people on B-4 were "talking about him." The very idea seemed to drive him nearly insane.

I could hear Bill yelling over and over again, "Do you have a problem with me?" I was lying in bed just reading a book and I could hear him coming down the hallway apparently stopping at each cell to ask his paranoid question. Suddenly Bill burst into my cell and yelled out the same thing. As I stood up, he used both hands to hit me in the chest. I could have recovered and fought, but I had stood awkwardly and his shove, innocuous under most conditions, had actually caused me to twist both of my knees. The pain came immediately and was searing. After calling me a "skinning bastard," he left, followed by Williams, his bodyguard.

For some reason, I decided to take a shower. In the middle of washing myself, I heard Bill's voice outside the shower stall. He was rambling on and on—basically, he was worried that I was going to turn him in. That's not something that anyone in prison would risk doing. Being labeled a rat could have serious consequences. I told Bill, "I'm not a rat," but I added, "What you did wasn't necessary." Strangely enough, Bill was able to admit that indeed his outburst was, in fact, unnecessary, but he couldn't bring himself to come anywhere close to apologizing. He even went so far as to basically call himself a "true con." Eventually he left.

After a couple of hours, when the knee pain still would not subside, I went over to the infirmary in the hope of getting some ice. I told the nurse practitioner that I had twisted my knees playing handball. She gave me Tylenol and a bag of ice. I returned to my cell and lay in bed with the ice evenly distributed on both knees. At the next movement, 4-5 came back to the block and stopped by my cell. He wanted to know everything, so I told him. Then I also told him that the matter was basically settled and over. 4-5 reluctantly agreed to let the matter go.

Fifteen or twenty minutes later, 4-5 returned to my cell. If we weren't good friends, his appearance would have terrified me. He was shaking all over, and pure rage was upon his face. "I can't get this out of my mind —and I'm fucking mad as hell!" he yelled. I tried to stop him, but he took off. He cornered Bill in the bathroom, and as luck would have it, Williams was also there. I heard 4-5 yell, "Tell me one reason why I shouldn't kill you right now?" Somehow, with Williams mediating, 4-5 was dissuaded from attacking Bill. It was just as well. I wouldn't want 4-5 to end up in the hole on my account. 4-5 told Bill that if anything like that happened again, not only would he kick Bill's ass but he would also start going after all of Bill's friends on the cell block.

Again, years after my release, I looked Bill up on the Internet. Not only is Bill a Level 3 sex offender but he, like Dennis, had been imprisoned before for the same type of crime. Most likely, his being worried about my turning him in was connected to his getting released on parole. An assault charge—even inside the prison—would most likely end any possibility for parole, or at least it would significantly delay it. So much for Bill's self-image as a "super con."

* * *

One night, after being one of the last guys through the medication line, I got trapped in the cement yard during movement. During my first few months in the cells, it had basically driven me crazy whenever I got "stuck" during movement. After a while, I just took my small prayer book with me and I would sit near the basketball court and pray for an hour. That particular night, a huge black inmate who was playing basketball walked away from the game and approached me. "I see you out here a lot with that book. Are you praying?" he asked. "Yes," I replied. His face took on a serious expression, and he said, "My grandmother is really sick, can you pray for her?" I really felt for the guy, and I answered, "Of course, what's her first name?" After he told me, I immediately said the prayer for the sick, inserting his grandmother's name in the appropriate place. In fact, I prayed for her every day. A couple of weeks later, I saw the guy in the school building, and he walked up to me, smiled, and shook my hand. "My grandmother got better. She's back home now. Thanks, man." I reminded him that I only prayed; it was God that had healed her. "That's cool," he said, then he went to his class.

A few weeks later, I once again got stuck in the cement yard during movement. My new friend and his crew were playing basketball as well. I looked to my left, and I saw a crazed-looking white guy walking toward me. There was no question that he was coming to see me for some damn reason. He walked up and said, "Hey, what are you in prison for?" I was surprised since I had never seen this guy before. Then I noticed that *all* the guys who had been playing basketball were now standing behind this lunatic-looking inmate. He must have *felt* their presence because he very slowly turned and faced the group that now surrounded him. My friend whose grandmother had been sick put his face about two inches from the crazy man's face and said, "Check it out. You fuck with the holy man and you die. Now walk away."

The guy who had been intent on messing with me scurried away with an amazing quickness. My friend looked at me and said, "I got your back, holy man." I don't think I deserve the title "holy man," but I can certainly say that more than one prayer was answered that month.

* * *

That night, I watched the eleven o'clock news, followed by David Letterman's show. I had developed a new habit; if I had an interest in Dave's guests on any given night, I'd watch the entire show. If the guests were of no interest to me, I'd shut the TV off right after the "Top Ten List." This was one of those "Top Ten only" nights. Despite being falsely imprisoned, things could have been worse. I had my own cell, a good, "clean" prison job (no washing dishes or cleaning toilets), a TV, and some very good, very loyal friends. I fell asleep quickly.

I awoke to the sounds of a woman screaming! I quickly checked my watch, and it was around 3:00 a.m. I was horrified—was a female guard being attacked? Yet all the inmate tiers, or floors, were sealed up for the night. I got out of bed and walked cautiously toward the end of the hall. I could then tell that there was definitely a fight going on, and the sounds were coming from the area of the guard's office on the floor above us. The noise lasted for only about ten minutes with the female constantly yelling, "Stop it!"

It wasn't like I could pick up a phone and dial 911. After things quieted down, I went to the bathroom then back to bed. I was surprised; every guard carried a two-way radio that had a panic button on it. If they pressed that button, every guard and IPS officer in the facility would come running to their assistance, and they usually sounded like a heard of elephants coming. Tonight? Nothing, not a sound. The next day I found out why. Two male guards had gotten into a fistfight, and the female guard was begging them to stop. I guess the guards could be just as bad as the inmates. I saw Matt Warren, an inmate who lived near me, the next day and asked if he had heard the "battle." He said, "Yup, but then I just rolled over and went back to sleep." I had to laugh. I was probably the only inmate that was worried enough to jump out of bed.

* * *

Eventually, the state realized that the cells we were living in were basically a Civil War era fire trap. It was decided that sprinklers needed to be installed. Anyone living in one of the cell buildings would be moved to a new "super-maximum-security" prison that had recently opened. It was said that only those inmates who had jobs "essential" to the operation of the prison would be permitted to stay. Ian knew that as a cook, he was not going to be moved. I had to wonder if my "chaplain's assistant" position would be deemed an *essential* job as well. Each week, some guys would be moved into the dormitories and guys from the dorms would be moved to a cell. As much as I would miss the privacy of my cell—not to mention having my own television—I wanted no part of, first of all, one of those late-night moves where masked guards basically roughed everyone up, and second of all, who the hell would want to go from medium security to a "super-max"?

Eventually, I was told to pack my belongings and move back to that old dormitory that I had been in after getting out of the Orientation Dorm. I ended up on the top bunk with an older black inmate on the bottom named Jim Manners. Jim was a Bible-quoting member of the Protestant chapel who seriously hated to hear people swearing. Sadly, since my arrival in prison, my vocabulary—at least the swearing section—was basically as it had been during junior high. (As always, though, I never used the Lord's name in vain.) Whenever something would frustrate me and my swearing would kick in, Jim would yell, "Junior, stop that cussing!" I had never heard the term *cussing*, and it struck me as quite funny—which tended to upset Jim all the more. He got even in a sense, because I really didn't like being referred to as Junior. I thought I had found a way to cure him of that habit; I started calling him Senior. As my luck would have it, Jim actually enjoyed being called Senior, so for the rest of my time in prison, Jim would call me Junior. (Maurice was still in that dorm, and every time Jim called me Junior, he would break out laughing.)

We had a corner section of the dormitory consisting of four bunks. Jim and I were against the wall. Roland had a bottom bunk next to Jim. On the bunk above Roland was a gentleman in his late sixties named Alex. Despite his being one of the oldest guys in the dorm, you could see that Alex was a powerfully built guy and a lot of that physical strength still remained. Yet he was a very mild-mannered person who was serving a second-degree life sentence. Alex had married very young. One day, when he was only nineteen years old, he returned home from work and found his wife in bed with another man. Impulsively, he retrieved a handgun from a dresser drawer and shot and killed her. There is nothing pretty about that story. However, in Massachusetts, it is the jury that decides if a person is guilty of first- or second-degree murder. The jury found Alex guilty of murder in the second degree. The implication of that is that the jury felt that at some point in time, Alex should be released from prison. No doubt that was due to his age and the fact that the crime was committed "in the heat of passion."

In fact, before Governor Bill Weld took office, Alex was confined at a type of halfway house in Framingham, Massachusetts. Every day, he walked about four miles to an apartment complex where he was employed as a groundskeeper. At the end of the day, he walked back. His only restriction was that he could not accept a ride in a car from anyone. Alex was a threat to no one at all. However, once Weld became governor, Alex and anyone in a similar position were returned to medium-security prisons. It made absolutely no sense. Alex had been in that halfway house setting for more than ten years without a single negative incident. And whenever Alex came up before the Parole Board, his deceased wife's sister came and testified that she was convinced that if Alex was released, he would find her and kill her. I can honestly tell you that forty-eight years after the murder, Alex had no desire to hurt anyone.

Pedro was also in the dormitory at that time. I had told Alex the story of Pedro and his friend Julio stealing my jacket and sweatshirt. At some point, I guess Pedro was unhappy that Alex and I were friends, and he approached Alex and said, "You know, that Kevin is a skinner." Alex quickly replied, "I'd rather hang out with a skinner than a thief." Pedro went away very unhappy. Apparently, Pedro was still angry that my threat against Julio had led to the return of my property. Really young Hispanic guys hated to "lose face."

I didn't know it, but whenever the electricity went out in the prison, the guards would *run* out of the buildings after having locked the inmates inside. While I understood that it was meant to ensure the guards' safety, it certainly made them look like a group of cowards. One night around 8:00 p.m., the lights went out and the evening shift guard bolted out of the building like he was shot out of a cannon. I didn't sense any kind of danger to anyone. I had been lying on my top bunk writing when the lights went out. Alex came from the bathroom and was standing in front of my bunk talking to me. It took me some time to figure it out, but I finally realized that he was standing there to protect me. I didn't feel any threat to my safety whatsoever, yet there was Alex guarding me like a Secret Service agent would protect the president. I almost made the mistake of telling him that I didn't need the protection, but I quickly realized that what he was doing was a great act of kindness, and it would have been wrong to reject that "gift." After a couple of hours, the lights came back on, and Alex went to his bunk and fell asleep. I think the poor guy was exhausted from standing in front of me for so long. I would never forget what he had done for me.

* * *

You would have to be an absolute idiot not to realize that if you were moved from the dorm to a cell block, you were slated to be transferred to the new super-max. As guys were told to pack up and move out of the dormitory, you could see the absolute sadness and sometimes burning anger on their faces. A morning came when Pedro was told to pack up and move back to a cell building. He was furious. As he left with all his belongings in a single trash bag, he looked over at me. I just looked back without any discernible expression on my face. When the door closed behind him, I burst out laughing—and so did Roland and Alex. The moment wasn't lost on Jim Manners either. Jim calmly said, "Good, one less troublemaker."

Roland had a definite skill of endearing himself to the really young inmates whom he was sexually attracted to. He had quite a bit of spending money, and he would offer to "help out" the younger guys with all types of canteen supplies. (Roland even used to get financial statements from investment firms mailed to him in prison.) I came back from the Sunday chapel service one morning and Roland was talking to a twenty-year-old inmate. I almost laughed because Roland looked like a professional counselor the way he was concentrating on every word the kid said. As I walked by, Roland said to the guy, "Tell

Kevin what you told me." I really didn't want to be involved in Roland's charade, but I was put on the spot. Essentially, the kid, in consultation with his mom on the outside, had decided that he should not remain in the dormitory because he was young and there were sex offenders living there. I was taken aback by his naivete. Didn't he realize that there were sex offenders living in the cell blocks? Or that there was always a guard inside the dorm but not in the cell buildings? And this kid was physically huge. Few guys would ever challenge someone as big as he was. (Furthermore, in all my time in prison, there were never any *forced* sexual encounters. The very few instances of sexual activity between inmates that I heard about had always been consensual.)

I knew that Roland wanted me to talk the kid out of moving. I wondered if Roland had explained about the upcoming move to the super-max. The kid told me that his mother had already contacted her state senator about their concerns. I don't know if I had any moral responsibility to try and dissuade the kid from a move that he obviously thought was in his best interest. In the end, I just wished him luck and walked away. He ended up at the super-max.

The night of the big move finally came. There was only slight tension in the dormitory. It would be a huge mass transfer of close to four hundred inmates. When it was over, rumors abounded about extremely rough treatment of the inmates by the guards. None of the remaining inmates had witnessed the move, so it was hard to tell if any of those rumors were in fact true. However, quite a few of the moved inmates were elderly, and three elderly inmates died within a couple of weeks of the move. The entire event was apparently just too much for them. I knew one of the deceased, an elderly black inmate that I really liked. His loss was extremely painful for me. Hopefully, God will take good care of him in heaven.

Also transferred were Julio, Williams, Bill, Sean O'Rourke, and very sadly, 4-5. I would really miss 4-5.

* * *

"Everybody, pack up your stuff! You're all moving to the Upper Rec." That was a day shift guard that I had never met before. All I could wonder was why the entire dormitory would be moved all at once. I asked another of the guards and he said that there had just been an inspection of the floor from downstairs looking up. "The whole place could come down at any minute," he said. "I'm glad you guys care about us," I replied. The guard got a nasty look on his face and said, "No one gives a fuck about you pieces of shit. We don't want the state to get sued—that's all." So I guess I had put my foot in my mouth. I should have known better by then, but I was always expecting some good to come from, well, everyone.

The Upper Rec was a much nicer dormitory that for some reason had gone unused since everyone was moved to the super-max. It was then that I realized that it was not just the cell buildings that had been moved. I had to wonder just how I had been lucky enough to avoid being transferred. Once we were settled, I was somewhat saddened that even though Jim and I had a really nice corner of the dorm, Alex was located at the opposite end of the building.

The door to the Upper Rec opened into a large room with a television and lots of chairs. For these dormitory televisions, it was necessary to purchase an AM/FM radio from the canteen. Tune all the way to the end of the AM dial and you had your TV sound. I guess that eliminated arguments over how loud the TV would be. The far wall of the TV room had wall lockers for each inmate. Through another doorway without a door was the sleeping area. The guard's desk was at the back wall and afforded him or her a view of the door to the outside.

What was important for me was that the guard had to walk to the TV room door at every movement throughout the day and the early part of the night, because next to the guard's desk was a small refrigerator with a smaller freezer on top. I needed my plastic bottles of Pepsi cold. Most guys would place their soda bottles in the bathroom sink and let the cold water run over it for close to an hour. That was a highly wasteful practice that yielded only limited results. In the cell building, I used to wrap two soaking wet washcloths around the Pepsi bottle and secure them with elastics. Then I placed it in the cell's open window. Since evaporation is also a cooling process, it did make the beverage cool, though not cold. Here in the Upper Rec however, I started my deceptive practice of placing my Pepsi bottles in the guard's freezer as soon as he walked out of the sleeping area and into the TV room. Then the bottles would cool off for an hour. At the next movement, I would go back and retrieve the now-quite-cold Pepsis.

The entire process went quite well until one day, during the early morning, the day shift guard inexplicably turned as he was walking to the TV room at movement and caught me. The thing was he had no interest in keeping me from using "his" freezer—just as long as I placed a bottle of Pepsi in there for him as well. I remember Father Jim being indignant about the whole thing when I told him. "He makes forty thousand a year and he's taking a Pepsi from you whenever you use his freezer!" Father Jim exclaimed. As I told the chaplain, "I consider it to be a 'rental' agreement." I simply had to pay to use the guard's freezer. It was still worth it to me. I could also freeze more than one bottle for myself as long as the day guard got his "payment." If necessary, I would place an extra-cold bottle in one of my boots and lace it up tight. The boots were insulated, and thus they would keep the Pepsi cold for a couple of hours—so long as they were laced up *very* tightly.

On Saturdays, there was often a female guard on duty. Once, she was in a huge argument—I have no idea what it was about—with a young Hispanic/black inmate. It became obvious that the stupid kid was about to get physical with her. I decided I had to step in. "You're siding with her against me?" the young kid screamed. "You can't get physical with a woman," I replied. Eventually, the kid calmed down. However, I had just defended a guard against an inmate, and that could spell serious trouble for me. The young kid went over and basically complained to the older Spanish and black inmates. If it wasn't such a serious moment, I would have laughed—it was like being on trial. Sadly, Jim Manners was away at his maintenance job. After about fifteen minutes, an elderly black inmate came out of the meeting and declared, "Kevin is right. It's just plain wrong to get physical with a woman." I was off the hook. Though the female guard never actually said "Thank you," she *was* in the habit of bringing in a bag of ice every Saturday. I had ice with my Pepsi every Saturday from that day onward.

* * *

Since we had moved out of the cell buildings, something was clearly bothering Dennis. He came over after dinner one evening and he seemed frustrated. "When we were neighbors in the cells, we used to hang out a lot. Now you spend all your time with Jim and Maurice. I thought you and me were you and me," he complained. I really didn't know what to say. Finally, I told him, "So just come over and hang out with us." I thought that was cool—you know, the more the merrier. Dennis got red-faced and shouted, "Then just forget it!" I never really knew what that was all about.

* * *

One thing I did know—I had fallen seriously out of physical shape since entering the prison. I wanted to get to the weight room, but there was a very long waiting list. Over a game of computer pin ball, I brought the matter to Ian's attention. "That's not a problem—put your name on the waiting list and I'll take care of it," Ian told me. "But how?" I asked. Ian laughed and replied, "Remember getting into this class? The gym is much easier than the school to deal with." The next day, Ian told me to meet him at the weight room at 7:00 p.m. True to his word, I was on the list. I decided not to ask any questions.

No one ever went to the weight room alone. It was always at least two guys and, most often, three or four. Ian had a friend named Al who joined us. Al was enormous. He worked in the "industries" section of the prison. The guys in industries were actual craftsmen—carpenters, wood workers, HVAC repairmen, and so on. They had separate living quarters that were far better than the rest of us had. They were also paid by the hour as opposed to being given the usual flat rate of either one or two dollars a day.

The guys in any gym often used encouragement, both positive and negative, to get their friends to lift more and more weight. Ian and Al were no exception, but Al had a nasty side that kept coming out. "Girls do more reps (repetitions) than you do!" he would often say. As time went on, Al was constantly on my case. To be honest, my bones, joints, and connective tissue are a certifiable disaster area. I developed knee problems when I was twenty-three years old. At twenty-four, shin splints developed. Despite the best efforts of the athletic trainers at Westfield State, I couldn't suppress the pain from the shin splints, and that eventually ended my six-mile-a-day running routine. At age twenty-five, I ruptured two discs in my lower back. The point is, I have had to be highly aware of my physical limitations. I was holding back for my own good, and it was viewed by both Ian and Al as my simply being lazy. Of course, they were both at least ten years younger than I was. Eventually I had had enough, and I stopped going altogether.

Maurice noticed that I had ended my workouts, and he asked me what had happened. As I told him, he shook his head knowingly. "That guy Al is an asshole," Maurice told me. Then he said that I could switch my gym days and work out with his group. And so I began lifting weights with an all-Spanish-speaking group. There were two other guys who spoke nearly no English, and Maurice was pressed into service as our interpreter. Things went quite well after that. Thankfully Ian never took my "group swap" personally, though I took care to impress upon him that it was Al and not him that I wanted to get away from. I think Ian knew that it was for the best.

I used to laugh at how Maurice would use language as an excuse for everything. If our group needed a certain piece of equipment, he would just go grab it even if it appeared that some other guys were using or about to use it. When the other group would start yelling at him, he would act as though he couldn't understand a word they were saying. Quite often, that would frustrate the other guys and they would simply let him take what he wanted. Then he would turn toward me with a sly smile on his face. It was hard not to laugh, but I had to control myself so as not to give away Maurice's "secret." (He used the exact same tactic in his interactions with the guards.)

One night, I was on my way to the gym, and as usual, I had a Pepsi bottle that I had filled with cold water. As I waited at the dormitory's door for movement, a guard asked, "Oh shit, you're not drinking the SECC water, are you?" I was scared at the way he had put that, and I replied, "What choice do I have?" The guard answered, "You can buy water from the canteen. I wouldn't drink this shit if I were you." Every time I took a drink during my workout, I was worried. Later, I asked the nurse practitioner. She didn't seem to want to answer my question. Finally, she said, "You have buildings here that date back to the Civil War, and the plumbing is just as old. You'll have to decide for yourself if the water is OK to drink."

There was really no way to avoid all contact with the tap water. The prison kitchen cooked with it and made Kool-Aid with it. And I was in the habit of drinking a lot of water—there was no way I could afford to drink the canteen's spring water all the time. The canteen's spring water came in soft plastic containers, and for some reason, it was the plastic that you tasted. It was sort of like the taste of water when you take a drink from a garden hose. I was worried about all the canteen's products anyway. It was as though they were some type of factory seconds. We got Bic pens for only twenty-one cents each. Yet sometimes those pens would write fifty or more pages—sometimes only five or six pages—and then the ink would run out. We got Aqua Fresh toothpaste—you know, with the tricolored paste. Except we'd only get two of those colors. It was hard to know what products you could trust.

I asked Maurice about it during our workout, but he just shrugged his shoulders and said, "We all have to die sometime." And then he laughed. While Maurice could become violently angry about some things, he was, for the most part, an extremely calm sort of guy. But not that night. When we returned to the Upper Rec, we saw that there had been a "shake-down." Shake-downs by the IPS officers usually came about for a good reason. They often received an anonymous tip that someone had a weapon or some other contraband. The IPS were rough on our property but not extremely bad. The regular guards, however, used to organize shake-downs when they were in a bad mood or if an inmate or inmates had pissed them off. What those guards did was usually an act of pure vandalism.

"Oh, fuck," Maurice whispered as we entered the Upper-Rec's sleeping area. There was a new night guard, a foul-mannered guy named Silva, and he was smiling from ear to ear. All our beds were on the floor with the blankets and sheets scattered about. Most of the sheets had boot prints on them—so many boot prints that it had to have been done on purpose. Yet that was nothing compared to what caught my eye next. In the center of the sleeping area was a huge pile of—everything from everyone's footlocker. "Bastards!" I yelled, starting to go off, but Maurice grabbed my arm and whispered into my ear, "They want you to go crazy. If you go off, you'll only make them happy." He was right, and I restrained my emotions.

It was a disaster. If you used Aqua Fresh toothpaste, well, there were at least twenty tubes of that brand in the pile. I had a red soap dish, and there had to be at least thirty red soap dishes in the pile. The same with toothbrushes, combs, socks, etc. It took everyone a couple of hours to sort through the pile. I was very surprised as no inmate seemed to try to take advantage of the situation and take items that he hadn't had in the first place. I got a soap dish and a new unopened bar of soap. As for my toothbrush, I just had to let that go. There was no way to tell one from another. It meant I would have to order a new toothbrush the following week then wait a week for it to arrive. I would have foul breath for close to fourteen days. The wall lockers were not touched at all. After that, I bought duplicates of everything—soap, toothpaste, shampoo—I even kept three extra toothbrushes in the wall locker. Of course, the fact that the wall lockers had not been searched pretty much proved that the guards were not looking for anything in particular. Silva had just organized the shake-down for his own amusement. The man was a flaming asshole.

In the middle of all this, an elderly white inmate stood looking at the group of laughing guards, and without any obvious anger, without swearing or becoming loud, he began to "curse" them. "I hope your first-born child dies of cancer. May your wives die young of tragic accidents. May all your children never have children of their own, and if they do, may most of them be stillborn…" And the old guy continued like that for a good ten or fifteen minutes. The guards were caught completely off guard. I was absolutely amazed. The old guy was like some prophet of doom straight out of a horror movie. While Silva looked angry, I could tell that some of the other guards were clearly horrified by the old man's "prophetic" soliloquy. One older guard mumbled, "Oh my god" then quickly left the dorm. The next time I got some Pepsi from the canteen, I sat down and drank a bottle with the old guy. He had made a bad night much better for me.

* * *

One thing that has always amused me is the enormous number of Americans who happen to be either white or black (though mostly white) who steadfastly assert that they have a great deal of American Indian "blood" in their ethnic makeup. Of course, now the "correct" term is *Native American*; however, any anthropologist worth a crap will tell you that *no one* was *native* to the Western Hemisphere. The "first Americans" migrated across the frozen sea from Siberia to Alaska then down throughout North, Central, and South America. That's why in Canada they have the term *First nations*.

The first person I ever met who claimed to be, as he put it, "more than half American Indian," was a kid in seventh grade who had a German surname. He had nearly clear blue eyes and his blond hair was so light that it came quite close to being white. He made that claim during our social studies class, and the entire class cracked up laughing. I could clearly see that our young female teacher was working overtime not to laugh herself. As I got older, the number of people claiming to have Indian blood seemed to increase exponentially.

Once, while on a trip through the state of Maine in the mid 1970s, I stopped at a small rural shop that said, "Native American Store." I had never encountered an establishment like that, having grown up only ten miles north of Boston. When I entered, I was somewhat surprised. It was kind of a junk shop. There were many little "Indian" statues, some peaceful, others featuring warriors whose painted-on facial expressions were borderline violent. Then there were some toy plastic spears with feathers attached as well, as some child-size bows and arrows. The arrows featured those rubber suction-cup tips. Just as I was about to leave, I heard a voice say, "Can I help you?" I turned to see a fairly large man wearing a blue plaid shirt and brown corduroy pants. In front and back of those pants the guy had what was supposed to be a red loincloth. I almost laughed; what was the point of a loincloth worn over full-length pants? Ethnically, the man appeared to be 100 percent black. His hair was in the style of a huge 1960s afro—like the guy in the old *Mod-Squad* TV show, and for authenticity, he had a long red feather sticking straight up out of the back of his hairdo. I looked at my watch for effect and told him that I was late for an appointment but that I would stop in on my way back. That seemed to satisfy him, and soon I was back on the road. I never saw that shop again.

So I was beyond amused in the fall of 1999 when Denis asked me if I wanted to go with him to a meeting of American Indians in prison. I tried not to laugh, and I said, "Denis, I'm not Indian." Denis said, "You're dark enough." At that point, I did laugh. Was he asking if I *was* Indian or telling me that I could "pass" as Indian? I said to Denis, "Look at the hair on my arms and legs, for God's sake." Denis looked perplexed and asked, "What's that got to do with it?" From there, I launched into a long description of a professor's lecture during an anthropology class at Westfield State College. The professor had asserted that the presence of facial hair—indeed, even the presence of most body hair—on either an American Indian or someone of African ancestry was "inescapable proof of the presence of white blood." Denis appeared both shocked and angry. He grabbed his AIP flier and stomped away. Denis had curly blond hair that was turning gray, extremely hairy arms, legs, and everything else and a full beard. He looked far more like Grizzly Adams than Hiawatha.

Yet I was genuinely curious. Why was Denis and another dorm resident, Andy, so intent on joining an American Indian support group? I decided that when the group was to be held that I would quickly check it out on my way to the athletic yard. When that early evening rolled around, I made certain that I arranged my travel so that I had to walk by the meeting room where the AIP group was to be held. It was just as I had thought—the room was mostly filled with guys who were painfully white; the majority, in fact, had blond hair. I stood outside the door completely alone, and I howled laughing.

And then a voice behind me asked, "Are you joining our group?" I was still laughing when I turned around only to come face-to-face with a gentleman directly out of central casting for a Western. I had always scoffed at the term "red man"—until that moment. The inmate's ID card read "Jonathan Cloud." He had long, dark braided hair, and his skin was the reddish-brown color of clay. His face was smooth without the slightest trace of a beard. I pointed into the meeting room and said, "I'm sorry—I thought this was AIP, but this looks more like the Swedish Olympic Ski Team." Without hesitation, Jonathan roared laughing. When he stopped, he said, "Yeah, you might be right about that." I probably should have just moved on, but I repeated to him what the professor from Westfield had said years before.

Jonathan asked me, "Did you watch *Dances with Wolves*?" I told him, "More than once." He laughed again and said, "Did you see the five o'clock shadows on the two main Indian characters, Kicking Bird and Wind in His Hair?" I just laughed, and he continued, "Your professor was correct. You never see old paintings or later photographs of Indians with mustaches or beards. And there was no Gillette Foamy shave cream or razors before the Europeans arrived." As he finished speaking, Denis and Andy walked by and into the meeting room. They both shot me a strange look. I looked at a clock on the wall and said, "Damn, I have to get to the yard before movement ends." Jonathan grabbed my arm and half jokingly asked, "What, you're not coming in?" I said, "I'm not Indian." Jonathan replied, "Too bad, at least you're normal."

Later that night, I was lying on my top bunk resting. I'm sure it appeared that I was asleep. Andy had the top bunk next to mine, and suddenly, I could hear Denis speaking to him. I decided to listen in on their conversation while keeping up thc appearance of sleeping. To be brief, Denis and Andy were worried about being "persecuted" after they were released from prison. Someone had put the idea into both of their heads that they would be able to go and live on an

Indian Reservation in Quebec after they were released. There is a sex offender registry in the Province of Quebec, but the information is only available to the police—not the public.

Eventually, I hoisted myself up onto my right side and interrupted their conversation. "There is just one problem," I began. "Canada will not let anyone with a criminal record enter their country—not even as a tourist." With an air of intellectual superiority, Denis countered, "But we're not entering *their* country—we're entering Indian land." I laughed and continued, "But the Indians are not guarding the border, the Canadian government is. So unless you intend to parachute onto the reservation, you're shit out of luck. And what makes you think the Indians want you on their land to begin with?" As they say, the silence was deafening. I never heard either of them talking about their immigration plans again. However, there was one notable result of our conversation: from that day on, Denis truly hated me.

* * *

The new year, 2000, was rapidly approaching, and I had a fairly good idea that I was going to get out of prison in the coming new year. I sent a note to one of the prison's administrators, a woman, and asked if she would calculate my "good time" and see when I could expect to be released. She quickly got back to me with the date of February 15, 2000. That was sooner than I had expected. I sent her a thank-you card for doing the calculation. That triggered an IPS investigation.

An IPS officer stopped me in the cement yard. "Kevin, did you send Carole a thank-you card?" I was taken completely off guard and muttered, "Yes." The officer looked troubled and asked, "Why?" I replied, "She calculated my release date for me, so I wanted to thank her." "Why the hell would you do that?" he continued. I finally got a bit angry and answered, "Because that's what civilized people do when someone helps them out!" The guy laughed a little and said, "Well, you scared the shit out of her." I was flabbergasted. "I scared her with a thank-you card?" I asked incredulously. The officer got more serious and said, "Look, this is a different world in here. Don't be nice or polite to anyone—it will just be misinterpreted. Trust me, you don't need the aggravation." All I could manage to say was "OK," and we parted ways. What a paranoid moron Carole must have been. When I told Father Jim what had taken place, he just shook his head sadly. At least he understood how I felt.

* * *

I returned to the dorm one Sunday after I had "conducted" the music for the Communion service. Basically, that meant telling the inmate congregation what page each hymn was on then playing a recording of it on a cheap boom box. I had to laugh; Father Jim always called it a *victrola*. It was amazing, I actually got requests for certain hymns to be played by various inmates during the week. Sadly, most of the tapes were of the modern "fruitcake" variety. Traditional hymns were even under attack in prison!

As I entered the dorm, I looked up only to see Roland talking to a nineteen-year-old inmate named Philip. Roland looked as though he was hanging on every word that came out of the kid's mouth. He may have been, but his real motivation was always sexual when it came to the younger-looking inmates, and Philip looked like he was sixteen. He was a good-looking kid with medium-length blond hair—just Roland's "type." I should have just kept my head down and kept walking to my bunk, but I was amused by the spectacle, and as I watched the two of them, I just cracked up laughing. Unfortunately, when Roland saw me, he motioned for me to come over and join the conversation.

I really wanted no part of Roland's game, but I walked over anyway. Roland looked at Philip and said, "Tell Kevin what you just told me." Philip started talking and talking and talking. He had come to SECC from another prison, and somehow, his television had been fatally damaged. The kid wanted to know how he could get the Department of Corrections to buy him a new one. It pissed me off that Roland had said anything other than "I don't know," which would have been the truth. All I could do was suggest that he contact the public defender's office for advice. I knew that inmates were constantly suing the Corrections Department, but I had absolutely no idea how a person would initiate such a suit.

One thing about Philip was that he knew he was good-looking, and he had a humorous habit. Whenever he entered the dorm's showers, if there were any other guys already in there, he would loudly announce, "Don't you guys be looking at my ass!" I have to admit, it was funny the first twelve times, but the "joke," after four months, was losing its comedic impact. I was in the shower one night, and as I began washing myself, another inmate, who had just moved into the dorm from Orientation, came along a few minutes after me. This guy was black, around 6'8", and he looked like a serious bodybuilder. He was in the process of placing his towel, soap, and shampoo in the stall when Philip walked in and loudly announced, "OK, don't you two be looking at my ass!" Without a second's hesitation, with the deepest voice I had ever heard, the new guy bellowed out, "I'm not *looking* at your ass! But if I *want* your ass, I will *take* your ass. As it is right now, I have no *need* of your ass, but that might change!"

Philip grabbed his towel, and without covering himself up at all, he *ran* out of the shower room 100 percent naked! He even left his soap, shampoo, and conditioner behind. I don't think I have ever laughed as hard as I did at that moment at any time prior to that incident—or after. I was almost doubled over, leaning against the shower's tiles with tears pouring out of my eyes. Then I noticed that it was getting much darker in the stall. The big man was now standing next to me sans clothing, and he looked pissed! Again, that deep voice shattered the silence. "You think that was funny?" he asked. I should have been terrified, but I just couldn't compose myself. All I could manage to say while still howling laughing was, "Oh God, yes!" The man started to laugh but stopped himself. Then he started to laugh again but stopped—and that made me laugh even harder. Finally the gigantic guy roared laughing and said, "I guess it was pretty funny, wasn't it?"

The two of us just finished our respective showers while off and on one of us would crack up laughing, which in turn would cause the other guy to do the same. When I was finished, I walked back to my bunk still intermittently laughing. I looked over and saw Philip complaining to Roland. Then I really started laughing. The two of them looked in my direction and shook their heads like I had been caught telling off-color jokes at a funeral. Philip said, "I can't believe you thought that was funny!" I just shrugged my shoulders and continued to get dressed.

While Philip and Roland were still talking, the big guy left the shower and walked over to my bunk. He had two bottles of Mountain Dew in his enormous hands. He introduced himself as Darren. I broke out a can of Pringle's Chips, and we talked, ate, and drank for quite some time. Every once in a while, I would look out of the corner of my eye only to see Roland and Philip watching the two of us. Much later, as I was brushing my teeth, Philip came in to do the same. He looked kind of hurt, and I sincerely started to feel bad. "Philip, he was just pissed off. He thought you were insulting him, calling him some kind of prison rapist. He wouldn't have touched you." Phil just looked at me for the longest time. Finally he said, "But you don't really know that." I could see that he was serious. "Phil, look, if he did try to hurt you, I would have tried to fight him with you—and he would have killed both of us—but I wouldn't let anything happen to you without trying to do *something*." That seemed to make Phil happier. I later thought about trying to get Darren to tell him he was just kidding, but I didn't think that Darren was the kind of guy who took back what he had said. What the hell—Philip got over it, and Darren and I became friends.

* * *

There was an inmate in the dorm named Matt Warren. I had known Matt ever since we were neighbors on B-3. Matt was able to do a myriad of different skilled tasks that kept him well stocked with the prison's number one form of currency—noodle soup packages. In addition to being able to repair radios and make hot pots boil, Matt could tailor clothing. I have very short legs, and like many inmates, I had to cuff my prison-issued jeans so much that they looked ridiculous. Most guys didn't care, but it was something I was highly self-conscious about. On the outside, I would leave a pair of pants with a tailor and then have to wait one to three weeks to get them back. Matt used to blow my mind. He would cut off the excess material and sew up the pant legs, all in less than ten minutes. Normally that would net him six soups, but he gave me a discount and only charged me four. It was well worth it.

However, lately, starting around October of 1999, Matt was spending most every night lying on his bunk listening to his radio. As the weeks wore on, he started to withdraw from interacting with just about everyone. Finally, in late November, I went over to his bunk one night and asked him why he was spending so much time alone.

"They're building concentration camps. Even worse, they're going to kill everyone who's now in prison," he told me. "Who?" I asked. "The federal government," he continued. "I've been listening to one of Ronald Reagan's sons, and he knows that all this is being planned for the minute we change to the year 2000. They will come for us on New Year's Eve." I said the first thing that came to my mind: "That's insane!" Matt looked resigned to some awful fate and told me, "It's going to happen."

I also had a radio, but I only used it for watching the dorm's television and to listen to Christmas music during December. I had to wonder how Matt had stumbled onto whatever wacko radio station that was putting out this huge conspiracy theory. As the fall turned to early winter, I could see that nothing I said could dissuade Matt from believing that we were all going to be shot on New Year's Eve.

As usual, the Christmas holiday was a subdued event. A priest came in to celebrate Christmas Mass with us—and so the deacon could have the day off. I was extremely grateful for that priest's taking the time to be with us. My sister Janice, my brother-in-law Jeff, and my mom all came in and had a vending machine Christmas dinner with me. I was grateful and extremely happy to know that this would be the last time we would be spending Christmas in a prison. It was also a very good thing that we ate in the visiting room. Earlier, what had been a fairly good turkey dinner during the past two holidays turned out to be something totally disgusting on Christmas Day 1999. The turkey smelled funny and tasted horrible. Virtually everyone took a sniff then a taste then threw the entire meal into the trash can. I thanked God for the vending machine hamburger I had later. That night Maurice, Jim Manners, and I had spaghetti out of Maurice's hot pot. I will always be amazed by Maurice's ability to cook up an exquisite meal out of a single cooking device.

As Christmas week went on, Matt was becoming truly depressed. I was very worried about the guy. I knew he wouldn't hurt himself, but I hated to see anyone so exceedingly convinced that his days on Earth were coming to an end. "You got thrown in prison for something you didn't do," Matt told me. "How can you have so much trust in the government not to kill you?" "I trust the national government," I answered. "But I would never trust this evil state." Matt looked at me sadly and replied, "The feds are worse."

As the week went on, I made sure that Jim and I would have some cupcakes and Pepsi to celebrate the new year's arrival. I had placed the Pepsi in the guard's freezer early in the evening. Since there was no "movement" during the overnight shift, there was no way to get it in any closer to midnight. (The midnight shift guards used to just sleep in their chairs at night anyway. They would be next to the fridge all night.) The two bottles were cold and tied up tightly in my insulated boots. The majority of guys had already gone to sleep. It was hard for me to "celebrate" the New Year. I guess I have never quite understood what it's all about. I used to do my best to wish my mom a Happy New Year, and now I had to basically do the same for Jim, but I considered the entire holiday to be total bullshit. If you're broke on December 31, you will most likely still be broke on January 1. The same with any other human affliction. There is nothing magical about changing from one year to the next. I suppose you could argue that I was imprisoned in 1999 and would be free in 2000, but I still cannot get into celebrating a number change. Maybe I would feel different about the holiday if I owned a liquor store.

Jim was listening to his radio so that he would know exactly when the New Year began—so was Matt, but for an entirely different reason. When the number change officially took place, I saw Jim's eyes light up like a kid seeing his presents on Christmas morning. We each said "Happy New Year," then drank our Pepsi. We offered to pour some into a cup for Matt, but he was not in a celebratory mood. After drinks and cake, Jim and I went to sleep.

* * *

Kurt Walther had a reputation; he hated sex-offenders. He had a job in "walks and grounds." That meant he did landscaping around the prison in the warm months and shoveled snow during the winter. Kurt also was suffering from some form of stomach cancer. He received pain medication from the infirmary, but it never seemed to be enough. (It turned out that he didn't have stomach cancer at all; he was having stomach pain because he was constantly afraid—of something.) Kurt tried to hang out with the young "thugs," but he always seemed to be slightly out of place. While walking by his bunk one day, I saw in his open footlocker a picture of a black German Shepherd. I asked if he had any other pictures of the dog. Kurt seemed agitated—afraid, actually—of being seen associating with me. However he did take out a couple of other pictures of his dog. It was a beautiful dog. Kurt was exhausted that night, since it had been snowing steadily for two days. The guys in "walks and grounds" were broken into two twelve-hour snow-shoveling shifts. It was extremely hard work for which they were paid an hourly wage.

In January, Kurt was released. He went over to the place where you sit in a cell until whomever is giving you a ride home shows up and your paperwork is set. Except it didn't work that way for Kurt. As he sat waiting in the cell, transport guards showed up, put him in waist and leg chains, and dragged him off to the Treatment Center. He had completed his criminal sentence, and now the state was going to try and have him civilly committed for life. The young thugs that he had always tried to befriend were outraged. One of them, a twenty-five-year-old doing second-degree life for murder, was beside himself. "This is the first time any skinner has ever fooled me!" he exclaimed. I found it hysterically funny. This young lifer, Ken, was nothing but a behind-the-scenes troublemaker. On the outside, he had gone to a bar and apparently taken a bar seat that belonged to someone who had gone to the rest room. When the guy came back, he kicked Ken out and a fight ensued. Ken got his ass kicked. So he went home, got a gun, and went back and killed the guy. Now he was crushed that someone had, in his mind, "pulled one over on him." Ken shouted out loud, "I wonder what kind of Christmas Kurt's victim had this year?" Without thinking, I yelled back, "A better Christmas than your victim had!" Ken stared at me for the longest time. I don't know if I could have beaten him in a fight, but I had come to realize that a second-degree lifer's only chance of getting out was via parole—and they wouldn't get parole with a fight on their prison record. He did nothing.

The public defender's office filed suit against the state on Kurt's behalf. It was a highly publicized suit. Luckily for Kurt, the action was filed as "John Doe vs. the Commonwealth of Massachusetts." Kurt eventually got out, but it took three weeks to happen. I was relieved that Kurt's name wasn't put out there for the entire state to know, but I was now quite worried about what might happen to me on my fast-approaching release date.

The next guy to be released was Matt Warren. While going into all the details would be both tedious and boring, essentially, Matt was also accused of a sexual crime that I'm certain he didn't commit. He had all his belongings in two plastic trash bags early one Monday morning. Jim Manners, in a rare explosion of humor, grabbed both of Matt's bags and threw them in the direction of the dorm's door as he exclaimed, "Get out and stay out!" Matt seemed more surprised than humored, but that's probably because no one would have expected that outburst from Jim.

As the day wore on, a lot of us were wondering if we would hear that Jim too had been grabbed up and hauled off to the Treatment Center. About a week later, one of the guys in the dorm got a letter from Matt. He was safely out of state custody. He wrote that he had enjoyed his first real pizza in ten years. Everyone was happy to hear that. Matt was an exceptionally nice guy. He was missed, but I'm glad he was out.

* * *

In the early spring of 1979, I drove to Westfield State College to register for the fall semester. I had attended one quarter at

Northeastern University after transferring there from a two-year school. Northeastern was a good school and well-known for its criminal justice program. Yet I could never adjust to the enormous size of the school. In one of my political science classes, we had a lecture by the professor twice a week and one hour in a small class setting with one of his many teaching assistants—basically doctoral students. The students were strongly discouraged from asking the professor any questions during the biweekly lecture. That was extremely difficult since the professor, Philip Reiser, was easily one of the most interesting lecturers on the planet. You were supposed to write your question down and pass it to your assigned teaching assistant, and he or she would answer your question days later in your small group session. It was a frustrating arrangement.

I also had an economics class taught by a gentleman from Africa. Some US Army units require its soldiers to read, write, and speak one foreign language fluently and be able to *make themselves understood* in one additional foreign language. This particular professor could read and write in English, but he was having terrible luck making himself understood by any of his English-speaking students. And those students were paying quite a high price to be in his class.

After that quarter, I applied to Westfield State to continue working on a criminal justice degree. The spring semester at Westfield was also a disaster for me. For better or worse, the two-year school had taught a real "nuts and bolts" criminal justice program. Westfield's approach to criminal justice was just the opposite. It was primarily theoretical. I found making the transition from practical to theoretical nearly impossible. In short, the classes were just plain boring.

Additionally, I was assigned to live in what was basically an all-male freshmen dormitory. I was twenty-three years old surrounded primarily by eighteen-year-olds. I made some great friends and I had a very good roommate, but I still considered the dorm to be unliveable. The excessive drinking went on nearly every night, and the smell of marijuana smoke was constantly present. (I hate that smell.) One Sunday morning, I went to take a shower, only to find the entire bathroom floor covered with broken beer bottles. On Monday morning, I withdrew from the school.

I was a very unhappy guy. Westfield, Massachusetts, is a beautiful city in a beautiful location. Westfield State University has a stunningly beautiful campus. I soon missed the place as well as the friends that I had made there. I spoke with the admissions people in early February and told them that I wanted to come back, this time to major in political science, and that I wanted to live in Lammer's Hall, which was a very nice co-ed dormitory. (Different suites were either all female or all male. Today, men and women at Westfield live in the same suites.) To my surprise, the school actually accommodated both of my requests.

As I was there in the early spring to register for the fall semester, I quickly looked up the old friends that I had made only a couple of months before and had lunch with them. Those friends introduced me to another student, Paul, who became the best friend that I had ever had. That fall semester, we became roommates. After school, we continued being roommates as we each chased after our first post-graduate jobs. That ended when I made the terrible decision to join the Holy Cross Fathers at Notre Dame.

It was Paul that I asked to give me a ride home from prison when I would be released. He quickly and very generously agreed. He would have to take a day off from work to pick me up. On February 14, I was preparing to leave SECC the following morning. I actually told very few other inmates that I was getting out. Jim Manners, Maurice, and Ian were the only guys that I told directly. The chaplain, Father Jim, mentioned it to Dennis. It was strange—Dennis was actually angry that I was getting out. (At the time, I had no idea that he was doing a second-degree life sentence for the forcible rape of young children. Nor did I know that it was his second time in prison for such crimes. I'm now sure he questioned if he would ever be released.) No doubt whenever someone was getting out, it made me wish that my own date would quickly come around—but I never felt any animosity towards the person who was leaving. I *was* quite surprised that Fr. Jim offered to hire Dennis as my replacement as the chaplain's assistant. In front of me, Dennis told Father Jim, "I don't think Kevin wants me to have the job." I was used to Dennis's bullshit by that time, so I just answered, "Dennis, for God's sake, grow up." I'm not sure if Dennis ever took the job or not.

I don't particularly like white T-shirts, so I had purchased quite a few navy-blue ones from the canteen over three years. It was time to give a few gifts away. Ian had asked me to give my watch to Jim Manners before I left and have Jim give it to him. I would have loved to have done that, but there was a fear hanging over my head—what if I was hauled off to the Treatment Center instead of being released? They wouldn't let me purchase another watch with one already listed on my property records. The same went for my hot pot. I really had wanted to give that pot to Jim. Still, I couldn't take that chance. I gave Jim a few of my blue shirts and most of my ballpoint pens. There was another inmate that was just an acquaintance but who had so very little that I also gave him a blue shirt. You would have thought that I had handed him a one-hundred-dollar bill. I checked on my books in the wall locker, but when I picked one up, a cockroach crawled out of the book's binding. I decided to leave all of my books behind rather than bring any bugs home with me.

The following morning, the day guard told me to take my stuff over to the holding cell building. I gave Jim Manners a hug, and he said, "Please don't forget me, Junior." That broke my heart. Jim was one of the nicest guys I had ever met—inside or out. I told him I would write. Except for Alex, Maurice, and Tom Ahern, all of my closest friends in prison were black. Though it surprised many of my friends on the outside, it never surprised me. People are people; that's just the way it is.

When I got to the holding building, I was immediately locked into a cell. I began praying the "Hail Mary" over and over again. The guard that had been running the holding cells eventually walked out, leaving me alone in the dungeon-like room. That struck me as odd. After about an hour, I was starting to worry. Then a transport guard walked in carrying a set of waist and ankle chains. My heart was pounding so hard that I seriously wondered if I was going to suffer a heart attack. He walked right up to my cell, dropped the chains, and asked, "Are you McCormick?" I was euphoric! "No! I am definitely not McCormick!" I happily replied, almost shouting.

The guard picked up the chains, scratched his head, and directing his question to no one in particular, asked, "Then where the fuck is McCormick?" Then he left the building.

A few minutes later, a corrections sergeant walked in. "Are you waiting to go home?" he asked. I replied that I was. "Let me see if I can light a fire under the administrators for you." He looked at my ID for my name, then he walked out. About ten minutes later, he came back and said that one of the secretaries would be right down. I couldn't thank the guy enough.

The secretary arrived, looking worried as hell. She told me to walk with her. "You must report to the Probation Department tomorrow as soon as possible in the morning," she told me. In fact, she told me that same thing four or five times as we walked through prison passageways that I had never seen before. Finally, we were buzzed through a thick steel door, and there was Paul sitting on a bench reading a newspaper. As the three of us walked out of that building into a parking lot, the secretary started in on Paul. "You must make sure that he reports to the Probation Department first thing tomorrow morning. The earlier the better." Paul's face showed a combination of bewilderment and amusement, but he quickly said, "OK." Just as she had with me, she told Paul that same thing again.

Paul opened the trunk of his car, and I threw the trash bag full of my belongings into it. I still wasn't entirely certain that all this was really happening. It was surreal. Once in the car, Paul looked over at me with a totally amused look on his face and asked, "Where to?" I looked out the window at the high wall topped with razor wire, then I looked back at Paul and said, "Paul, please get me the fuck out of here!"

* * *

# Going Home

As soon as the three prisons were well out of sight, I began to relax—just a little. Then I asked Paul, "Do you know if there's a McDonald's around here?" "Are you hungry?" Paul asked. "No, I want a huge Coke from a tap—with a lot of ice," I replied. Paul laughed, and soon we were in a McDonald's drive-through. After ordering the Coke, we pulled up to the window. Paul paid the woman, and as the drive-up window began to close, Paul yelled out, "Hurry up, I've got a con in the car!" It was vintage Paul, and we both cracked up laughing. It was my first "fountain" Coca-Cola in three years, and it tasted like heaven on earth.

Paul had a few errands to run in his old hometown. One of the stops was to a bank where he had been taking care of my personal account. I had given Paul legal power of attorney. I had to wonder how many other people had a friend that they trusted that much. Our next stop was at a gas station mini-mart. I decided I would go inside and see what they had for candy. They sold candy in the prison canteen, but there were very few items that I liked. When I entered the store, I came face-to-face with the largest assortment of candy that I had seen in a very long time. Without thinking, I blurted out, "Oh my God! Look at all this!" A very surprised female store clerk looked at me and asked, "Good heavens, where have you been?" I quickly answered, "In Asia… with the Peace Corps." That instantly relieved her curiosity. I bought a Nestlé Bar. As I was leaving, the woman shouted, "Welcome home!" I thanked her and left. My first shock was that the Nestlé Bar tasted different. Something had changed in the formula between 1996 and 2000. I was extremely disappointed.

Our next stop was to Paul's parents' home as he had some small things to leave off there. I picked up the phone and called my mom. As soon as I told her it was me, I added, "Mom, I'm free. I'll be home soon." I wanted to cry, but I held myself in check. A quick ride down the Massachusetts Turnpike and then north on Route 128, and soon we arrived in Wakefield, Massachusetts, and again I wanted to have another Coke. I was very surprised that Paul didn't join me in having one, but then again, he was always a Pepsi man.

I had spent many hours at that McDonald's. It was fairly new since they had recently closed one down in the Greenwood section of town in order to move closer to the town's center. I had been one of the older store's first customers when they opened in Greenwood. I was sixteen at the time. (And gasoline was twenty-eight cents a gallon!) During that awful year while waiting for my trial, I had often just sat in the new McDonald's looking out of the window at the Southern skyline. As I walked back to Paul's car, I stopped and asked, "Do you mind if I stand here for a minute and just look around?" Paul replied, "Stay here as long as you want."

After a few minutes, we got back into the car, and I must have been too exuberant because Paul decided to caution me. "I know you're real happy now, but don't go overboard. Things will probably get hard for you as time goes on." I fully understood his concern, but to this very day, I wish he hadn't said that. There *were* rough times ahead, but it would have been better to let me have that one afternoon of unrestrained happiness. Even as I write this fourteen years later, I wish I could go back and capture that day's mood once again.

When we pulled into the driveway of my home, my mother opened up the front door. Our dog Brittany was standing behind the glass outer door, and instantly, I knew something was very different. Brit's orange and white face was now almost all white—she had aged while I was gone. I felt a surge of anger, knowing that Ray's lies (and others as well) had robbed me of three years with a dog I very much loved. Truthfully, I think Brittany had forgotten me and basically was meeting me as though it was our first encounter. There were just certain games that we had played that she seemed to have forgotten. In short order, we began playing new games with new dog toys.

I hugged my mom like I was six years old again. I still cannot imagine how painful this entire tragedy had been for her. Then she looked at Paul and me and said, "Let's go to Kowloon for lunch." Kowloon is a great Chinese restaurant in Saugus, Massachusetts—there was no way I could argue with her suggestion.

It's strange, but even after as short a time as three years, going into a beautiful restaurant again was the most amazing experience. A table with an actual tablecloth. A waiter that brought the food to that table. It was the first time in three years that I didn't have to stand in a long line for my meal. And there were plates! No stainless steel tray to eat off of. I haven't ever enjoyed a meal more than I did on that first day of freedom.

That evening was incredible. No, nothing earthshaking occurred; I just sat and watched television with my mom. Brit was still looking at me with a bit of suspicion, but as soon as I picked up one of her toys and threw it, we were playmates once again.

# *Probation*

Driving south on the McGrath–O'Brien highway toward the city of Cambridge, there is a sight that turns my stomach. It has to be one of the ugliest buildings ever to mar the Cambridge–Boston skyline. It's the Middlesex Superior Court building with the Cambridge Jail near its top. An orange band circles near the summit of the building—that's the jail. It was the scene of my undoing by a pathological liar. (Not to mention a "testi-lying" cop.) I could avoid the sight of the state's prisons—who the hell would ever visit Bridgewater? However, there is virtually no way to enter the city of Boston from the north and avoid seeing this architectural disaster. You can see it from Route 93, McGrath/O'Brien, and the Tobin Bridge. It's even visible from the Orange Line and the commuter rail trains entering and leaving North Station. The only uglier building is Boston's City Hall. Though I've never experienced any life-altering injustice in the city hall.

I found a parking space and made my way to the court's entrance. There was a small line going through the security check point, which was manned by Middlesex County Deputy Sheriffs, a.k.a. "jail guards." You never knew what you were going to get with those guys. One day a grouch, next time an amateur "comedian," and at very rare times, a fairly nice guy. The only thing all three types have in common is that they're all fairly dumb. This time, the jail guard almost had a stroke when he saw that my keychain had a handcuff key. "Are you in law enforcement?" the man asked. "Not anymore," I replied. "That's the first handcuff key I was issued as an Army MP back in 1975." The guy was at a loss for what to do. "Okay," he finally said, "Next time leave it at home. We can't have you releasing prisoners." I faked a smile and said, "I wouldn't want to do that." The guy answered, "Amen, brother." If only he knew that I was on my way to probation, he never would have called me *brother*.

I took one of the building's notoriously unreliable elevators to the probation department's floor. There was a huge counter separating visitors from staff, and there was a stack of forms on top. A highly pleasant older woman greeted me. I had to wonder where they got her from. Though I never learned her name, she was extremely nice and obviously quite intelligent—a far cry from the typical county employee. She told me to fill out one of the forms and then wait for the department's supervisor.

The supervisor, Greg Turner, was your typical Irish-looking leprechaun-sized guy. He invited me into his office and launched into a long diatribe about this being my third incarceration for drunk driving. I kept trying to stop him, but he continued to wave me off with his raised right hand. When I was finally able to get a word in, I told him, "I'm not here for driving drunk." That infuriated him. "Well, if you're going to start denying your many drunk driving offenses, then I think we have a serious damn problem!" He was almost screaming. Then he went on and on about my "drinking problem." Finally, I yelled out, "I'm here about a sex crime." That instantly shut him up. After all, who would ever admit to that? "Oh," he said. "Take a seat outside and I'll get Mona."

Mona was a dark-haired Italian girl. She had a small St. Anthony prayer card on her desk and a corkboard on her wall with a collection of various police department patches. As we conversed, it became obvious that she wasn't the county's brightest bulb. She was pleasant enough—in a firm sort of way. She told me that I had to make an appointment with a sex therapist in Brighton, a section of Boston. She also stated that she would be visiting me at home every two weeks. The final insult—I had to pay the probation department $65 a month. (I realized then just how diabolical Ray Swanson had been. I now had a sex therapist, just as he had. That was probably part of his plan from the very beginning when he, with help, concocted his elaborate lie.) And that was it. Mona said she would see me at home the following week and to call this therapist as soon as possible.

# *John "Billy" Kohl, Therapist*

When I got home, I called Mr. Kohl at his office in Brighton. It's funny—if you had a physical pain somewhere and needed to see a physician, it would probably take a week to get an appointment, but if you were required to get therapy for a problem that you didn't have... "How about two o'clock tomorrow afternoon?" he asked. "Great," I answered unenthusiastically. "Good, I'll see you then!" Kohl replied. He seemed far too excited for my taste.

The following day, I walked the 150 yards from my front door to the commuter rail station. When I was a kid, the trains were from the Boston and Maine Railroad and the engines were painted a really nice blue and white. Then the railroad went bankrupt, and a guy named Guilford took over. After some time, the state itself took over the rail system. The "blue and white" lasted for a while, then some idiot decided that the rail "line" should be called the Purple Line, and all the train locomotives were painted a ghastly purple color. The really cool B&M symbol was also replaced with a white circle that featured a big black letter *T* in the middle. Brighton is served by the MBTA's (Massachusetts Bay Transportation Authority) Green Line. Like all of Boston's subway trains, the green line also ran above ground.

As far as Boston neighborhoods go, Brighton is a fairly nice place. (Someone told me that Tyler Cohen lived in Brighton until she moved to Florida.) Boston College is there, along with the Archdiocese of Boston's Saint John's Seminary. I located John Kohl's office. It was in an older building. Kohl's office was on the second floor. Inside the office, there was a waiting area that was also the place where Kohl held a large sex-therapy group session at night.

There were two smaller offices. Kohl's inner office was his alone. The second office was shared by two therapists, one of whom had a PhD.

I sat in the outer office and waited. Finally the door opened, and a man with a young blind boy came out. I wasn't sure which one of them was the patient. Kohl came out and called my name, and then I realized that John Kohl was himself a blind man. Normally, that would have triggered a lot of respect from me, but if I had learned anything from Moreau Seminary at Notre Dame, it was to not *ever* give anyone *automatic* respect for any reason.

His office had a large window on the back wall, in front of which was a desk. Then against the left wall was a very comfortable couch. In front of the right wall was a big easy chair. I sat on the couch while Kohl took the chair. "As you can see, I'm blind," Kohl began, "and if that raises any questions in your mind, feel free to ask them." (What kind of question could I possibly have?) And then he said, "I'm Billy Kohl." I didn't get it. His first name was John, so I might have expected him to call himself *Jack* or even *Johnny*, but why *Billy*? I figured it was best not to ask. (I used to joke with my family and friends that I had an appointment with "Jacky William.") Billy also had a bookcase, and on it was a toy airplane and truck. They seemed out of place, but what the hell—I still had a toy oil truck and an electric train engine on my bookcase. They were both from my childhood; I could never bring myself to throw either of them away.

Once, I saw a great movie, entitled *Peter and Paul.* It was about the two great Apostles of Jesus. In the film, St. Paul was speaking to a group of Greek men. When he said that Jesus had risen from the dead, all the Greeks cracked up laughing, then they all walked away. I gained a deeper appreciation for how St. Paul felt every time I had to tell someone that yes, I was convicted, but no, I was not guilty. There really was no choice involved—if I didn't tell the truth, then Billy would have started trying to "cure" me of the problem that I didn't have. I could see that professing my innocence disturbed him. What I failed to realize was that that set in motion a "game" that would take place for one hour every week for the next five years. Billy would "interrogate" me in the hope of trying to get me to admit to committing a crime that I hadn't even ever conceived of in my mind.

As the years wore on, I would become sort of an "entertainer," just keeping Billy occupied while he was trying to wear me down.

We talked about my time in prison. When I mentioned that I had worked as the prison chaplain's assistant, he said that one of his guys from the evening group had said that he had quit going to church in prison because guys were engaging in sexual acts with each other in the pews during the services. "Not at SECC," I told him. "Yes," Billy replied. "At SECC." I wondered if he was just saying that to see how I'd answer him. "It's impossible," I replied. "Your patient is lying to you." I could tell he didn't like that at all. The thing is, it *was* impossible. It would have meant that the chaplains and the other inmates at the services were ignoring what was happening. The chaplains would have lost their jobs. The inmates involved would have been physically attacked by the other guys in the chapel. Finally, when what had happened came to the attention of the prison administration, the sexually involved inmates would have been transferred to a higher-security prison. So was Billy that naïve, or was this his idea of an "intellectual provocation?" As time went on, I'd come to understand that this type of asinine bullshit was just part of the game Billy was playing. He was a frustrated cop. Billy wanted to be enforcing laws, and his interrogation games were simply a manifestation of that hidden dream that would never come true. (Months later, he would tell me that his job was to "protect the community." I wonder if that had been his intent when he first decided to study psychology.)

Every once in a while during our sessions, Billy would start poking holes in some type of brail notebook. I found it very distracting. Eventually, he felt his brail watch and told me that we were out of time. He asked if the same time next week was OK with me. I was shocked! Next week? I thought that I'd see this guy once a month—maybe twice a month—but every damn week? Was this standard practice, or was it a fee-driven thing?

As I left his office, I checked the time and the train schedule. There are huge gaps in train service during the early afternoon. It would be a long wait at boring North Station. Since there was a small Chinese restaurant across the street from Billy's office, I stopped in for lunch. It wasn't the best food, but it was acceptable. When the server asked if I'd like a cocktail, I was truly tempted. A Vodka Collins would be awesome after an hour with Jacky William. "I'll have a Coke," I replied. Afterwards, I could see that while the street was somewhat congested, there were a few parking spaces. Next time I'd skip the train and drive there.

# *The Job Search*

One thing was certain: I needed work. I quickly found an ad in the *Boston Sunday Globe* for "call center customer service representatives." The company was located in Waltham, Massachusetts, and they qualified credit applicants for cell phone service. On Monday, I quickly got an interview by calling the number in the ad. In fact, I had an interview that very afternoon.

The person who interviewed me was a young woman who could not have been older than twenty-five. She was also one of the most beautiful women that I have ever seen. She told me that she had immigrated to the United States from Russia with her entire family only six months earlier. I asked her, "And you studied English in school in Russia?" She shook her head and replied, "Oh no, I learned English once I got here." I was entirely blown away! Not only could this woman speak English as well as my college English professor, but she spoke with out any trace of a foreign accent. It was a though she had been born and raised in America. I left the interview feeling really good about my chances.

Back home that night, I told my mom all about Natasha. I had to laugh; all Mom said was, "Russian people are very smart." Then she handed me a local newspaper that she had bought for me. There was another call center CSR ad, but this one was more local and the company was Comcast Cable. I called that number as well, and they told me to come in at 9:00 the next morning for an interview. This time, however, there was a far more complex application form. And there it was: "Have you ever been convicted of a felony? If yes, please explain." How do you approach something like that especially if you know that you were, in fact, *not guilty*? I just sat there in Comcast's Malden, Massachusetts, call center and debated what to do. I knew if I answered *yes*, then I most likely would not get the job. Yet if I answered *no* and they *actually* did a background check, I also would not get the job. I decided that 1) I had not actually been guilty, 2) I had a active appeal, and 3) maybe they wouldn't actually perform a background check at all. I checked *no* and went on to the interview.

The woman who interviewed me actually liked me so much that she had a supervisor give me the second interview minutes after the first one concluded. Then the two women spoke for a few minutes and offered me the job. I was absolutely euphoric! They told me to return the following morning to complete some additional paperwork. I thanked them both and went home.

Back at home, the answering machine's little red light was blinking. It was Natasha—and she too wanted to offer me a position with her company. There was nothing to debate. Comcast paid nearly seven dollars more per hour than the other company. The benefits were awesome as well, including free cable, phone, and Internet. That would be the first gift that I could give to my mom. I called Natasha and turned down her offer. It was hard since I really liked her as a person and I was greatly impressed by her intelligence—and her beauty. Natasha was nice but seemed let down.

The next morning, I returned to Comcast and met the woman who had been my first interviewer. Immediately, I could see in her face that something was very wrong. She said, "You lied on your application." I was dejected, and even though I knew it would not alter the situation, I explained that I had *not* been guilty, that even the first probation officer said that I "didn't have a prayer with a jury deliberating on the Friday before a long weekend." Then I told her that the conviction could very well be overturned on my active appeal. I knew she felt bad and that she believed that I was telling the truth, but it didn't help. Rules were rules. She told me to wait while she was writing down the names of some companies that she did not believe actually ran background checks. I was sad, but I was also grateful and I told her so.

I took her list and went home. I needed the advice of someone in business; I called my best friend Paul. Some people wouldn't understand Paul as I do. Certainly he felt bad for me, but as usual, before more than five minutes had passed, Paul had me laughing with his awesome sense of humor. He told me that there was a character on the TV show *Seinfeld*, who was either fired or not hired from/for a job, but he simply showed up for work anyway with his lunch bag and briefcase. I had watched *Seinfeld* once, hated it, and never watched it again, but this was truly funny. Then he told me to call Natasha back, tell her something "fell through," and ask if the job she had offered me was still available. Personally, I thought he was nuts. However, Paul made the point that I had nothing to lose. I told him I would try his idea. Paul replied, "And if that doesn't work, like I said, just show up at Comcast for training tomorrow morning with your lunch, pens, and notebook." I laughed, and we both hung up.

It was mid-afternoon when I reached Natasha on the phone. She told me that I should come down and see her. I jumped at the chance! As I headed towards Route 93 for the short trip to Route 128, I checked the traffic report on radio station WBZ. As the guy described "heavy traffic on 128 southbound, and increasing traffic on the northbound side," I realized that I couldn't be traveling Route 128 at a worse time. I had covered the trip from Stoneham to Waltham late at night—it usually took about ten minutes, though I generally drove well above the speed limit. This time, around 3:00 p.m., the trip took about forty-five frustrating minutes at between fifteen and twenty miles per hour.

When I entered the building, Natasha was out in the hallway. It was as though she had been waiting for me. With a highly satisfied smile, she told me that the position was no longer available. I guess not simply telling me that on the phone was her way of getting back at me for turning down the job in the first place. And yet I was so happy to see her again that I really didn't care! God, I was like an infatuated seventh grader. I told her how impressed I was with her "journey" to America and at how exceedingly well she spoke English. And I told her how my mother had said, "Russian people are smart." I concluded by telling her that I had greatly enjoyed meeting and conversing with her, and then I wished her continued success. Natasha looked downcast. I don't know if she felt bad about having me drive all the way down there in heavy traffic or if she was saddened that her "revenge" had been a failure, but I wasn't angry at all. In fact, I'm still not angry—and it was a *very* long ride back home.

A few weeks later, another ad appeared in the *Globe*. This one was for a company called E-Support Now. It said, "Call center reps needed to provide customer service via e-mail, phone, and live chat. You must be Internet savvy." Hmm, *Internet savvy*. I had learned everything about Microsoft Office in Herve's prison class, but the Department of Corrections wouldn't let *any* inmate connect to the Internet. I didn't even own a computer at home, and I hadn't ever been on the net—not even for a minute. I called the number and spoke with a woman who said she was a personnel representative. She asked, "Are you computer literate?" I quickly and honestly replied, "Yes." Then she inquired as to how many hours a day I spent on the Internet. And then I lied, "Some days two, on other days, I often lose track and sometimes spend as much as four or five hours surfing." (I was glad that I had heard the term *net surfing* on television.) The woman on the other end cracked up laughing and said, "Then you might be just the type of person we're looking for. Can you come in for an interview tomorrow afternoon?" I had an appointment with Billy at two, so I said, "Well, anytime after 3:30 would be great for me." The lady replied, "Good! Then how about four o'clock?" "That would be perfect," I told her.

Now what the hell was I going to do? I knew absolutely nothing about the Internet. Then I remembered that there were computers at the local public library. I'd ask the librarian there for some help. Fortunately, the Melrose Public Library was about 175 yards down the street from where we lived. I got in my car and drove down. (Yes, I know I could have walked.) When I arrived, I walked through the front door, took a left into the Reference section, and there to my right were around ten computer workstations. I cursed under my breath when I saw that most of the computer desks were occupied by middle-school-aged kids. I never reached the point where I *disliked* kids, but after Ray Swanson, I no longer trusted anyone between the ages of two and twenty. (With the exception of Paul's kids, they were quite "normal" and thus trustworthy.)

I started toward the reference librarian, but I stopped as soon as I heard her give a woman what I considered to be a less-than-friendly response to a question. Now what the hell was I going to do? The clock was ticking down toward the next day's interview, and I was completely ignorant of the Internet that I had professed to love so much. I went around and sat down at the only open workstation—with a young girl on one side and a boy on the other.

I tried everything I could think of to get online, but I was beginning to see that I was in real trouble. Perhaps I could reschedule the appointment, I thought to myself. Then I realized that would probably require an even bigger lie—and I just didn't want to do that. "God, am I screwed," I whispered to myself. God bless kids and their supersonic hearing. The girl looked at me, laughed, then got up and left. *Great*, I thought silently to myself. *Now even twelve-year-olds are laughing at me*. After a few more failed attempts to get things going with that damn computer, the boy to my left leaned over, looked at my screen, and asked, "What are you trying to do?" In my frustration, I had lost all my inhibitions to speaking with a kid, and I just explained my entire predicament to him.

"OK," he replied. Then looking at his watch, he said, "This will take at least an hour." And then this middle-school kid launched into talking and showing me stuff—and then he had me do a bunch of things as he told me what to do. After quite a while, I heard a buzzing sound—it was his phone. He looked at it and told me, "My ride is here. I got to go. Don't worry, you can pull this off. Keep playing with the Net and do it every day. And tomorrow, *act* like you know *everything*!" Then he grabbed his backpack and left. I knew that you were supposed to be quiet in the library, but screw it, I yelled out, "Thank you!" He looked back, smiled and waved, then he disappeared through the door. I never even knew his name. I never saw him again. Looking at my watch, I could see that he had invested about an hour and a half in a total stranger. I knew I should have stayed there longer, but I was exhausted, so I too got up and left.

The next day, I had to fill out an application at E-Support Now. Their application had the most unique statement that I have ever seen: "You will not be asked about any prior criminal record on this form or during your interview." Sadly, I would not ever encounter a company with that policy again. The woman that I had spoken to on the phone told me that there was a computer terminal right next to where she was working and that I should feel free to "surf" while she finished up what she was doing. Then we would talk.

I began playing with the Internet, looking up people from politics, looking at pictures of everything from dogs to fighter planes, and then I began reading news stories on CNN's website. What I didn't realize was that the personnel lady was surreptitiously watching my online activity. When she had "seen enough," she began talking to me. E-Support Now provided customer service to the customers of many, many online companies. It was just plain cheaper for them than hiring their own CSRs. (At least E-Support Now was located in the United States!) The biggest client was Priceline.com, but there were easily close to thirty different companies that E-Support Now served. And then out of nowhere, she said, "A training class starts next Monday. Be here at 9:00 a.m." I couldn't believe it! I was hired! Herve from the prison school and that middle-school student had gotten me my first job since my release. I will always be grateful to both of them.

Training began with a couple of day-long classes, and a field trip was planned. The day before the trip, the entire class was ushered into the executive meeting room. This was odd since all of the classes had thus far been held in traditional-looking classrooms in the basement. Two guys entered and stood at the head of the class. They were high-energy types, and they seemed genuinely pleased to be among us. They began.

One asked the group, "When you hear the words *outdoor living*, what comes to mind?" One young woman answered, "Camping!" Both of our presenters smiled as though she had just said something truly dumb, and the younger of the two said, "That's not it." A trainee in his early twenties enthusiastically yelled out, "Canoes and kayaks!" "No," the older man responded. I could see that the smiles on our two guests were becoming harder and harder for them to maintain. One of the women in our class, Kate, was very pretty and bursting with energy. She was a recent high school graduate. She got an idea and she jumped up out of her seat like a submarine launched cruise missile, saying, "I know! You're selling outdoor furniture!" Now our two presenters seemed not so much annoyed as worried. The second oldest of our group—I was the oldest at forty-four—shook his head at the rest of us and said, "You guys *really* don't get it." The older presenter smiled from ear to ear and said, "Ah, *you* get it. Tyrone, tell the rest of the class!" Our guests were looking at him like he was the Messiah, and he blurted out, "These dudes are selling sporting goods!" Both presenters in unison said "No." But our colleague continued, "Football stuff." "No." "Baseball, basketball…" "No," the two men said a little louder. Our classmate was on a roll. "Hockey for you white folks, maybe even a little tennis…" "*No!*" the older presenter practically screamed. "We're talking about outdoor cooking! You know, grilling over a fire!" The man who had just recently been reeling off all the sporting possibilities said, "OK, I guess it *could* be that."

"It's exactly that," the older presenter replied. I knew instantly that these two men were the ones who most likely not only came up with the idea of a large home appliance company branching out and selling grills and accessories online, but they had definitely been the ones who had sold their bosses on the name "Outdoor Living" as well. That a fairly young group of people had heard the name of the new website and had no idea what they were actually going to be selling was obviously weighing quite heavily on the two of them. It took a while for each of them to "recover" from our first few minutes together.

There seemed to be nothing all that wrong with the idea though. People would be able to view a good variety of high-end grills on the new site. There were grilling accessories, i.e. cooking utensils and spices, and they even had contracted with a well-known food provider to ship steaks carefully packed in dry ice to the customers. Personally, I'd rather buy my food at the local supermarket, but I guess it could work out for some people. The grills could either utilize the traditional propane gas tanks or they could be permanently installed at a fixed outside location and connected to the home's natural gas source. They even had a network of handymen in every part of the country who would come to the customer's home and assemble the grill—for an extra charge of course.

At the end of the class, our two guests looked both exhausted *and* worried. I don't think things had gone quite as well as they had hoped. They told us that the next morning a bus would be provided to take all of us to a location forty miles west of Boston where we would watch a grill being assembled. After assembly, the same person who put it together would cook up some food and allow us to sample it. It seemed like an easy thing to actually be paid for, and I was looking forward to the trip. They gave each of us a good-sized binder with all their products described and pictured. I spent that night memorizing the binder's contents. This job was very important to me, and I wanted to do it well. As I read, I was taken aback by the prices for the grills that ranged from around $800 to $2,500. When I finished my "homework," I discussed my concerns with my mom. She just said, "There are lots of people with plenty of money—don't worry. Besides," she continued, "when the people that buy them have their friends over for a cookout and they see how nice the grill is, they will probably want one for their own home." I knew she had made a good case, but still the high prices scared the hell out of me.

The next morning, as I drove to the company on Route 93 South, I was absolutely horrified at just how much traffic there was. It was 8:00 a.m., and the short ride took close to thirty minutes to complete. I thanked God that I had asked for the second shift. (The ride home after 11:00 p.m. generally took me eight to ten minutes.) As I pulled in, I saw our bus parked out front. I was about the ninth person aboard. An E-Support supervisor was up front with a list of just who would be on the trip, and I had to laugh—this was starting out exactly like a grade school field trip. After twenty minutes, the only employee missing was Kate. She pulled into the parking lot just about the time the driver and supervisor were about to give up. She jumped on board with the energy of a ten-year-old. I started laughing, and she caught me. She came down the aisle all smiles and took the seat next to me—deliberately banging into me as she sat. "You're late," I told her. "They were going to leave without you." She looked up at where the supervisor was sitting and whispered, "Asshole." We both cracked up laughing.

We made small talk during what seemed to be an endless ride. Eventually, after heading West for some time, we exited the Massachusetts Turnpike and began to roll through some of the smaller "Metro-West" towns. Kate looked at me and asked, "Can you imaging living out here? There's absolutely nothing around." I laughed and said, "It's not that bad. I used to live in Holliston—not all that far from here." She laughed and said, "Oh, bullshit!" I replied, "It's not that bad. Everything we have around Boston is just a short ride away in Framingham and Natick. Then at the end of the day, you can go back to a nice, quiet town and relax." Kate laughed, shook her head, and said, "And to think I had such high hopes for you."

Finally, we arrived at what I guess was a "club" type high-end appliance center. As we walked through the showroom building, I was amazed that all the cooking appliances were doing just that—cooking stuff. Customers who came here didn't just look at a cold, albeit very expensive, oven—they actually saw it cooking a turkey or some other roast. One oven was even baking chocolate-chip cookies. One of our cruder women co-workers blurted out, "So this is how rich people buy shit!" Kate turned toward me with her mouth open. I said, "Carol is a class act, isn't she?" We both laughed.

Finally, we followed a middle-aged man out to the back of the building. There was a large box and a set of tools that took up almost as much space. The man began unpacking and assembling the huge-ass grill. Kate moved closer and whispered into my ear, "All this excitement might give me a heart attack." We both laughed and got a dirty look from the guy putting the enormous grill together. The supervisor, who was as recently hired as the rest of us, walked over and told Kate and me to "control ourselves." I looked at him and said, "We're just enthusiastic, Henry." The guy looked surprised and said, "Oh, I'm sorry," and walked away. Kate whispered, "God, what a moron." I had to bite my tongue to keep from laughing all over again.

As soon as the grill was fully assembled, the man attached a huge propane tank and grabbed a long-stemmed lighter. I jokingly pulled Kate backward and said, "Watch it blow up." Again, we both died laughing and earned a new round of dirty looks from both the assembler/cook and Henry. The cook pulled out a drawer on the grill and said, "I'm going to add some wood chips from an apple tree for a smoky-apple flavor." Kate and I looked at each other with equally blank expressions on our faces. The cook then started placing chicken breasts on the grill. He yelled out to the entire group, "There isn't enough chicken for everyone to have their own piece, so pair up and split a breast."

I grabbed two plates off the table and told Kate to stay with me and stand right next to the grill. She looked slightly confused, so I told her, "The first two cooked pieces are ours—and we're not sharing them with anyone." Kate quickly nodded her agreement. She was as deadly serious as a soldier who had just accepted a dangerous assignment. As soon as the first cooked pieces of chicken were placed on a platter, I rapidly nailed one followed by another with my fork, and Kate and I basically left the group and sat under a tree to eat. I was thoroughly amazed—no one seemed to have noticed what we had done! About ten minutes later, Henry looked over at us, then he walked over to a barrel full of ice and Coca-Cola, grabbed three cans, and brought Kate and I each a Coke. We sincerely thanked him. He talked for a while then asked, "How did you each get a whole piece of chicken?" I responded, "I don't know. It's what the guy cooking handed to us." Henry chuckled and said, "Oh, you two got lucky," then he walked away. With feigned disgust, Kate looked at me and said, "God, you're such a liar." Then she laughed.

On the way back to E-Support, Henry got the bus driver to stop at an ice cream stand in Natick center. I paid for Kate's cone as well as my own. Kate started to talk to one of the other women in our group. Tyrone walked up to me and quietly said, "Oh man, Kev, Kate's beautiful *and* she fucking likes you. You going to do her tonight?" I was shocked. "God, Tyrone, we're just friends." Tyrone gave me a "don't bullshit me" look and said, "Oh, c'mon, man, you ain't going to tell me you don't want a piece of that." I was really saddened that he was talking like that. I told him, "You know, chances are I'm older than her own father." At that point, Kate walked back over. Tyrone held up both of his hands and backed away. Kate looked puzzled and asked, "What was that all about?" I quietly answered, "Now *he* wants to know how we each got a whole piece of chicken." Kate looked amused and asked, "Should we tell him?" I shook my head and replied, "No, screw him." We both just laughed and got back on the bus.

# *Nightmares and Dr. Marc*

I had started having terrible "prison" dreams shortly after getting out. The prison had sent me home with a few of the sleeping pills that I used on the inside, but I was running out. Once the pills ran out, the dreams increased in both frequency and intensity. They were not violent dreams; they were about not getting released.

The first dream was mostly an accounting nightmare. I was back in SECC, and I knew that my release date had come and gone—but no one was saying anything. I couldn't figure out if it was a conspiracy against me or just state corrections department stupidity. Over and over again, Jimmy Manners was saying, "Junior, you have to tell someone about this!" As the dream would end, nothing was ever resolved.

In the second dream, I was walking through the cars of an old passenger train. It was all sleeper cars. Everyone in the bunks were inmates. Some cars had female inmates; some had males. I kept walking through the cars hoping to find a way out or, better yet, a way *off* the damn train. I slowly came to realize that the Department of Corrections was not transporting us to another prison. We were all on a train that would never stop so that we would never be released. The frightening part was that all the inmates on the train were very sick with—something. I was the only passenger that wasn't sick, hence the heightened need to get off the train to nowhere.

Attempted escape could get ten years added on to your prison sentence. The final two dreams involved being in the wrong place, i.e. outside the prison or in a restricted part of the prison, and saw me trying desperately to get back *inside* without being caught. And so the third dream, strangely enough, featured skiing. I hadn't been skiing since 1979, which made the dream all the more strange. In the dream, there were two side-by-side ski trails. It was an extremely gentle slope—even beginners would have found each run to be way too easy. The trail on the right was within the prison, while the trail on the left was on the outside. After skiing down the trail, I suddenly found myself on the "outside" trail. I had no idea how I got there. I was terrified that the people from the outside world would notice how I was dressed and turn me in. The dream would end with my having no idea how to get back inside the prison. I was thoroughly terrified.

In the fourth and final dream, I suddenly realized that I was in the administrative offices of the prison where no inmate is allowed to be. It was like running a maze. I kept following stairs, hoping that they would lead to a door—any door that would lead back to the area where inmates were allowed to be. After a series of uncountable errors, I did finally make it back to an inmate-authorized area. This was the final dream that began in my sixth year after being released. I have often wondered if the fact that my probation was over after five years in any way accounted for my getting back safely inside the prison. I suppose I will never know.

However, one thing was clear. I was unable to sleep through the night, and I was becoming deeply depressed. It was only two months after my release from prison. I made the decision to see a psychiatrist. I had a relative whose husband had been seeing a Dr. Marc Konic. Dr. Marc was affiliated with the Melrose-Wakefield Hospital and had an office in his home in next door Malden. I was hesitant at first but only because of the location. Malden as a city was more congested than Melrose, and I feared either not being able to secure parking or worse, having to pay for it. I was somewhat surprised to find that the doctor's home office, in fact, had enough space for two cars. In front of the office, there was a small convenience store with about six parking spaces. On those rare occasions when the doc's two spaces were full, I'd simply park at the store, go into the store and buy some small item—a newspaper or candy—then walk over to my appointment. The store owner never seemed to notice.

Dr. Marc's wife was also his secretary. She was from India. She could be friendly unless you crossed her in *any* way, then the diminutive woman turned into a raging Rottweiler. My mother was the first one to find this out. I was late for an afternoon appointment once, and Indira called the house. Unfortunately, my mom picked up the phone when she should have let the answering machine get it. Indira basically chewed my mom out because *I* was supposedly late. When I arrived at the office for my one o'clock appointment, it was 1:04 p.m. according to the digital clock on Indira's desk. Almost pleasantly, she said, "Oh! I just left a message with your mother." According to my mom, Indira was quite unpleasant, and my mother was neither in the habit of exaggerating or prevaricating. Back at home, I checked the caller ID log. Indira had made her nasty call at 1:03 p.m.—one minute before I arrived—and after I was presumably three minutes late.

Indira also kept what she called her *black book*. She told me that if I ever missed an appointment without giving her a twenty-four-hour notice, she would put my name in that dreaded book. Once your name was in the book twice, she would no longer make appointments for you. You were "out." Indira also had the bizarre habit of lining up pens of a similar make on her desk in groups of three. There were usually five or six groups of three pens on the top of her desk at all times. All the pens were gifts from visiting pharmaceutical reps. She also sold vitamin supplements to the patients and, at one time, was even selling books of poetry authored by some unknown man from India.

Dr. Marc, by contrast, was one of the nicest guys I have ever met. (I often wondered why the hell he had married Indira.) Our first session lasted an hour and a half as I described the state of my life starting with the false accusations in 1996 and everything that had taken place right up to my first appointment with Billy Kohl. Marc looked puzzled and asked, "If his name is John, why does he call himself Billy?" I laughed and told him, "I don't think anyone knows." The doctor leaned forward and joking asked, "But does *he* know?" When we finished, I got a prescription for a mild sleeping pill and an antidepressant. Marc said that he would see me in two weeks just to see how the medication was working. He said once we were certain that the medication was working, we could move to once-a-month visits. I told him that beat the hell out of seeing Billy

Kohl every damn week. Dr. Konic was visibly blown away. "What in the world are the two of you going to talk about every week?" he asked. "I have no idea," I replied.

Neither of the medications worked all that well for me. We tried different combinations, and finally, the depression I was experiencing came under control. I never really got a handle on my constant insomnia. Eventually, Dr. Marc and I saw each other every six weeks.

* * *

I was working the 3:00 p.m. to 11:00 p.m. shift at E-Support Now, and I was really enjoying what I was doing. I was playing video games, chatting with strangers from all over the world, and surfing the Net in general. Sadly, only a few days after our field trip to see a grill assembled, Kate stopped coming to work. Although the woman from personnel who hired me was restricted in what she could tell me, I was able to find out from her that some other job offer came to Kate, but she had to take it right away. She quit without any notice whatsoever. I could tell that it really aggravated the woman from personnel. I just hoped that Kate was happy. I definitely missed her.

I had responsibility for five different online companies, but I was only receiving two or three inquiries during each eight-hour shift. Only the CSRs handling Priceline.com were actually busy. I was making $11.50 per hour. There was a group of young guys who always sat near me that had only one client—a women's apparel company based in Germany. There were four of those guys, and they worked from noon until 8:00 p.m. Their ability to speak German fluently netted them a starting wage of $16.50 per hour. In the five hours that we sat together, those four men took around three calls—collectively. (And they made $200 a week, more than everyone else.) One of them was a painfully serious guy who actually was from Germany. Late one afternoon, one of the group, a guy named Greg, turned to the German and asked, "What's the best way to say 'I'm sorry' in German?" Before the other man could answer, I quipped, "Try turning off the coke-oven." Everyone howled laughing—except the man from Berlin. I really didn't care what he thought.

I was absolutely shocked one night as a gentleman from Georgia was speaking to me about Outdoor Living's most expensive grill. I had thoroughly studied the product line, and I could sense that this customer really wanted to buy what he kept calling "the best grill on the market." Suddenly, while we were speaking by phone, my computer screen indicated that a person wanted to have a "live online chat" with me about a wallet from one of my (American) apparel companies. The chat questions sounded less like a curious customer and more like some kind of a test. I stood up, and about forty yards away, I could see Akmed, one of the supervisors, typing away on his computer. I quickly shot an answer to the "wallet" question and saw Akmed start typing again. As soon as he hit the Enter key, another question showed up on my screen.

"Kevin, are you still there?" the man from Georgia asked. "Yes," I told him, and we continued our conversation. Now the wallet guy was upset. "Are you paying attention to me?" the chatter asked. "Of course," I replied.

"Kevin, give me a second—I want to go get my credit card," the gentleman from Georgia told me. Then the chat lit up again. "Sir, I think you're ignoring me." I stood up, and I could see Akmed looking at his screen waiting for my answer. I quickly typed, "Akmed, I'm making a sale, and if I lose that sale, I'm going to walk over there and kill you." The very second I hit Send, Akmed froze, then very slowly he turned his head and looked in my direction. Then over the phone, the grill customer said, "Look, Kev, I think I'll call back later. You seem kind of busy." I started to speak but he hung up.

I pulled the headphones off my ears, and I started quickly walking over to Akmed's workstation. I was out of control. "You stupid fucking prick, you just lost Outdoor Living *and me* a twenty-five hundred dollar sale!" Shaking and stuttering, Akmed got up and almost fell over his own chair. I was screaming right into his face. "You have to play your bullshit supervisor games about a twenty-dollar-wallet while I'm making a huge sale." Akmed stammered, "God, it's not like you'd get a commission." "You idiot!" I screamed. "I want Outdoor Living to succeed!" I suddenly looked around, and quite a few of my co-workers were watching—and most seemed to be thoroughly enjoying my meltdown. I got close to Akmed and very quietly told him, "I swear, the next time this happens, I *will* kill your ass." Then I walked away.

There was a really big, really tough black CSR named Ronnie who sat near me. (Strangely, I have no idea what companies he worked for.) Ronnie looked at me seriously and asked, "You OK?" I quickly told him the entire story. Ronnie smiled and said, "Damn! Now that's what I call dedication!" It was only then that I was finally able to sort of laugh at what had just happened, though I was still furious. At mealtime, Ronnie and I had Chinese food delivered. No matter what the situation, Chinese food always improves my mood. While we were eating, Henry came into the lunchroom and got a bag out of the fridge. He took out a Tupperware like container and threw it in the microwave. It was full of chili. Unfortunately for Henry, he didn't loosen the cover at all. When he finally took the container out, the microwave's heat had basically welded the cover to the rest of the container. Ronnie and I nearly died laughing. Henry wasn't amused at all. Both Ronnie and I offered Henry some different Chinese appetizers, but he wouldn't take anything. Henry just sat there for thirty minutes staring at his now-inaccessible chili. I sincerely felt bad for the guy.

* * *

It was a brutally hot day when I arrived in Brighton for a 1:00 o'clock appointment with Billy Kohl. If May was going to be this hot, I was not looking forward to June. It was only a few minutes after noon, so I went across the street to Han's Village, the small Chinese restaurant. The older couple that ran the place were nowhere to be seen, but a young Chinese woman in her early twenties was waiting tables, and as I sat down, she was locked in an argument with an older black woman. The waitress was telling the older woman that she shouldn't come to a restaurant unless she was prepared to leave a tip. "I have no obligation to give you a tip!" the older woman barked. The waitress seemed extremely angry and shouted, "You have no class." The older woman sat down and began looking at the menu.

Suddenly, she jumped up out of her seat and said, "Oh no! You'll probably spit on my food!" As she was going out the front door, the waitress screamed, "Don't come back here—ever!" Then as though nothing at all out of the way had taken place, she walked up to me and asked, "Would you like something to drink?"

While my brain thought *Coke*, my mouth said, "A Vodka Collins and a number 3 please." I had three of those before my food arrived, then I asked for a Coke. As I was eating, I was somewhat surprised that the three drinks were having a profound effect on me, then I remembered that I had taken a tranquilizer just an hour earlier. I was taking Xanax again. I figured there was nothing I could do at that point but eat my lunch and drink a few Cokes. As I looked across the street, I saw Billy Kohl tapping his way down the street with his white cane. He went into the office building while I continued eating. A few minutes later, he reappeared at the front door and taped a paper sign to the inside of the door. I ate as slowly as possible to kill the time before my appointment. When I finally left the restaurant and entered the building where Billy's office was located, I stopped and looked at the sign Billy had posted. It read, "Please do not lock the doors. The doctors have appointments tonight." I blew out laughing. Only Billy had an appointment that night—with his large sex group—and Billy did not have a doctorate.

Billy had a tactic that I quickly became aware of. He always began with small talk, then he would try to drop a "verbal bomb." I'm not really certain what it actually was that he hoped would result from that. I usually either made a curt comment about what he said or asked—or sometimes I would just change the subject. In a very short time, I had become quite adept at controlling what we spoke about. (Of course, Billy's main hope was to somehow secure an admission of guilt.) Today, however, I was exceptionally calm, owing no doubt to the combination of Xanax and vodka.

Billy leaned forward in his chair and asked, "Since we last met, have we masturbated?" "We?" I asked, "Are you asking if you and I have masturbated?" Billy's face turned a bright red, and he sternly said, "I mean you." It was obvious that he was angry, and I thoroughly enjoyed seeing that. Quoting the Universal Catechism of the

Catholic Church, I said, "You know I can't do that, Billy. It's a gravely disordered act." Billy was clearly agitated, "Says who?" he demanded. "Says the Church's catechism," I replied. "God, Billy, you don't want me to go to hell, do you?" He quickly changed the subject. I slipped off my moccasins and laid down on the couch. It was extremely comfortable. I really don't remember what else we talked about that particular day, but I now had a new habit. I stretched out on Billy's couch every time we met from that day onward. I'll always wonder if he knew about that.

* * *

My first home visit from my probation officer, Mona, was on a Wednesday morning at 11:00 a.m. I set up a comfortable recliner off to the right of our living room couch for her to sit in. She was prompt, knocking on the front door at exactly eleven o'clock on the dot. My mom was none too happy that she was about to miss *The Price is Right* so that Mona could "hang out" with me. I let Mona in as my mom was ascending the stairs to her bedroom. "Hello, Mrs. DeCost-a!" Mona yelled out as if my mother were deaf. Between Mona's preemption of her TV show, along with her Mediterraneanizing our French surname, my mom wouldn't answer her.

She sat in the chair and glanced over at the coffee table in front of me, and she saw that I had a movie video from Blockbuster. As if she were about to make the bust of the century, she snapped up the tape saying, "Anything good?" Trust me, that wasn't a question. I wanted to laugh and tell her that Blockbuster never carries pornographic films, but I decided to stay silent. Obviously disappointed over picking up a Jet Li film, Mona said, "I'd like to see the upstairs." I gave her the tour of my bedroom and a room that I used as a prayer chapel. Passing my mom's bedroom, she looked at the door, and I just said, "Not a good idea." She said nothing. Some time a year or two later, I saw an open file in her office—it was my file. The top sheet read, "I checked out his room looking for pornography but found none." I didn't know whether to laugh or scream; I have never possessed porn in my entire life.

One framed picture did catch Mona's eye. It was a picture of my friend Alexei sitting at the controls of an airplane. One early morning at Boston University's George Sherman Student Union building, I was having breakfast before my classes began. I was still wearing my Emerson College Police uniform, having come directly to school from my overnight shift. A young undergrad approached with his breakfast tray and asked if he could sit with me. A conversation ensued—mostly about my department and about Alexei's home in Russia. He was studying journalism at BU. I laughed and reminded him that being a journalist in Russia could be a very dangerous job. He told me that because he was "in university," as he put it, that he had avoided the compulsory army service back home. He was happy about that but saddened that he had never gotten to do any shooting. I told him that I was going to my gun club's range on Saturday and offered to take him along. Alexei was ecstatic. We were close friends until he returned home. We stayed in touch via e-mail and the phone, but eventually, we just grew apart.

Now Mona was captivated by his photograph—most likely because at age twenty, Alexei still looked as though he was sixteen. "Who is that?" she asked. Not wanting to drag Alexei's name into Mona's "realm," I told her it was Alex from school and that we were target shooting partners. "And the plane?" she asked. "His parents have a small charter business." I honestly told her though I didn't mention that the business was a few miles outside St. Petersburg, Russia. Mona had served some time with the Air Force. She went up to the photo and, with the air of a military advisor, pronounced the plane as being a "DC-10." After she left I took a magnifying glass and looked closely at the photo. The instrument panel was covered in Russian words in the Cyrillic alphabet. I later called Alexei and asked if the plane was an American-made DC-10. "Where would we get that?" Alexei asked while laughing. "It's a Russian plane."

The following week at Billy Kohl's office, I could see that "Jacky William" was trying desperately to "hold back" on something until just the right moment. Had we been friends, I would have sarcastically screamed, "What?" Billy began with his usual bullshit small talk. "Since we last met, have you socialized?" Although I knew exactly what he was asking, I feigned ignorance and asked, "What is *socialized*?" Billy explained that he wanted to know if I had spent any time with friends. Quite truthfully, I told him that I had visited a married couple that I knew and that they had, much to my dismay, produced a Monopoly board game. "I hate board games," I told him. "Jacky William" took on the facial expression of a Poker player about to lay down an insurmountable card hand, and with a great flourish, he said, "I guess you'd rather be target shooting."

"Oh," I replied. "You've been talking to Mona." Billy's face reddened, and he said, "We hardly ever speak. No, never." I was pissed and asked, "Then where did 'target shooting' come from?" Billy was angry now and stuttered,......... just... you know, with your military and... you know... your background." Then he just stopped talking. After an uncomfortable silence and owing to Billy's "frustrated cop" mentality, he asked, "So when *was* the last time you went target shooting?" I knew what he wanted. Firing a gun—even an air rifle—would be a violation of probation and, as a convicted felon, a crime. Trying to control my anger, I told him honestly, "In June of 1996. Now after I leave, make sure you call Mona and let her know." Always the consummate liar, Billy replied, "I never talk to Mona."

I had added a specialized track in pastoral care and counseling while at Boston University. There were two professors that were psychologists as well as ordained ministers. I greatly liked one and disliked the other. I had run into many "therapists" during my life. (Good God, what does that say about me?) Some were OK; some were amusing. The psychologists that gave me my psych tests for both Moreau Seminary and the Emerson College Police were both amusing guys—in differing ways. However, many therapists/psychologists seemed to feel that outright lying was part of their job. They also presumed that they were always the "intellectually superior" person in the room. As much as I hate arrogance, I hate a liar even more. And this wasn't just some guy in a bar saying that he had once defeated twelve other guys in one fight then successfully wrestled a bear, this was strategic/tactical lying meant to entrap. In the early 1980s, after I had ruptured two discs in my lower back, a surgeon sent me to see a therapist with a master's degree to see if the pain was psychological. I had a back support pillow, and the label had fallen off. I told the guy that without the label, it was hard to know which end of the pillow should face upward. He said, “The strap on the back should always be on the bottom.” A few days later, the surgeon told me that the support pillow was upside down. I told him, “Kenneth told me to put it this way.” The surgeon looked surprised and replied, “I wonder why? He knows better than that.” Intense pain has a tendency to make me blunt, and I shot back, “It’s probably because he’s a professional fucking liar.” The doc was no longer surprised—he was shocked.

I have faith in a few psychiatrists, MDs. However, with the exception of my aforementioned BU seminary professor, I absolutely abhor nearly all therapists/psychologists. Jacky William tops that negative list.

* * *

Things at E-Support Now were continuing quite well. The pay wasn’t great, but the atmosphere was fun. One of our co-workers, Marisa, a woman in her mid-twenties, was sitting in the lunch room one night, and she looked as though she was ready to kill someone. She had dyed purple hair and a ring in her nose, but what the hell—I liked her.

“What’s up?” I asked all the while, knowing she was angry as hell. “Some asshole ate my lunch for the third time!” she exclaimed. “What was it?” I replied. “I made a lasagna, and some son of a bitch took all four pieces and left me with nothing!” I really liked Marisa; her “blue” vocabulary would put some drill sergeants to shame. I had just returned with a large Italian sub, so I split it in half and shared it with her.

“Here’s what you do,” I began telling her. “Next week, make another lasagna and leave one layer empty. When it’s almost cooked, lift up the ‘empty’ layer with a fork and add a can of dog food. If they steal it, they probably won’t do that again. If they start screaming—even better—then you’ll know who the thief is.” Marisa’s smile went from ear to ear. She promised that not only would she do that, but that she'd let me know which day it was happening so that I could, as she put it, "enjoy the moment as well."

After we ate, I went back upstairs to my workstation. As creatures of habit, we all pretty much used the same workstation every night. The only time that changed is if you or someone else was asked either to come in early or stay later. Then grudgingly, you might have to take another desk if "yours" was occupied. As I have said, we didn't exactly have a ton of work to do, so everyone was usually engaged in net surfing. As I made a right turn toward my desk, a painfully serious woman named Ruth stood and started in on me. "When I got to my computer today, there was an army tank as the screensaver. I had pictures of babies on there when I left for my days off!" I realized that some prick had ratted me out. "Sorry Ruth, but workstations are not assigned and someone had mine," I told her. "So how do I get my babies back?" Ruth yelled. "I don't know," I replied, "where did you get them from?" Suddenly, our section supervisor, Tommy, stood up and said, "Ruth, you didn't get them from the Net, did you?" Tommy was one of the few supervisors who actually tried to enforce the rule against Net surfing.

Ruth was too frustrated to think clearly, and she said, "You're gay, Tommy, so of course you don't care about babies!" Tommy was furious. "Excuse me! Let's talk in the office, Ruth." Most of the employees were in their early twenties and four or five of them began humming the music from the old TV show *Dragnet*. I just quietly laughed and got back to work. A co-worker named Ronnie leaned over to me and asked, "Is Tommy really gay?" I told him, "I seriously don't know, but it all worked out good for me—at least Ruth is off my back." Ronnie just shook his head and laughed. Fast as lightning, a kid named Dave, who was a total computer geek, ran over to Ruth's computer and in seconds left her with a female Great Dane and her puppies as her screensaver.

A few minutes later, Ruth and Tommy returned to their places on the floor. Ruth saw the dog picture and shot me a vicious look. To his extreme credit, Dave spoke up, "I got a picture of babies back for you, Ruth." The whole section of about twenty-five workers cracked up laughing at the same time. "Back to work!" Tommy barked. Some smart ass in the corner shouted out, "What work?" At that, even Tommy laughed.

The following week, Marisa's dog food lasagna was again stolen. Although she had given me a "heads up," we never found out who the food thief actually was. Marisa's lunch was never stolen again.

* * *

After I graduated from high school in 1974, I had enlisted in the Massachusetts Army National Guard. Although I had joined in July, the day-to-day unit administrator wouldn't allow me to go to training until the following January. That made me *very* unhappy, but it was an intentional lifesaver. The AST (administrative supply technician), Sergeant Russ, knew that unless you grew up in the deep South, you'd probably want to die at Fort Polk, Louisiana, in the hot months of July and August. When I returned home the following May, I took a series of real dead-end jobs, mostly as a security guard. When Christmas 1975 came around, I was scheduled to work a security shift at Simmons College in Boston. There was no way I was going to work on Christmas Eve or Christmas Day, so I simply quit. However, in 2000, as the holiday season approached, I knew I would probably be working on both Thanksgiving and Christmas and that there was nothing I could do to change that.

I guess I had underestimated the inventive creativity of the people that ran E-Support Now. The way they set it up, every employee would have to work for two hours on each of the holidays. It was the absolute most fair holiday scheduling that I had ever seen. On Thanksgiving, I went in for my two-hour shift from 5:00 to 7:00 p.m. The management had the restaurant chain Boston Market set up a huge table with turkey, stuffing, vegetables (for those so inclined), and two huge cakes. The stuffing tasted like Stove-Top brand and the gravy was passable, but the turkey itself was absolutely perfect, as was the cake. What the hell, I even ate some corn. At my desk, I did some online Christmas shopping—from E-Support–related businesses when possible—and I also had an online chat with someone claiming to be from Thailand. I think the person was the real deal, but who knows. All in all, it was a great Thanksgiving.

The next day, when I came in, all the office talk was about the upcoming Christmas party. I kind of felt that I would be out of place with a twenty-something crowd, and I told the workers in my section that I was going to skip the party. I was thoroughly unprepared for the avalanche of reactions that followed. Ronnie said, “Kev, you have to go.” I quietly shook my head. Dave popped up from the other side of the desk partitions and, like a twelve-year-old, sadly announced, “If you don’t go, I’m not going.” Marisa walked over and said, “Fuck you, you are too going.” I became inundated with pretty much the same sentiments from about twenty people. Tommy appeared and handed me back my form that said I wasn’t attending, then he handed me a blank one and said, “Now fill this one out correctly.” I took the form, signed it, and said, “OK, OK, I’m going.” The entire work section started clapping. I was embarrassed, yet it also made me feel extremely good inside. The party was awesome.

* * *

I absolutely love giving Christmas gifts, but since I don’t exactly have a ton of money, many people outside of family and extremely close friends simply get a card from me. Yet writing out Christmas cards is something that I greatly enjoy. I usually put on a recording of Christmas hymns while I write out my cards. My cards are *always* religious and most often Eastern Church. In the Christmas spirit, I also sent cards to both Mona and Billy Kohl. Billy seemed genuinely appreciative; Mona, not so much. Billy was one of those guys who would shake your hand once a year—at Christmastime. (There was a guard at SECC who did the same.) I’m not exactly sure how to take such once-a-year gestures of civility. It’s kind of like the Roman Catholic “sign of peace” handshaking. Most Catholics would gladly do without it. (Recently I was at Mass, and a man, woman, and their two children made a big deal of shaking the hands of everyone within reach. The husband even slid across the pew to shake hands with a couple who were somewhat far away. Then when the moment was over, the wife reached into a big bag she had with her and pulled out a huge bottle of liquid hand sanitizer. She shot a glob into the hands of every member of her family, then she did her own hands. I felt deeply insulted. Later, from the same big-ass bag, she pulled out bottles of spring water for herself and the kids. I wanted to tap her on the shoulder and ask, "Got any chips in there?" I didn't.

Christmas was the one time when Billy Kohl seemed to realize that he was supposed to be a therapist and not the state's Grand Inquisitor. He always wanted to know if the Christmas season caused me to suffer from depression. As I told him, nothing makes me happier than the Advent/ Christmas Season. (Lent in the Eastern Church. The period before Easter is Great Lent. Observant Eastern Orthodox and Easter Catholic Christians do not eat meat at all for forty days before Easter and Christmas.) I love the lights, the store decorations— everything. I may not have a ton of material possessions, but that's really not what the season is all about anyway.

Christmas 2000 would be my first Christmas in freedom after three years of false imprisonment. I greatly enjoyed everything from buying a Christmas tree, cleaning and cooking the turkey, writing out my cards—both Christmas and Chanukah—and I especially liked going to church. I attended both the Melkite Divine Liturgy as well as a Roman Catholic Mass. Our house also had electric candles in each window with the *very* traditional orange bulb. I absolutely *love* those orange candles! When I was growing up in Melrose in the 1960s and '70s, nearly every home, church, municipal building, and business had those candles *and* the orange bulbs. My childhood doctor had those big C-9 orange bulbs—they were awesome. However, starting in the 1980s, under the influence of a surging yuppie class, many, if not most, homeowners changed to white bulbs for their window candles. I continue to find that very sad.

One other sad thing also took place. Many of the "friends" that I used to exchange cards with simply did not reciprocate for the first time that year. The most striking absence was from both my former co-workers from the Emerson College Police and from former Emerson students who had been my friends. Three former student/ friends changed their address without telling either me or the post office. One former student friend wanted to have lunch with me after I was released, but our schedules never aligned to make that possible. I think he wanted to assess firsthand if I had been "damaged" by my three years on the inside. After getting a "no forwarding address" stamp on his Chanukah card, I performed an Internet search and mailed the card again. There was no response. I used to receive around fifty cards each Christmas and I sent out about sixty. On Christmas 2005, I had received about five Christmas cards and had sent out around twenty. I guess adversity *does* let you know who your true friends are. The hell with it. I had my family, my dog, my tree, candles, and two different Christmas church services—and I was extremely happy!

Again I had two hours of work at E-Support. Just like at Thanksgiving, there was a ton of food from Boston Market. I had a set of three orange-bulbed candles on my desk. They had been there since the day after Thanksgiving. I had given Ronnie a set for his desk as well, but he liked them so much he brought them home to display in his apartment's window. (One day, he smiled and told me, "You know, Kev, I'm the only guy in my neighborhood with Christmas candles.") About two minutes into my Christmas shift, I got a call from a woman on one of my apparel company's lines. I'm not certain if she knew exactly what number she had dialed. She told me that she lived in elderly housing and that it was so depressing that on Christmas night someone had just been taken away in an ambulance. I got her to talk about her Christmas memories, and she insisted on hearing mine as well. We spoke for two and a half hours—past my two-hour shift—but I wasn't going to be the one who ended the call. Finally, she told me that she was getting tired and needed to go to bed. I wished her good night and a very Merry Christmas. Then I went home and watched two TV recordings that I had made: *The Grinch* and *A Charlie Brown Christmas*. Christmas 2000 was absolutely awesome!

# *Father David Ziomek*

I met Father David when he was assigned as the assistant priest (parochial vicar) at Saint Joseph's Parish in Wakefield, Massachusetts. The pastor there had already basically infuriated me by assuming my guilt in the false charges that were brought against me. The pastor was so typical of many Roman Catholic priests in that basically, he never truly listened to what anyone actually said. He would hear the first three words of a sentence and be off and running. Once, in Confession, I half jokingly told the him that if I should go to hell, it would most likely be due to my computer. The guy launched into a prolonged speech about the evil of Internet pornography. I had to shout, "I don't look at porn!" just to stop him. Then I calmly told him that whenever my computer malfunctioned, I would swear at it for ten minutes without using the same word twice.

The first time I returned to St. Joseph's after getting out of prison was the resumption of my problems with the pastor. At the end of Mass, while my mom and I were leaving, he stopped me in the end-of-service "handshaking" line and asked, "How long were you inside?" I knew what he meant and answered, "Three years." As if he were making some great philosophical pronouncement, he declared, "I think that was long enough. Yeah, that was long enough." I wanted to scream, "You fucking fool, I was innocent!" Instead, I just silently walked away.

In all truth, I wanted to leave there and never return. However, I had made many acquaintances there and I liked those people a lot. And the music ministry was excellent—and by *excellent* I mean "traditional." (I want traditional Catholic hymns accompanied by an organ. I do not want guitars, pianos, drums, etc.) However, I cannot tell you how mind-ravaging and soul-destroying it is to be falsely accused of something and be thought guilty by the very people in your life who should actually know better. For God's sake, that pastor had listened to my Confessions for years!

The following week, I took my mom to my second "spiritual home," Annunciation Melkite Cathedral in Boston. (I say "Boston" because it was once listed as being located in the Roslindale section of the city. Now, after a zip code change, its address is listed as being in the West Roxbury section.) I love Annunciation Cathedral. It is one of the most beautiful churches that I have ever seen—and I've seen a lot. It was also where I experienced my first Eastern Catholic Liturgy. When I lived at St. Gregory's Seminary, we often attended the Sunday Divine Liturgy there.

Yet this time, something was amiss. The elderly deacon looked out of the sacristy entrance and seemed to be staring at me. I had known this guy fairly well since 1987. Then I saw him bring each of the altar boys to the same door. And then it hit me—he was warning them to stay away from me! All during the Liturgy, each of the four altar boys would turn and stare at me. When the Liturgy ended, my mother, who was oblivious to all that was taking place, wanted to go downstairs for the coffee hour. Now there were many parishioners there that I knew quite well, but none of them came over to talk to us. We were being shunned! Later, as we drove away I said, "I'm never going to church there again." My mom was shocked and asked, "Why not?" I was exceedingly happy that she had not noticed what had just taken place.

The entire Melkite event, as well as the St. Joseph's debacle, were essentially both my fault. I never should have confided in the pastor at St. Joseph's after I had been accused. The Melkite situation? I had caused that too. During my time living at St. Gregory's, I had spent quite a bit of time (albeit not voluntarily) with Melkite Bishop John Elya. When I went to prison, I was seeking out the spiritual advice (and support) of the people I had known on the outside, and Bishop John received a letter from me. He sent a rather nice letter back to me, but apparently, even though I truthfully proclaimed my innocence, he must have decided that I was guilty—or at least someone to be avoided. Yet it's a total shame when you cannot even seek out spiritual comfort from those who hold pastoral positions within the Church.

In the midst of all this, I was at Wakefield's 7-Eleven Store one evening when I ran into a parishioner from St. Joseph's. The man asked me, "Did you hear we're getting a new priest?" I asked him if the pastor was being transferred, and he replied, "No, he's just getting a helper." All I could think was, *Good luck to him with that guy.* The following week at the Saturday four o'clock Mass, I got my first look at Fr. David Ziomek (pronounced "zha-meck").

First of all, Father David called himself just that: *Father David.* While all Eastern Catholic and Eastern Orthodox priests are addressed as *Father* followed by their first name, very few Roman Rite priests are, the majority being heavily influenced by Protestant formalism. In the Eastern Churches, even bishops and patriarchs are addressed by their first name. I happen to like that.

Father David was about my height, 5 feet 7 inches, though he was quite thin. He wore glasses that looked quite good on him. However, there was something absolutely staggering about this man, and no one who ever knew him would disagree—*he radiated holiness.* Over the next few years, I would be present when people would either tell him he was saintly, or more often, they would tell him that he *was* a saint. Father David would usually turn red, lower his head, and say, "No." It may well be the only thing that I would ever believe that he was ever wrong about.

I recently read a book on the Sacrament of Confession where the priest-author wrote that only around 5 percent of Catholics ever go to Confession at all. I would have to disagree and say that it depends upon the parish. In some parishes and chapels, I have waited in a long line for my turn in the Confession Room. In other parishes, the priest is lucky to see three people each month—and it's usually the *same* three people each month! At St. Joseph's, very few parishioners seemed to approach the Sacrament. Yet after Father David arrived, on the days when he was hearing Confessions, the waiting lines began to grow. After a couple of years, I actually would make an appointment with him for Confession because the Saturday afternoon lines were simply too long.

It happened that after an absolutely brutal week between putting up with Mona and listening to the absolute bullshit of Billy Kohl, I went to Confession to Father David, and I was in bad shape—not so much in great sin but in a really bad place mentally and spiritually. The bottom line was, I didn't want to live anymore. And while I hadn't tried to hurt myself, I had made a major mistake in taking my medication, and when I realized what I had done, even knowing that the result could be fatal, I decided not to seek medical help. Having survived, I was now worried that my lack of action and concern might actually have constituted sinful behavior.

Father David was exceedingly understanding, though he pointed out several "errors" in my thinking and lack of action to preserve my life. We talked for well over an hour, and when we had finished, I doubt that there was much of anything that Father David did not know about me. Then he asked, "Have you had lunch yet?" Since I hadn't, we walked over to a local pizza shop and ate. Not since Father Weiher had any priest cared that much about me. After that day, we went out for lunch every couple of weeks—and we became very good friends. We would often have long theological discussions that were thoroughly stimulating. Most Roman Catholic priests "looked down" on my theological degree—because it was earned at a Protestant university—but Father David did not. (Few priests from either of the two Boston Archdiocesan seminaries could have survived the academic rigors of Boston University's School of Theology.) I was extremely lucky to have him as my friend.

* * *

Mona and Billy Kohl genuinely were a pain in my ass, so I was somewhat happy when Mona passed me off to a different probation officer—Luis. Luis was in his twenties and, unlike Mona, actually seemed to possess a sense of humor. I have no idea if he got his position as a result of affirmative action—he was Hispanic—but I don't believe he was hired for his political connections. He was just too intelligent to be a "political hack." He was the only Spanish-speaking probation officer; there were no black POs.

The change in style was refreshing. Since we were little kids, my sisters and I were brought up to Weir's Beach in Laconia, New Hampshire; sometimes for the day and at other times for a full week. Sadly, my dad could only be there on Sundays. Despite that fact that he and his brothers owned their own business, none of them over the span of close to forty years ever took a single vacation day. It was incredibly sad that the only time off that my father ever took was during the last year of his life when he was battling cancer. Anyway, after my release from prison, I wanted to take my mom to the beach that she loved as soon as I could. (I knew no one else had taken her there during the three years that I was locked up.) Mona told me that I needed permission and a "paper license" just to leave the state. I got that from her and traveled the ninety miles from our home to the beach. However, while we were parked at the beach, a Laconia, New Hampshire, police car pulled in and parked behind our car for about ten minutes. It was painfully obvious that Mona had called them beforehand and "warned" them that I would be there. It was borderline absurd. (Though I do understand the reasons, the knowledge of my own innocence was the cause of my anger.) After swimming, we had dinner at Hart's Turkey Farm Restaurant in the neighboring town of Meredith before heading home. If you're ever in the area, not having dinner at Hart's would be a huge mistake.

The following fall, I was at Walmart and saw a winter coat that I particularly liked. Though available in blue, green, and black, it was the green color that looked the best. The only problem was that I couldn't find a green one in my size. Over a couple of days, I checked for that green coat at three Massachusetts Walmart stores and never found one. Finally, I called Luis and told him what I was looking for, and I asked him for a "license" to travel the twenty-one miles to the Walmart in Salem, New Hampshire. Luis asked, "Can you go there today?" I answered in the affirmative. Luis then told me, "OK, go now and just call me when you get back home." I did just that, and even though I never found the item that I was searching for, I greatly appreciated Luis's common-sense approach toward my travel desires.

It would only figure that the first time a wedge was driven into Luis's and my working relationship that it would be because of Billy

Kohl. Billy wanted his tentacles into every facet of my life. He wanted me to tell him which people I had contact with, what we did, what we spoke about, and on and on ad nauseum. He was trying to do the probation department's job rather than his own job as a therapist. As I have said, Billy was a frustrated cop.

At one of our weekly "interrogation" sessions, Billy produced two identical forms and asked me to sign them. He was asking for my permission to be able to speak to Dr. Marc as well as Dr. Hanson, my primary care physician. "Why do you want this?" I asked. Billy answered, "For collaboration." "Collaboration?" I snapped back. "That's a word usually associated with those Jews who assisted the Nazis in the persecution of their fellow people." Billy's face turned the brightest shade of red that I had ever seen. I tossed the papers onto his lap and said, "I'm not signing anything." I had never seen Billy so frustrated nor so obviously angry —and I greatly enjoyed the moment.

Two days later, around ten in the morning, there was a loud knock at the door. That sound reminded me of my old perjury-committing pal, Detective Ron Callahan. It was Luis, and he looked awfully serious. Never one to beat around the bush, he placed the same two forms that Billy Kohl had tried to force on me on my coffee table and simply said, "You have to sign these." I probably still should have refused, but I didn't. I signed the damn papers. Luis thanked me and left.

At my next meeting with "Jacky William Kohl," I said, "So now you send a two-hundred-pound gorilla to do your dirty work." Billy sort of mumbled that it wasn't *his* idea, but that was obviously pure bullshit.

At various times during my probation, I would become aware that I was being followed when I drove around in my car. I don't think that they were probation department employees but rather part of some private security company contracted by the department. I woke up one morning and I just plain felt sick. I called Dr. Hanson's office, and they offered to see me in the afternoon—which was very generous. However, I felt way too sick and I was vomiting severely. I thought about going to the local hospital, but generally, a trip to the emergency room would take up three to four hours. Instead, I traveled to the Walk-in Medical Center in Framingham, Massachusetts. I had seen the doctor there quite frequently since 1984 when I lived in the area. The physician and his staff were great people, and despite the long drive, I knew that I would be seen within fifteen to twenty minutes after my arrival. It was an ugly drive there since I continued to throw up—into an old, large McDonald's soda cup.

When I entered the doctor's office, a new secretary said to me, "Sir, drinking beverages is not allowed in here." Half ready to fall over, I replied, "I'm not drinking out of this." And then I vomited into the big cup again. I was immediately placed into an exam room. Eventually, the doctor gave me a shot and a couple of prescriptions. I was feeling better when I left, but again I could see in my rearview mirror the same ugly white Honda (cube-shaped, like a Nissan Cube but the Honda version) that I thought was following me on the way down. I remembered some of my colleagues in military intelligence talking about how to see if someone is following you. So when I exited the Massachusetts Turnpike and got onto Route 128 North, I entered the far right lane and traveled at forty-five miles per hour. Sure enough, the white Honda did the same. When I got off at the Wakefield exit, I went around the rotary (roundabout) three times—so did the Honda. As much fun as the game was, I still felt too sick to keep playing, so I made for the Walgreen's Pharmacy and filled my prescriptions.

The following week, at my appointment with Dr. Marc Konic, the doc handed me a note that was obviously written by his wife, Indira. It read, "Billy Kohl says that Kevin DeCoste is obtaining medication from a doctor other than you." I then told Doctor Marc about my sickness and my trip to Framingham. He took the note back and, shaking his head, tore it up. So I wasn't exactly shocked when the same thing happened the next time I saw Doctor Hanson. What was funny was that in both cases, each doctor handed me the note that had been passed to them by their secretaries. Billy Kohl just didn't "get it." Both of my personal doctors knew me well enough to know that I had been falsely accused, convicted, and imprisoned. Neither of them were willing to play Billy's little game.

Nearly two years later, Billy complained—or should I say he *whined* about the fact that he was consistently "ignored" by both my personal physicians. Sounding like an eight-year-old who had not gotten what he had asked for at Christmas, Billy whined, "Neither of your doctors will talk to me" (sniffle, sniffle). I told him, "You can force on me all the forms you want, but both of those guys respect my privacy." Again, Billy cried, "Even Dr. Konic?" I couldn't resist, so I replied, "Konic thinks you're a thief for scheduling an appointment every damn week." (Konic actually did say *exactly* that to me.) Billy was crushed. So much for sending a two-hundred-pound gorilla to get what you want.

* * *

Eventually, I was handed from Luis back to Mona. It was too bad; I actually liked Luis. I think that Mona and Billy must have thought they could trap me some other way because I was told that I would have to go to a certain floor in the Cambridge Court Building for drug testing. The testing was conducted by Middlesex County sheriff's deputies, and they were unprofessional flaming assholes. There were chairs in a room and three huge pitchers of water on a table. Everyone came in and basically starting downing cup after cup of water hoping to get things "going." When you were ready to give a urine sample, a deputy would go into a bathroom with you and stand there and watch you piss into a plastic cup. So that they wouldn't stare directly at your bodily "equipment," there were mirrors on the ceiling and on three of the walls. It was a humiliating experience.

Nearly all men have problems urinating under such "conditions," and that used to infuriate some of the deputies. The guy at the desk was the absolute worst. He used to point at a sign that said, "Failure to produce a sample in forty-five minutes will constitute a violation of your probation" and say, "Piss or go back to jail." That only made things worse. I always made it after around thirty minutes. I never "failed" the drug test either. Once when Mona was out sick, I saw Luis and he said, "It would be better if we knew what your medications were, but your doctors won't tell us." I wanted to ask,

"Won't tell you or won't tell Billy Kohl?" I never asked the question since I already knew the damn answer.

* * *

One afternoon I got to my workstation at E-Support Now and began signing onto each of my five online companies. When I got to Outdoor Living, I was shocked. There in big letters were the words "Thank You," followed by a short message that the site was now permanently closed. Although I hoped and prayed that this was not the beginning of the end of E-Support, deep down inside, I knew that it was. I saw Tommy heading my way and I asked, "Did you see that Outdoor Living is gone?" He just shook his head and kept walking by. I began to wonder just how many client companies E-Support could actually lose before drastic cuts would need to be made—or if E-Support could survive at all.

It didn't take long to find out that things were going horribly wrong. Personnel began laying people off—permanent layoffs. A young woman named Carly went absolutely insane. She left the personnel office then went on a rampage, tearing as many wires out of the computers on the floor as she could before the police arrived to stop her. At least the IT (Information Technology) people would be secure in their jobs for a while. It was sort of amusing, but I felt really bad for Carly—she had just bought a new car on credit.

After that, my women's apparel company decided that they didn't like how I responded to customer's email questions, and I personally lost them. I have to admit it—that blew me away! I went to Tommy and had him go over all my work for that company. Tommy said that he would have answered the e-mails exactly as I had. Then as a joke, he added, "Though I probably have more fashion sense than you." I was angry as hell, and even a gay joke made by a gay guy couldn't alleviate my sour mood. A week later, when that fashion company also went out of business, I have to admit, I celebrated their corporate demise. However the, "dot-com boom" was now going bust, and it was going to take a lot of us down with it.

My turn came the following week. I too was permanently laid off. After the Carly incident, when they told us in groups of two that we were finished, they made a supervisor go out onto the floor and get our belongings. I guess they wanted to keep the wiring intact. The person who was laid off with me was only eighteen years old, and he put up a huge argument. Though I admired his fighting spirit, it was a useless battle.

At about that same time, a horrific tragedy took place at an office complex in Wakefield, Massachusetts. A disgruntled and arguably insane worker smuggled an AK-47 assault rifle into the workplace. Then in cold blood, he gunned down more than twenty of his co-workers. I got a call from a guy that was still working at E-Support, and he told me that the Wakefield incident had absolutely terrified the management of the company. They wondered if one of the laid-off E-Support workers might "copycat" what the evil nutcase in Wakefield had done. Tragic as it all was, it did become somewhat useful to me. I had applied for unemployment compensation, and when I called the state office that handled such claims, the woman told me that E-Support had still, after a week, not sent along my paperwork. I called personnel at E-Support and got an answering machine. I hung up. Then I got a thought. I called back and left a message: "Hi, this is Kevin DeCoste. I just heard from the unemployment office that my paperwork has still not been faxed over to them. I guess I should drive over and talk to you. I'll be there in an hour." Less than ten minutes later, I got a call from the same woman from the state that I had spoken to earlier. She told me that E-Support had just faxed everything necessary over to her and that they had attached a note asking her to "let me know."

Just a week after that, I got a call from Tommy. He was at a local bar and asked if I wanted to join him for a drink. I told him that I was pretty much in for the night. Then he told me that he too had just been laid off. We spoke for a short time then said goodbye. As soon as I put the phone down, I got on my computer and went to E-Support's website. It was still operational. Two weeks after that, the site was gone. It was incredibly sad. I had loved working there.

# *The Sex Offender Registry*

Detective Sergeant David Murray left me in the fingerprint room and stepped into the Chief's office. I stood at the doorway trying to see and hear what they were talking about. Sergeant Murray came back to the entrance of the Chief's office and looked at me. He was obviously concerned about something, and I had a fairly good idea of just what that was. I tried to act as though I hadn't a care in the world.

Actually, at that time, I didn't. This was February of 2001, and I had taken two Xanax tablets prior to coming to the police station. In 2000, there was no sex offender registry in Massachusetts. Some type of legal battle had broken out involving a passage in the state constitution that read in essence, "A person has the right to be left alone." Of course, this was up against the federal offender registry law that was signed by President Bill Clinton. One of my friends, a life-long Democrat, had once said, "Clinton really didn't want to sign that law." To which I had quipped, "And he came close to being the first president to have to register himself." My good friend from the "left wing" really didn't like hearing that. Yet if Monica had said in any way that their relationship was *not* consensual, it could have happened. Anyway, eventually, the federal law carried the day.

I'm not entirely certain if it's hard to get an appointment outside of the city of Melrose to register as a sex offender, but it had taken me a couple of weeks in my city. I had imagined walking into a very hostile environment at the station, so the two-week delay only added to my nervous state. I had spoken to an old friend who had served in the 26th Military Police with me about my fears. He had said, "You've been through way worse than this. The drill sergeants at Fort Polk's Infantry School, the school desegregation riot duty in South Boston as an MP—this should be a piece of cake." "Yes," I told him, "but back then, no one was assuming that I was a criminal scumbag." He couldn't understand that regardless of my past experiences, this situation placed me entirely outside of my element. Others had said that having the knowledge of my own innocence should have helped. It didn't.

Sergeant Murray was a very professional cop. He had told me when we first sat down that when I come into the police station to register that I should "look at the clock and write down your arrival time and do the same thing when leaving." I think he was referring to the fact that there was a video camera filming the lobby of the station. Thus, if my paperwork ever was lost, at least I would have some type of proof that I had been there. People that failed to register ended up on a state police "Wanted" poster and were tracked down and arrested.

At that moment, I was a bit concerned that I was going to get into some type of trouble for being obviously tranquilized. I should have realized that Murray was way too experienced a cop not to have noticed. However calmed I was though, I was not what could be seen as "impaired." Finally Sergeant Murray came back to me and said, "You're all set." I left the station greatly relieved that I wouldn't have to come back again until the following year. What I didn't know was that it was either a policy or a practice for the detective who had taken the registration to stop by the registrant's home the next day to verify the address. Over the next thirteen years, some of the cops did come—early in the morning—and I was never awake. I was just in the habit of staying up very late at night either reading, writing, or surfing the Internet, and seldom was I ever awake before 10:00 a.m. It never caused me any trouble.

Eventually, there were some type of personnel problems in the Melrose Detective Bureau, and while that was going on, getting an appointment to register became very difficult. At the absolute worst, one year, it took me six weeks to get an appointment. As I told one police lieutenant, "I don't want to end up on a state police Wanted poster."

Every year, it was the same ritual. Fill out a form, get fingerprinted, and have a new photograph taken. One year, Sergeant Murray didn't take the fingerprints. As he put it at the time, "I know it's you." Later, another detective would tell me that the state had *demanded* that the prints be taken faithfully every year. I guess in a big city, a guy could send someone else to register in his place, but who the hell would volunteer to do that? At least in my mind, there wouldn't be enough gold in Fort Knox to get me to go through the registration process for someone else. And despite the fact that the Melrose Police had a digital fingerprint machine, the state insisted that the prints be done the old-fashioned way—on cardboard forms with ink. (One detective once told me, "The state just wants to break everyone's balls.")

You had to go through this process in the city in which you lived as well as in the city where you were employed. Though having a criminal record kept getting me turned down for every job that I applied for after E-Support Now had closed, I couldn't possibly imagine going through the registration process twice. Because every business seemed to run a background check, for better or worse, that never became a problem.

The state sent out the registration form about two weeks prior to the month in which you had to register. At least that was helpful. By law, you technically have to register on your birthday each year, but seldom are you at the police station on your exact date of birth. (I had to laugh as one attorney once said to me, "It's the state's warped way of saying "Happy fucking birthday.") In 2002, I was in Billy Kohl's office a few days before my February 23 birthday. I could see that "Jacky William" was practically bursting at the seams with some self-perceived, verbal bombshell that he wanted to drop on me.

Looking like a game show contestant that was certain he was about to win the grand prize and grinning from ear to ear like a jackass, Billy said, "Well, your birthday is almost here, so I want to remind you to go to the police station and register." And even though I didn't think it was possible, when he finished those words, his silly grin became even more pronounced. He was obviously relishing his prospects for making me feel bad. I waited to see how long his smile would last, but when he just kept on grinning, I said, "I already registered two weeks ago." Suddenly, Billy looked like a ten-year-old who had just discovered that his parents, not Santa Claus, had been buying his gifts every year. He didn't even recover all that quickly. That was the only "good" that ever came from having to register for a crime that I hadn't committed. Happy fucking Kevin's birthday, Billy!

# A Great Loss

About six weeks after Christmas I went to the post office to pick up my mail, there in my box was the Christmas card that I had mailed to Father Weiher way back in November. I knew that I had addressed it correctly, so what could be the problem? Then I saw it—across the front of the envelope someone had written, "Deceased." I tried to call a priest that I had known at Notre Dame, but I kept getting his answering machine. Finally I ran Father Weiher's name through Google, and sure enough, I found his obituary.

I guess what infuriated me was that someone among the Holy Cross Fathers had written "deceased" yet never considered writing a short note explaining what had happened, how his funeral had gone—anything besides just writing "deceased" on the front of my Christmas card envelope and getting the post office to return it. I had lived among these priests so trust me, they weren't exactly burdened by a lot of work. In fact, with the exception of those priests who taught at the university, most of them had more free time than your typical retiree.

My first thought was that I needed to have a Mass said for Father Weiher as soon as possible. With the Catholic doctrine of Purgatory, we are taught that we can assist those who have died but may not as yet entered heaven by our prayers and, most importantly, by the Most Holy Sacrifice of the Mass. I immediately took off for a local parish to schedule the Mass. The secretary was very understanding and sympathetic. As she wrote out the Mass request, she mispronounced Father Weiher's last name. I told her that *Weiher* is pronounced as *wire*—like electrical wire. What I didn't know was that she wrote that down as well.

When the day came for the Mass, I approached the priest and told him how to pronounce the name. He took an absolute fit! He pointed to a small index card with the instructions that the secretary had written down. "I've been told a million times how to pronounce his name!" he snapped at me. I guess out of further anger when he said Father Weiher's name during the Mass, he simply referred to him as Charles Weiher, not noting that he had spent his entire adult life serving the Church as a priest.

I guess I should have known better. At one time, I had belonged to this guy's parish. Every single year after a particular Gospel reading, he would say, "You know, my brothers and sisters, there may be life on other planets, we don't know, and Jesus would have to redeem them too. Exactly how we don't know." (Try hearing that once a year for about twelve years!) I had also interviewed him for a class at Boston University, and I had come away with the impression that the man was borderline insane. I had known two other priests that had been assigned to his parish as his assistants. In each case, they both eventually made arrangements to sleep somewhere else and basically "commute" to work at their assigned parish. This guy also was convinced that the other two priests were hitting his car doors with their car doors when they used the parish's two-car garage. I used to drive by and howl laughing because the crazy priest would place huge pieces of cardboard up against his car's side that faced the other priest's cars. He was thoroughly "gone."

Shortly after that Mass, I had another one said for Father Weiher at a different parish. I spent some time before the Mass with the priest who would be celebrating the Liturgy. He told me that it was the very first time that anyone had ever told him all about the person for whom the Mass would be offered for. He said he greatly appreciated it. What a huge difference a "sane" priest can make!

* * *

Not long after the two Masses for Father Weiher, it became apparent that our dog Brittany's health was also rapidly deteriorating. Brit stopped playing and began having trouble walking. She wasn't sick or injured—she was just plain old. She got a lot smarter at the same time. When she wanted something—water, food, or cookies—she would look at the object, then at me, then back at what she wanted again. I did whatever I could to make her comfortable. Eventually, I would have to carry her outside so that she could relieve herself then carry her back into the house.

Every day, she would just lie in exactly the same area doing nothing at all. When she first got sick, Luis was my probation officer. He was terrified of dogs—all dogs—but he had come to like Brittany. He had also recently married a woman who already had a son. Once he told me, "My wife's son wants a dog so bad. If I do get him one, it will only be because I've seen how nice Brittany is." Luis would always speak to Brit in Spanish, and she would just lie there wagging her little two-inch tail.

I left for McDonald's one Sunday afternoon to buy a Coke. (I don't like Coke in cans or bottles.) I told Brit that I would be right back. My mom was sitting at the dining room table reading the Sunday newspaper. When I returned, I found that Brittany had died. I felt intensely guilty for not being there for her last moments. My mom actually bought a grave at a pet cemetery for Brit. It was a sad burial. We placed her favorite toy in the little wooden coffin with her. When any of my dogs have died, the impact has been just as great as a human family member's death. The day after Brit's burial, Mona came for a "home visit." I couldn't bring myself to engage in conversation with her at that time. She stayed a short while then left. I don't think I said more than two sentences to her. I was reminded that by his lies, Ray Swanson had "stolen" three years from Brittany and me. May God in His justice punish him.

* * *

Once a dog has died, a house becomes unbearably quiet. After a week, I knew that we needed to fill that horrible void. A new dog is never a "replacement"; he or she is just a new family member. There's an animal shelter north of Boston that we had gotten a dog from before, and I thought it might be a good thing to adopt a homeless dog. I packed my mom into my Explorer, and we made the trip to the shelter.

I had been at different dog shelters before, but this time it was extremely hard for me. These dogs were in small cages. In many cases, the dogs were too big for the cages they were in. Yet that wasn't the worst part. What was eating me up inside was the knowledge that these dogs were basically "incarcerated," just as I had been. There was a distinct relationship between the cells that I had been locked away in and the cages that these dogs were locked in. Looking at them, I felt somewhat sick.

My mom was funny; I think she wanted every last one of them. However, I made a turn and there she was—a Norwegian Elkhound! We made an instant connection. The sign on the cage read "Jasmine." There was a smaller sign warning visitors not to stick their hands into the cage, but it was too late; Jasmine was licking my hand right through the bars. While this was going on, my mom asked me to look at a dog in a cage a few feet away. I turned slightly away from Jasmine to look at the other dog, and Jasmine freaked out, barking insanely as though I had suddenly rejected her. I quickly turned back, and Jazz resumed licking my hand.

We went to the office to tell the woman there that we wanted to adopt Jasmine. The woman, Alice, got the dog out of her cage and we all went to Alice's desk to talk. According to Alice, Jasmine had come up to their shelter from Tennessee. The dog allegedly had a "barking problem," and the family that had her lived in a condo complex and the condo association had "voted her out." We also found out that Jasmine had been adopted once from this shelter and that those people couldn't handle her—I don't know why—and returned her after a couple of days.

There was something else going on. This woman, Alice (not her real name), was a total bitch. There was a dog in a cage across from her desk, and for no apparent reason, Alice got up and covered the cage with a blanket. She said that the caged dog was "annoying" her by looking at her. She then told us that Jasmine "hates men." While she was telling us that, Jasmine was endlessly licking my face. I wasn't certain why we were getting the third degree from this woman, but

I resented it. She also wanted three references and an adoption form filled out. We did this and left. The only person more angry than I was that we had to wait to take Jasmine home was Jasmine herself.

The following afternoon, we were told that the adoption was approved. My mom and I were way beyond happy. When we got there, there was the matter of making the "donation." According to the shelter's literature, they did not charge money for the dogs; you just had to make a donation. Yet each dog had a different "donation" price posted on their cage. So how the hell is that a donation? Alice said, "It's seventy-five dollars for Jasmine's donation." My mom took out her check book and was interrupted by Alice, "Cash, MasterCard, or Visa?" I looked at the woman and told her that I couldn't get to my bank and be back before the shelter's closing time. So I said, "I'll bring the cash tomorrow. Can we just take Jasmine home?" Alice got really nasty and snapped, "No! No dog leaves without the donation!" I was nearly destroyed. I asked her, "Can you just hold her until I come with the money tomorrow?" Again the nasty bitch snapped at me, "No, if she's still here in the morning, then it was meant to be." Jasmine cried as Alice took her back to her cage. Neither my mother nor I slept very well that night.

The next morning, I was at my bank before they even opened. I cursed myself for having a passbook savings account with no ATM access. As soon as I made the withdrawal, with my mom alongside me, I sped up to the shelter. It's funny, Jasmine seemed to know that she was being sprung from her undeserved jail cell, as she began jumping up and down wildly. As we were paying Alice another female worker entered and asked, "Jasmine's going home?" She sounded surprised. I wasn't sure what to make of that.

As we drove away with our new family member, I said, "I hope that bitch Alice falls down a flight of stairs." My mother said, "That's a dirty word." Then after a slight pause, she added, "I hope she does too."

* * *

Mona came the following week and was thoroughly startled by the size of Jasmine. Jazzy was easily five times the size that Brittany had been, and Mona was *not* a "dog person." One of the strangest sights in the world is when a dog genuinely seems to like someone who's afraid of them. The dog keeps trying to get close, and the fearful person keeps pulling back. It's sad in a way because the poor dog just doesn't understand the problem. Jazz was very quick to offer Mona a toy, which she wouldn't take. I asked Mona, "Where's Luis?" She said that they were "switching back" for a while. I was saddened and replied, "I wanted him to meet Jazz." Without thinking first, Mona said, "He'd have a fatal heart attack." Then she turned a couple of shades of red. I had to laugh. Mona always made such a big effort to never say anything about Luis or Billy Kohl in front of me. I know it didn't exactly make her happy, but I quickly added, "I forgot, you're afraid of dogs, but Luis is terrified of them."

Mona went through her usual litany of inane questions. It was too bad, under different circumstances, I would have really enjoyed meeting Mona and having an occasional conversation with her. I often wondered about her educational background. I had a feeling it wasn't all that extensive. She hardly ever displayed any sense of humor nor did she ever really show interest in worldly affairs. However, it was apparent that she favored the Republican party. We both disliked a particular Democrat politician—but that's about all we had in common.

Before leaving, Mona told me that the following week she was bringing a computer specialist named Sam to check out what web sites I frequented online. All I could think was, "Oh great some other asshole sticking his face into my life." However, looking at Mona, I simply said, "OK." It was painfully obvious that she was just waiting to see my reaction.

The next Monday, right on schedule, Mona and Sam were at my door. I brought them to my bedroom where my computer was, and then I realized that there was only one chair. When Sam took the chair at my desk, I offered to run downstairs to grab another chair for Mona, but she declined. So there we were, Sam and Mona at my desk and Jasmine and I sitting on my bed. Sam inserted a disc into my computer that apparently helped him examine it. I was dying of curiosity, and I would have loved to see what that software actually did, but for me to run over and look at what Sam was doing would have made it look as though I had something to hide. I lay down on my bed with Jazz at my side.

Sam kept looking over at Jasmine, and Jasmine, for her part, kept eying him with what appeared to be great suspicion. "I don't think that dog likes me," Sam said. "She's just protecting her territory," I shot back. "I think the dog is racist," Sam added. (Sam was Spanish.) That pissed me off, and I started to shoot a harsh reply back, but before I could, Mona said, "Not Jasmine." I cooled down, but I told Sam, "Dogs don't hate different races—unless some evil bastard trains them to." Sam ignored my comment, but it's true—dogs don't dislike certain groups of people, but people often *train* dogs to hate the people that they hate.

Off and on, I had to get up as Sam would ask where a certain picture came from. Then he stopped on a picture of a very young boy. "Who is this?" he asked. I blew out laughing, "That was me in kindergarten. I'm going to blow it up for my mom." At that point, Mona whispered, "Even I could tell that's Kevin." Sam seemed greatly perturbed that I was laughing at him.

Then Sam looked like he had discovered a definite criminal conspiracy. He began pointing to the screen and directing Mona to look at different places. "Why do you have this Window Washer software?" Sam inquired. Webroot's Window Washer is a software program that removes all the cookies that Internet sites place on your computer. The more cookies you get on your computer's hard drive, the slower the computer performs. The cookies also allow Internet sites to spy on your online activities. It's mostly done to tailor advertising to the user's particular interests—but why the hell allow that? Also, in advertising online, every picture that pops up in an ad also remains on your hard drive, and nothing takes up more space than a photograph. Window Washer removes those photos and overwrites them, making it impossible for anyone to ever "resurrect" them again. Additionally, the software erases your browsing history after each Internet session. I could understand why that would upset both Sam and Mona; however, I wasn't using the program to hide anything. After they were done, the two of them left after saying that they would be doing this "from time to time." A few hours later Mona called me on the phone and told me that I had to uninstall the Window Washer program.

I took the program off the computer. A couple of years later, when my probation ended, I reinstalled the Washer and ran it. It actually took over three hours to remove all the accumulated cookies that had been placed since the day I had been told to remove the program. Sam checked my computer two or three more times. What a waste of time.

* * *

Mona and Luis were both terrified of dogs, but Mona overcame her fear enough to conduct home visits under Jasmine's watchful eyes. Over time, Jasmine seemed to develop a liking for Mona even though she always worked to keep the dog at arm's length. Even though I have had seven dogs during my lifetime, only Jasmine ever tried to scratch her butt by sitting on a carpet then pulling herself forward with her front legs while remaining in the seated position. At the time, there was a television commercial for a carpet cleaning company featuring a dog doing exactly the same thing. While my mom thought that it was a disgusting sight, my sister Joan and I would howl laughing whenever Jazzy "did her thing."

So it was beyond difficult to suppress my laughter when Jazz sat about fifteen feet away from Mona then started dragging her ass across the living room carpet toward where Mona was sitting. Mona groaned with utter revulsion during the butt-dragging incident. Through my muffled laughing, I said, "I guess I'll have to rent a carpet steamer." I was actually quite impressed with myself for not simply collapsing onto the floor and rolling around while laughing. But Jazzy wasn't finished. She walked right over to where Mona was sitting and looked up at her face, which was contorted with complete disgust, and then Jasmine sneezed, and snapping her head as she did so, she covered Mona's right arm with her "nasal mist." The look on Mona's face was worth millions. Her facial expression would not have been any different had she accidentally fallen into an open septic tank. I'm certain that she left that day disliking dogs a lot more than she did when she had first arrived.

When Mona left, I called Joan and recounted the entire story for her. We both convulsed with laughter for a good fifteen minutes. After that, I drove to the post office to buy some stamps. I stopped at McDonald's on the way back to grab a coffee for my mom and my usual medium Coke. My friend Bev was at the cash register, and after ordering the two beverages, she asked me, "Would you like anything else?" I began to say no, but I stopped to think. "You know what? I'll have four plain double cheeseburgers." Bev's eyes widened, and she asked, "Hungry today?" I just chuckled and answered, "They're not for me."

Jasmine loved the cheeseburgers. "Good dog!"

# Post-Release Police Harassment

A few months after I was released from SECC, a very disturbing thing began happening a couple of nights a week, every other week or so. Someone was driving into our home driveway just after 11:00 p.m., and with their high-beam headlights on, they would sit there until either my mom or I would look out the window. It was a red Ford pickup truck. After we looked, the truck would back out of the driveway and speed away. On one such night, I ran out onto the front stairs and at least got a look at which direction the truck had gone. The truck was headed onto a seldom used, very quiet road that, with either a right or a left turn, would take the driver in the direction of where Detective Ron Callahan lived.

I figured that since the truck was appearing shortly after 11:00 p.m., it was a good bet that Callahan was working the 3:00 to 11:00 shift. A few days later, I spotted a similar truck parked across the street from the Melrose Police station. Just to be sure, I made the same observation on three different nights over the course of two weeks. Although we had a garage at home, it was always occupied by my mother's car. My car was parked outside all the time, so it wasn't a case of Callahan's wanting to know if I was home or not. He just wanted to screw with me. What was really hateful—even evil—was that he was frightening my elderly mom. This went on over the course of several years.

I was at Walgreen's Pharmacy one afternoon, and they were having a sale in what they humorously called their "hardware section." Most of the tools were incredibly cheaply made. Still, I found myself looking over all their offerings. And then I saw it—a huge handheld spotlight! It worked on batteries. Instantly, I decided that I would buy it and then use it to "blind" the driver of the pickup truck when he next trespassed on our driveway. I brought it home and charged up its batteries. Then I sort of rehearsed shining it through our front picture window down upon the driveway. For whatever reason, weeks went by without the truck showing up. One night, I was using it to make sure there were no skunks in the back yard before letting the dog out, and the damn cheap-ass "made in China" spotlight just plain stopped working. I was so angry. A few days after that, the red pickup was again in our driveway lighting up our living room with its eternally damned high beams.

This time, when the truck took off, I ran out to my car and gave chase following what I believed would be the quickest route to Callahan's house. When I arrived at his address, the truck was parked in his driveway but he was not outside. I just idled in front of his home and steadily blew my car's horn. Then I left. As I turned onto West Wyoming Avenue, a main road, a Melrose Police cruiser passed me and made the turn that would take him onto Callahan's street. I suppose I could have gotten into trouble, and perhaps I should even have been worried, but instead I laughed out loud. Why? Because even though I couldn't be certain that the police car was going to Callahan's street because of my horn blowing, I realized that if he was, he was taking his sweet-ass time getting there.

After a few years, two notable events took place. First, for some reason, it was reported in the local paper, the *Melrose Free Press*, that *all* of the detectives on the Melrose Police force had been moved back to patrol duties and all new officers got the detective positions. It was even reported on a site called Wickedlocal.com. However, neither source ever explained the reason or reasons for the highly unusual move. The second event —my mom got to the point where she could no longer drive and we got rid of her car. And so my car was no longer parked in the driveway; it was now always "hidden" in the windowless garage. The red pickup never showed up in our driveway again.

* * *

Today, most police cars are equipped with on board computers that allow the officers to access every bit of information that they used to need the police dispatcher to look up for them. That includes criminal records. Additionally, just checking the status of a driver's license in Massachusetts will tell the cop if the person is registered as a sex offender. So trust me, if you have a criminal record and also drive a motor vehicle, you'd have to be a fool not to invest in a radar detector. In a traffic stop, as an ex-con, you will never get off with a warning—verbal or written. And so one morning, I stopped at the end of my driveway and waited as a Melrose Police car passed. As I pulled out onto the road, suddenly my radar detector went off. I wasn't driving over the speed limit anyway. Then the signal stopped. As I came down a hill, I could now see the cruiser about one hundred yards ahead of me. Once again, my detector picked up a signal that lasted about ten seconds. Was he trying to catch me? Well, all the local cops knew where I lived, and this time the cop and I pretty much had the road to ourselves, so I would say "yes."

Then there was a day when I was in a downtown Melrose pizza shop. I had frequented that shop ever since I had returned home from Notre Dame in 1987. I was on very friendly terms with all of the restaurant's staff. Everyone who worked there spoke some East European language—I used to know *which* language, but I have long since forgotten. While I was waiting for a pizza, a uniformed Melrose cop entered the shop and picked up an order that he had apparently phoned in. The cop paid for his food and left. A short time later, the shop's phone rang. As one of the workers spoke on the phone, he kept looking over at me. When he got off, he began speaking to his co-worker in their foreign language and now they were both looking at me. There would be a long unintelligible stream of words, and each sentence would end with the English words "children. What can you do?" It was painfully obvious what they were talking about and who it was who had just called them on the phone. The state had classified me as a level 2 offender. Massachusetts law allows any resident to go to the police station, sign a form, then they can view the information on any level 2 offender that lives within a certain mile radius of that person's home. The information on level 3 offenders is posted right up front in the police station's hallway. Regarding level 2 offenders, the state says, "There will be no community notification."

So did that cop violate the law by calling the pizza shop? I'm not really sure. However, once again, knowing that I was not guilty of the offenses made me both depressed and embittered by all these events. I never got a pizza or anything else from that shop again.

* * *

The health of my knees seemed to deteriorate more and more with each passing year. At first, I was sent to a really young orthopedic surgeon by Dr. Hanson. It was weird; this young guy didn't want to do anything for me at all. Not even a cortisone shot. Next, I wanted to see the same surgeon who had successfully operated on my brother-in-law's knee, but before I could get an appointment, that surgeon was arrested for writing himself multiple prescriptions for painkillers. Finally, I saw a Dr. Burr. I had met Dr. Burr briefly in 1982 after injuring my back. To my mind, he was the only doctor at the time who had been honest with me. Three orthopedic doctors had told me that my discs would "eventually heal." When I asked Dr. Burr if my back would "eventually heal," he replied, "Not until someone goes in there and fixes it."

Dr. Burr scheduled me for arthroscopic knee surgery in late January. As Dr. Burr told me, "It's a small scar, but it's major surgery." First the right knee would be done, then a few months later the left. I was told that I would need to use crutches for seven to ten days. That wouldn't be a major problem—unless it snowed. The surgery was performed on a Monday morning. Unfortunately, it was going to snow Monday night, and I was supposed to have my weekly appointment with Billy Kohl at 1:00 p.m. on Tuesday. I called Billy after I got home from the hospital in the afternoon. I asked if we could skip our appointment for that week. Kohl's answer was an emphatic "No." Then I asked him to reschedule the appointment until later in the week. He indicated that there were no other openings. When I told him that there was a danger of seriously injuring myself in the snow, he made a veiled reference to "the importance of following my probation requirements." If the painkillers weren't keeping me calm,

I probably would have exploded in anger. Instead I just told the prick that I would see him the next day.

It began snowing around 10:00 p.m. on Monday night. By 9:00 a.m. the next morning, it was still steadily snowing. It slowly tapered off then finally ended by 11:30 a.m. I had thought of calling Kohl before he got in at noon and leaving him a voice message saying that I wasn't coming, but I was truly worried about having a problem with Mona—Billy's evil accomplice. I would have to go.

Because of my surgery, I couldn't shovel out my driveway, and the city plows had really packed us in. Fortunately, I had an old Ford Explorer with four wheel drive. After fully warming up the engine, I simply hit the gas and rammed through the huge snowbank. I had always loved doing that.

The streets in Brighton were a total mess. The plows had done their job, but between the road and the sidewalk, there was a four- to five-foot snowbank. Even the ubiquitous Boston parking meters were thoroughly buried. None of the stores or office buildings had even attempted to shovel out an opening from the street to the sidewalk so that their employees and customers could get through, and the nearest intersection was at least a quarter of a mile away. There was nothing left to do but try to climb over. At first it wasn't all that bad, but at the summit of the snowbank my right leg suddenly sank in—all the way up to my hip. I couldn't even hang on to the crutches.

Being stuck that deep in a snowbank would be a pain in the ass for anyone over thirty years of age, but with just twenty-two hours since knee surgery? It was horrific. It took me several agonizing leg pulls to finally work my way out, then I just collapsed onto the sidewalk. The pain was beyond belief. Finally a UPS delivery guy came by and helped me to my feet. He picked up my crutches, and as he handed them to me, he said, "Dude, you shouldn't be out in this shit." What could I say? I simply answered, "I know." I thanked him for his kindness. Then I staggered down to a local CVS store and bought myself a can of Coke, which I used to down two codeine tablets, then I hobbled over to Billy's office.

Of course, Billy's office was on the second floor of an old, rundown office building, and the way up included a climb of about thirty stairs. As I waited for Kohl to show up, I was seething with anger. I even fantasized about waiting for him at the top of the stairs and then throwing him, crashing down the entire steep flight. Eventually Billy showed up and remarked, "What a day!" Gritting my teeth, I frostily replied, "You don't know the fucking half of it." Instantly, Billy put on his little pouting "anger face." No matter what the situation, Billy always felt that because of his being blind, no other person on Earth had things as rough as he did. I wanted to tell him about what had just happened to me. I wanted to tell him that it was his fault and that he was a self-centered, flaming asshole. However, I realized that my pain would mean absolutely nothing to the little prick. I knew that, as I said, that he would feel that it was nothing compared to his "suffering." Most of all, I didn't want him to enjoy the thought that he had the power to cause my reinjuring myself by forcing me to keep my appointment. But from that moment on, I hated Billy Kohl with a burning passion that would never be extinguished.

The pain was so bad that I had to see Dr. Burr the following day. Burr was extremely angry. "What the hell were you doing out in a damn snowstorm the day after surgery?" he demanded. I told him I had an appointment that I couldn't reschedule. I didn't give him the details because I really didn't want him to know that I was on probation. I had already called Dr. Hanson and filled him in—Hanson knew the entire deal. Dr. Burr called him while I was there, and I could understand just from hearing half the conversation that they were talking about my entire legal "situation." At one point, Burr said, "Of course I know he'd never do anything like that—I've known him for more than twenty years." When the conversation between Burr and Hanson finally ended, he took the x-rays and put them up on the lighted display. Still looking at the films, Dr. Burr said, "We're going to have to go back in there." Then he added, "You should sue that son of a bitch!" Then turning toward me, he asked, "Do you want the name of a good lawyer?" I explained to him that I really didn't want to see the inside of a courtroom again. Dr. Burr replied, "You should seriously think about it." I just could not file suit against Kohl. I was way too afraid that the media might pick up the story and then my name and face would be everywhere.

Two weeks later, the surgery was successfully repeated. We purposely scheduled it for the day *after* my appointment with Jacky William Kohl.

# *Probation Ends*

In January of 2005, the end of probation was rapidly approaching. As if they were trying a last-ditch effort to catch me committing some crime or violating probation, the vehicle surveillance increased dramatically. I was becoming less and less amused by it all. Exactly what was the point? Prevention? Prevention of what? Catching me doing something illegal? I always knew when these clowns were around.

It was a very cold night after a snowstorm when I drove up to my sister Joan's apartment in Wakefield. Some mail had come for her at my place, and I had called to let her know I'd be bringing it up. As I drove through downtown Wakefield, I noticed a large white Ford pickup truck closing in on me from behind. The truck had a greatly beefed-up suspension system. It reminded me of something out of those famous desert truck races in Baja, California. The driver appeared to be quite young—probably in his early twenties. What bothered me was that he was driving aggressively—way too close to my rear bumper given that the road was covered with snow and ice.

Joan had been patiently waiting for me behind the frosty glass storm door of her apartment. I pulled over, and the white truck raced past me. He drove to the next intersection and wildly spun his vehicle around, ready to continue his pursuit. Joan came out, and we stood in the street talking. I told her to turn around and get a look at my "tail." It was priceless. When the guy noticed that we were both looking at him, he revved his engine like a sixteen-year-old who was having his first night out in his dad's car.

When I left, I drove up toward the truck with my window down. The kid's window was also open. Though he never uttered a word, he banged his hand on his truck's door like he was encouraging a horse to run. I just laughed and headed to McDonald's for a Coke.

As I went through the restaurant's drive-up, my "follower" waited in the parking lot. Then he followed me home. I wondered how long he'd stay in my neighborhood. It was so cold that he'd have to keep his engine running just to stay warm. It was something I'd never find out.

The next day at Billy Kohl's office, I asked him what the purpose of vehicle surveillance was when the person being watched knew that he was being followed. What genuinely surprised me was that Billy wasn't playing dumb, which was his usual modus operandi. Instead, Billy shocked me by saying, "You know a lot of backwoods trails, don't you?" It was a rhetorical question. It was then that I realized why I had been followed by the kid in the "monster truck." Earlier in December, I was followed around by an older man in a boxy Honda Element. (Not the same vehicle as the white Honda that had previously followed me.) At that time, I had noticed that the Honda had an extremely low ground clearance. I had allowed the guy to follow me onto US Route One in Saugus, then I abruptly turned onto a steep, unpaved road that climbed up into a forested area. The Element would have gotten hung up before reaching the summit of the road. I had watched the guy stop halfway up and laughed as I continued my journey back home.

I looked at Billy and answered, "I know a hundred different trails." It was an outright lie. There were only two trails in the Melrose area where my Ford Explorer could "ditch" a regular passenger sedan. Billy dropped the subject. I was never followed again. However, our verbal exchange did confirm one important thing for me: that Billy was highly involved in absolutely *everything* that the probation department did.

* * *

January slowly gave way to February, and my probation would end on February 15. At the end of January, Mona again switched off with Luis. At first I was surprised that Luis wanted me to keep my last few appointments with him at the Cambridge Court House. Only later did I realize that he was avoiding seeing me at home because

Mona had told him that our new dog was "huge." I guess Luis would spend the rest of his life being afraid of dogs.

Finally, the day came for me to have my last appointment with Billy Kohl. It was the culmination of 260 hours of Billy's bullshit interrogations. There wasn't a single thing about the man that I liked. From our very first hour together, Billy had established and maintained an adversarial relationship with me. It didn't have to be that way.

Suddenly, Billy started waxing nostalgic, talking about the past five years as if we had been on some wonderful male-bonding adventure together. "Wow, five years is a long time," he began. "Yeah, really long," I added curtly. Billy went on, "Lots of things change over the years." OK, he was sort of right, so I said, "Yup, the record store downstairs is gone and Han's Village closed. Your whole neighborhood is in decline. When there's no Chinese food around, what's the point of coming around here anymore?"

"Well, there are many good restaurants and stores still within walking distance," Billy interjected with a big smile. And then I realized what he was up to. This unofficial grand inquisitor of the state wanted me to voluntarily keep seeing him! I wanted to scream at him, *"Are you shitting me?"* Instead I simply allowed the deafening silence to do the "talking" for me. Finally, his smile disappeared and Billy broke the silence saying, "I have to write a final report to Luis. Does his name end with the letters *es* or *ez*?" Being highly sensitive to the proper spelling and pronunciation of a person's surname, I told him, "*Ez*." Billy asked, "Are you sure? I think it's *es*." I knew that Mona and Billy had always worked as a "tag team" and that Billy was quite fond of her, so I said, "Billy, it's spelled with an *ez*. Don't go around screwing up everyone's last name like Mona does." Instantly, I could see the anger on Billy's face. He ended our last meeting by saying, "Well, I have to run over to Walgreen's and get some paper for my report." And that was it. I would never see Billy Kohl again. I was glad that my last "in-session" comment about Mona had thoroughly pissed him off.

I went to the Cambridge Court House to see Luis for the last time on a freezing cold Tuesday morning. Instead of talking to me in his office, Luis simply came out to the reception area to say goodbye. He handed me his business card and said, "If you ever need anything, give me a call." Except for the incident over signing Billy Kohl's permission notes to talk to my doctors, I had sort of liked Luis. Had we met under different circumstances, we might even have been friends. I shook his hand and said, "You're a good guy, Luis." Luis added, "It was never personal, just business." I had to laugh at his quote from *The Godfather*. And then I left for the elevator. When I got outside I looked at the Court building and reflected upon all the injustices that I had endured there. Then I walked back up to the building and kicked my shoes against it so that the dust my shoes left behind would "bear testimony against them." All of them!

* * *

Despite knowing that a thoroughly undeserved legal black cloud would continue to follow me wherever I went, I felt as though a huge weight had been taken off my shoulders. Each month had featured at least four hours with Billy Kohl and two with either Mona or Luis. The following Thursday, Janice, Jeff, my mom, and I had dinner at China Moon to celebrate. I told the waiter that I would not be driving and that I wanted plenty to drink. He didn't let me down.

As much fun as that night was, I still wanted to do something—anything that would reflect my change in status. The cold winter of 2005 afforded few possibilities. Finally, in the middle of March, I decided to take my mother out to see the campus of my alma mater, Westfield State University. I had graduated from there in 1981, but since the graduation ceremony was held in the neighboring city of Springfield, my mom had never actually seen Westfield's beautiful, sprawling campus. On the way out, we stopped for lunch at the Hu Ke Lau Chinese restaurant in Chicopee. Paul, myself, and another student had enjoyed dinner there twenty-six years earlier. Those years had definitely taken a toll on the place, but the food was quite good. Afterwards, we took off for Westfield.

Since my mother now had quite a bit of difficulty walking, I had to show her the school from the inside of my car. She absolutely loved seeing all the places where I had lived and studied. There were a few more buildings. I showed her the new chapel that wasn't there during my time. There had been some fund-raising for that chapel during the Catholic Masses while I was there. We had to rent a Protestant church located nearby. The majority of Westfield's students were and still are Catholic, so it was sad for me to find out years later that the new chapel was too small to accommodate the number of students who would attend each Mass. I'm not sure how they handled that situation. It reminded me of the infamous "vote" for the football stadium. Just before I entered Westfield State, the students were asked to vote on whether they wanted to see a football stadium or an ice hockey rink built on campus. At the time, the school had a men's hockey team and they were division champions—and no football team at all. The students voted for a football stadium. It never made any sense.

After our tour, I headed back on a route that would cause us to head northeast and force us to cross through New Hampshire on the way home. It was silly, but it felt good to cross state lines without having to obtain someone's permission. Yet it wasn't entirely satisfying.

The next month, in mid-April, I got an idea. I asked my mom if she would like to travel to Hart's Turkey Farm Restaurant in Meredith, New Hampshire, for lunch. She quickly accepted my invitation. Instead of underwear, I wore a pair of black gym shorts under my sweatpants. Dinner as usual at Hart's was absolutely perfect. Afterwards, I drove to the Weir's Beach section of Laconia and parked above the docks where tour boats left from during the summer. I looked at my mom and said, "Wait here for one minute."

I hurried down to the dock area. It was around forty degrees out and a light rain was falling. I quickly took off all my clothing except for the gym shorts. Because of the overcast sky, the water appeared to be black in color. I thought about the nuts in South Boston who ran into the ocean every January 1. This would be much easier, I reasoned, since once I dove in, there would be nothing left to do but climb back out—it would be over *very* quickly.

I made my jump, and I was quite surprised that the water didn't feel all that cold. I swam back to the long dock and reached up—and it was way too high for me to grab onto! I had to swim about thirty yards back to shore. With about ten yards to go, I noticed that my legs were starting to feel like useless rubber prosthetics. I was greatly relieved when I finally felt the lake bottom beneath my feet. I walked back onto the dock and retrieved my clothes. Once I reached my car, I spotted a police cruiser right behind it. The cop's window was down, and he looked at me, still dripping with water. He shook his head and said, "You're insane." Then he simply drove off. I quickly put on my sweatpants and got back into the car. My mother looked at me as though I was in need of serious psychological help but said nothing. I drove home finally satisfied that I had properly celebrated the end of probation.

* * *

I confess that I don't really know the inner workings of the Roman Catholic Church in Boston. Cardinal Sean O'Malley would come one spring after my probation had ended to Saint Joseph's in Wakefield to administer the Sacrament of Confirmation. When he left, it was announced that the pastor was being transferred to a North Shore parish and that Father David would become the pastor of a church located in Milton, south of Boston. I wondered if Father David was in any hurry to be the "boss" of his own parish, but it was something I never asked him. Thankfully, we still met for lunch at least once a month. Still he would no longer be at my parish, and seeing him for Confession would basically come to an end.

After a new priest came and left after less than a month, a new pastor finally took over at St. Joseph's. He was a fairly nice guy and, like myself, theologically conservative. Shortly thereafter at a Sunday Mass, he announced that the woman who was the music cantor was leaving the parish to take a new job. I was deeply saddened as this woman, Michelle, had the voice of an opera star. Together with the lady who was our organist, they provided the best church music in the area. At the end of Mass, I noticed Michelle standing in a corner.

Many people were stopping to wish her well. As I approached her, she began crying, and I knew it had to do with something other than her taking a new job. "What is it?" I asked. Between sobs, she told me, "I don't have a new job. He's just getting rid of me." I was thunderstruck. "But he—" I began, but she cut me off saying, "I've been fired." I gave her a hug, and I left the church exceedingly angry.

I suppose if you're going to terminate someone's employment that it might be "charitable" to lie about what was really happening, but this was a *termination without just cause!* Had there been a legitimate reason, she would not have been allowed to complete an entire weekend of services. It didn't take long before the organist, who was also the parish music director, was said to be moving on to a new position somewhere else.

And then it happened. Slowly the organ was being replaced by piano music, and the musicians began coming in from neighboring St. Patrick's parish in Stoneham. That was the new pastor's former assignment as an assistant. I tend to think of the use of a piano in churches as relegated to those poorer parishes that simply cannot afford an organ. However, when a church musician walks by a perfectly good organ in order to play the piano, it's like a professional race car driver passing by an available Ferrari in order to drive away in a Hyundai. From a qualitative point of view, it simply makes no sense. Yet the same thing was taking place at St. Patrick's for years, and they actually had a beautiful, fully functional pipe organ! I realized what was happening. Michelle and our organist had been replaced in order to change the music to the kind of folksy, iconoclastic garbage that the new pastor liked. To paraphrase Pope Benedict XVI in the book, *The Ratzinger Report, that type of music is fine for church social events but not for worship.*

Through the summer and fall, I continued to grit my teeth and attend Mass at St. Joseph's with my mom whenever she was strong enough to attend. However, a Christmas Eve Mass brought an end to my patience. There were no traditional Christmas hymns at all. And as the Mass began, some high-school-aged kid started pounding away on a set of bongo drums. This was absolutely absurd! I realize that in some cultures, the church music is quite different from what

I am used to, but this was an entirely Eurocentric parish. The ethnic ancestry of the people in the pews was predominantly Italian, Irish, French, or Polish, but this was music with a Latin American theme.

When the Mass ended, I left the church violently angry. That nontraditional, totally out of place "music" had ruined my Christmas celebration. It was as though the very Church that I had grown up in had been cruelly taken away from me. My brother-in-law Jeff told me, "It's modern music. That's to get more people into church." But that's simply not the case. Every Mass at St. Joseph's was already packed with people. Catholic people are traditional by nature—most of them wouldn't *ever* consider changing parishes under any circumstances. These very good people were essentially trapped in those pews by family history. Many had received all their childhood sacraments there. Many more had been married there, and their children were being raised in the faith at St. Joseph's.

Thankfully, my rage was gradually assuaged by sitting at home that Christmas Eve and watching the highly traditional Mass being televised from the Vatican. Now those folks knew their music!

I didn't fully reach my breaking point until a few weeks later. My mom had been rather ill all weekend, and I was afraid of leaving her alone. She seemed to be doing better late Sunday afternoon, so I headed out for the 5:30 p.m. Mass at St. Joseph's. As soon as I entered the church, I was aware of the electronic synthesizer that was doubling as the piano. Then there was some guy playing some type of horn instrument. I knew it was my last hope of attending Mass that weekend, and I tried to steel myself against the awful sound the two "musicians" were making. Then a guy walked in and sat at a set of drums. He looked like some barely recovering alcoholic. He began pounding on the drums as though he thought he was Ringo Starr. I could feel my blood pressure rising, and my heart was pounding against my chest. This didn't sound like church; it sounded like some sleazy nightclub! I got up out of my seat and began to make my way to the exit doors. I noticed that at least twenty to thirty people were watching me closely to see what was up. I was so frustrated that I yelled out above the horrific sound, "I can't stay here and listen to that jackass pound away on those drums! I thought I was in a church!"

Suddenly, more than half of those watching me began applauding. My face was probably redder than a fire truck, but at least I now knew that the people in the pews disliked that poor excuse for music as much as I did. Soon I began "making the rounds" and attending Mass at many different parishes.

* * *

As the years passed, my mother's physical health continued to decline. I began spending more and more of my time at home taking care of her. Eventually, I took over all the cooking and laundry duties. She fell a few times, and I had to pick her up. A few years later, I would end up tearing both of my rotator cuffs lifting her. Both shoulders would require surgery. Because of her decline, I basically had to go to any parish church that would fit into my thoroughly unscheduled free time. To that end, I basically covered our refrigerator with church bulletins. Sometimes I simply had to give up on the weekend and attend a weekday Mass.

The most convenient daily Mass, as luck would have it, was at twelve noon at St. Patrick's in Stoneham. That Mass was held Monday through Saturday. Nearly every Mass is offered for a deceased person, and there is a small "fee." At St. Patrick's, if you wished, you could pay a little extra and have an organist and a cantor as well. Since it was in the smaller, less formal "lower Church," there was thankfully no piano or any other bizarre instruments.

After a while, there was a new priest at St. Patrick's who had come over (incardinated) from a religious order. Diocesan priests take the vows of chastity and obedience. Those in religious orders take an additional vow of "poverty." I'm not certain just how a priest from a religious community (order) obtains his "release" from, not only from the community itself but also from the vow of poverty. I can't imagine that the religious order would be too thrilled about a priest's leaving—especially since the order would have paid for, at a minimum, four years of the man's theological education. Most dioceses in the United States are suffering from a priest shortage, so I can sort of understand the willingness on the part of bishops to take these guys in. (Though I can imagine that a community that wanted to be rid of someone might also give the man an acceptable, or even a glowing, recommendation.)

However, over the course of a couple of weeks of seeing Father Bob at the twelve noon Mass, I got the impression that he was most likely an OK guy. Since Father David was no longer in my local area, I made an appointment with Father Bob for Confession. When seeing a priest for Confession at the rectory, there are usually no time constraints; there is no other person waiting in line behind you. Furthermore, the relaxed, informal, "living room" atmosphere tends to encourage a bit more conversation. Somehow, during my Confession, I mentioned that I had been falsely imprisoned. We talked about how it had all taken place, and Father Bob seemed sympathetic. At the end, he gave me the Sacramental Absolution, and the celebration of the Sacrament ended. And then Father Bob asked, "There, do you feel better?" I was seriously taken aback by that question. It seemed to divorce what had just taken place from the spiritual plane. True, most people *do* experience some kind of psychological relief after Confession, but that's sort of a side effect of the very *spiritual healing* that takes place in the Sacrament. It reminded me of a few of the Holy Cross Fathers from Notre Dame that seemed to view their primary role as social workers who just happened to wear Roman Collars. I had to seriously wonder if Father Bob believed in the spiritual efficacy of the Sacrament or if he was just going through the motions because he thought it was part of his job. I would not have to wait long to find out.

With my mother's health steadily declining, I was hard-pressed some weekends to get to church. On the weekends, whenever she seemed to be safe to leave alone for a while, I would run into the kitchen, check my many church bulletins for the next available Mass, then race up to that parish. Even when I was able to get to Sunday Mass, I would often still attend the daily Mass a few times each week. At the end of the twelve noon Mass on a Monday, as I was leaving, Father Bob asked if I would step into a side room in the church. We both sat down, and he began.

"Why were you at the 10:00 a.m. Mass on Sunday?" Not thinking that this was some type of Bobby Kohl–like interrogation, I launched into a discussion of my troubles getting to Mass when my mom was so frail and how, whenever an opportunity to get out of the house arose, I would consult my many bulletins and then go to the nearest church. And then Father Bob absolutely stunned me. He said, "No. You were there because you *knew* it was a family Mass and you were there checking out the children." I looked directly into his eyes and said, "That's an absolute lie." He replied, "No it's not." Then I said, "I have a Master of Divinity the same as you. I told you I was falsely accused and falsely imprisoned. Do you actually think I would lie during the Sacrament of Confession and risk going to hell?"

Without answering my question, he asked if I was aware that a priest from St. Patrick's had been arrested for stalking late-night talk show host Conan O'Brien. "What's that got to do with anything?" I asked. He said, "If after that incident the people of the parish find out that *you're* at Mass here, it could cause the parish a lot of problems." As I was about to speak, he interrupted me saying, "You should go to church somewhere else." I looked at him and said, "You know, on the Last Day, you're going to owe me an apology." He got angry and shot back, "No, I won't." Then abruptly, he said, "I think you should go. I'm feeling threatened right now." I stood to leave saying, "That's because you're a major league wimp." Bob got out into the hallway first, and with quite a few people around he said, "Go to church, Kevin." I turned toward him and fired back, "The only reason you're here is because you couldn't keep your vows to your community!" My words had their desired effect—Bob looked like he had just been hit in the stomach by a cannonball. I left the church vowing to myself never to return.

> Given the delicacy and greatness of this ministry and the respect due to persons, the Church declares that every priest who hears confessions is bound under very severe penalties to keep absolute secrecy regarding the sins that his penitents have confessed to him. *He can make no use of knowledge that confession gives him about penitent's*

> *lives* [emphasis mine]. This secret, which admits of no exceptions, is called the "sacramental seal," because what the penitent has made known to the priest remains "sealed" by the sacrament. (Catechism of the Catholic Church, second edition, sect. 1467).
>
> The *secret of the sacrament of reconciliation* [emphasis in original document] is sacred, and cannot be violated under any pretext. "The sacramental seal is inviolable; therefore, it is a crime for the confessor in any way to betray a penitent by word or in any other manner or for any reason. (Catechism of the Catholic Church, second edition, sect. 2490).

It should be noted that I did not confess to having committed any sin regarding the false accusations that were made against me. However, *nothing* that is told to a priest during the Sacrament of Confession may be used by that priest in *any way* after the confession has ended, and that is *exactly* what Bob did. I no longer refer to him as Father Bob because the man is not fit to remain as a priest.

When I got home, I was surprised that there was a message on my answering machine from Father David. He wondered if we could get together that week. I quickly returned his call, and we agreed to meet for lunch the following day. I guess God does work in mysterious ways!

Father David and I sat in his office at Saint Elizabeth's in Milton. While I never saw the interior of the church building, the rectory was beautiful. After some general catching up, I began to tell him about the incident with Bob at St. Patrick's. Throughout my recounting of the incident, Father David slowly shook his head. A man may feel sympathy. A good man will have empathy. However, this went beyond all that. I could see that Father David had been hurt by what had happened to me nearly, if not just as much as I had. As I went on, I was becoming both angry and emotional. I finished speaking with the words, "You have no idea how painful it is to tell people the absolute truth and have absolutely no one believe you!" In less than a split second, Father David replied, "Well, I believe you." His heartfelt belief in my innocence made me cry then and still brings me to tears years later.

At the beginning of my life, God gave me two great parents. I lost my beloved father way too early in life—he was fifty-eight and I was twenty-two. Then in his extreme kindness, God sent me a spiritual father in the person of Father Weiher, and later, he sent me a spiritual brother in Father David. Yet the evil that had afflicted me was so overwhelming that I would not realize all that for many years.

A week later, Father David suggested that I "try out" the parish of Saint Maria Goretti in Lynnfield, Massachusetts. A seminary classmate of his, Father Tom Powers, was pastor there. It was a very welcome change. Father Powers was certainly an orthodox Catholic as well as a good liturgist, preacher, and confessor. And praise God—there was traditional Catholic music accompanied by an organist! I worked overtime at home to try and get to my new parish every week.

* * *

Once you become a "caregiver" for an elderly family member, you tend to lose track of time and even people. Father David and I still got together for lunch but with far less frequency. Fortunately, the state eventually provided two home health aides—one to clean the first floor and another to give my mom a bath six days a week. My sister Janice bought her a small bed that we placed in the living room as my mother could no longer climb the stairs to the second floor.

As the years continued to pass, I guess we all got older—my mother, me, and sadly, even Jasmine. On a freezing-cold late winter day, I let Jasmine outside in front of the house. Even though it was so cold that you'd have to be borderline insane to be out walking, I still had to stand in the doorway and watch for pedestrians as Jasmine never really looked kindly on those who walked upon "her" sidewalk. And then Jasmine's butt hit the ice. It looked as though she were just trying to sit down, but it was so rapid that I knew something was terribly wrong. I tried to coax her into standing up, but she couldn't. She was a very big dog, and I couldn't lift her. I expected her to have either an expression of panic or pain but far worse, she looked as though she wanted to "give up."

I got my now old Subaru Wagon as close to her as I could in the neighbor's driveway, and sadly, I had to drag her as gently as I could toward the car. Yet there is nothing gentle about being dragged. Finally, at the car, I made a monumental effort and lifted her into the back. Jazzy used to cry when riding in a car whenever I had to stop at a Stop sign or traffic light. Her vet had told me it was probably her fear of being returned to the animal shelter. This time, she was totally silent. The silence hurt me far more than the previous crying ever did.

I drove as quickly as possible to the nearest animal hospital, though it was not Jasmine's usual health facility. I ran inside, and there was a receptionist and a nurse at the desk. I told them that Jasmine was in the car and I believed that she was badly hurt. In a dry monotone, the receptionist asked, "Is your dog one of *our* patients?" I completely lost it, and I angrily screamed, *"My dog is outside in my damn car and I think she's dying! Now please help me!"* Instantly, a vet ran out of her office and told the nurse to grab a stretcher, and they both followed me outside. Jasmine's face was pathetic and I fought the urge to cry—the dog would have instantly picked up on my emotions.

After x-rays and an exam, the vet called me into her office. Both of Jasmine's hips were broken (shattered), and she doubted that she would ever walk again. I had to make that most dreaded decision. Jasmine had to be euthanized. I don't care how "humane" the process is, the reality is that a beloved member of your family is going to be killed right in front of you, and worst of all, with your permission.

What made it harder is that I could tell that Jazz *knew* she was going to die, and even though I spoke to her and hugged her till the very end, she would not even look at me. I know in my heart that she believed that I had thoroughly betrayed her. When it was over, the vet told me that I could stay with her as long as I wanted. I lay on the floor with my arms wrapped around her, and I cried until I simply ran out of tears. It was Friday and a really horrific start to the weekend. It was almost as hard explaining to my mom that the big, beautiful dog that we both loved wouldn't be coming home. Jasmine was going to be cremated, and I paid the extra eighty dollars to have it done "separately" and the ashes returned to me. (I guess it's usually done in a "group" and the ashes disposed of.)

I prayed that night that the Lord would take good care of my "puppy." Although I hadn't as yet read Father Boris Bobrinskoy's books at that time, I still firmly believed that our animals went to heaven. (When Father Boris laid out that fact with beautiful theological reasoning, he became my favorite theologian.) Now, for the fifth time in my life, our home had that horrific silence that came whenever a beloved dog had died.

The next day, I kneeled in deep prayer before the four o'clock Mass at Saint Maria's parish. I was again begging God to take care of Jasmine—and to see to it that my dad and her met. As I continued my prayer, Father Powers came out to place a few things that he would need upon the altar. He looked over at me and began walking over. I thought it unusual that he would interrupt me while I was obviously praying. "Hi, Kevin," he said softly. "I wanted to tell you something before I announced it from the altar. Father David died last night. I know you two are friends and I wanted to tell you personally."

I don't remember if I said anything in reply. I hadn't known that Father David was sick. Thinking back on that moment, I wondered why I hadn't asked, "How?" Maybe I did. I don't know. My closest friend and my awesome dog had died less than twenty-four hours apart. I do remember that I then prayed asking Father David to take care of Jasmine until I saw them both again.

That Monday, a letter from Father David arrived. It was a one-page handwritten note. He said he was sorry that we hadn't had the chance to talk and go out for lunch as often as he would have liked. He also wrote, "We will have to get together as soon as I get this cancer taken care of." I was heartbroken. If only he had told me sooner, I could have at lest been at his side while he fought his final battle. I also realized that he most likely wanted to spare me any worry over his illness. Still, I wish I had known. Looking at his writing, it was obvious to me that he had written it when he was very weak, or possibly while in great pain. The handwriting was all over the place, and he had always had very nice penmanship.

Just as with Father Weiher, I knew that I would painfully miss Father David for the rest of my earthly life.

# *Yuri*

In our neighborhood, when I was very young, there was a woman who, quite sadly, had been widowed twice. When she got married for the third time—that I knew of—I remember asking my father why she kept getting married when all her husbands just kept right on dying. He told me, "I guess she just can't live without a man." That was pretty funny to a twelve-year-old. Forty-one years later, I realized that I just couldn't live without a dog in my life. It made sense. I no longer had any friends to speak of, and sadly, my mom's mind was slowly closing down. I began searching the local newspapers for "puppies for sale."

When my mom was a young kid growing up in Boston, she was chased home one day by two German Shepherds. She said she just barely escaped into her home. While she always continued to love dogs, she hated the entire German Shepherd breed. Yet there was an extremely nice one down the street when I was growing up, and I had always wanted one. I figured that now was my chance, and I answered an ad from a breeder in southeastern Massachusetts. All of our previous dogs had been spayed females, and all of them had battled unhealthy weight gain. I decided I wanted a male puppy.

I had had three online pen pals from Russia, and one of my electronic friends had a son named Yuri. I decided that my new dog would also have that name. (One thing I didn't know was that in Russia, animals are *never* given "human" names, and my naming my new puppy Yuri greatly angered my friend. But he got over it.)

It was a long ride down to the breeder's home. I was told on the phone that there were only two puppies left, one male and one female. (The puppies were four months old.) On entering the basement of her house, I saw two really cute puppies. One walked over, sniffed me, then walked away completely uninterested. The other was jumping all over my legs. I asked, "Which one is the male?" In a deadpan voice, the woman replied, "The one that's mugging you." It was love at first sight!

I paid the breeder, and then she really surprised me by saying, "Don't you put him in your car, I'll do it." I have never been able to figure out why she said that. I climbed in. Yuri was sitting in the front passenger side bucket seat. I started the car and put on my seat belt. And then Yuri crawled over and lay down in my lap. I said, "No, Yuri. If I get pulled over by a cop and you're in my lap, I'll probably get a ticket." As I finished speaking, Yuri looked up into my eyes with the cutest look I had ever seen. I said, "OK, I guess I'll have to take my chances," and off we went.

I felt like a proud new "father." When we got off the highway in Wakefield, I first stopped at McDonald's drive through for a Coke. Dan, the manager, told me, "I'd like to steal him from you." I just laughed. Next, we stopped at the Greenwood branch of the post office where I had my PO box. I brought Yuri inside with me and put him on the counter, much to branch manager Agnes's delight. She said, "You know, Kevin, if we weren't friends, I'd steal him from you!" I cracked up laughing, telling her, "You're the second person who's said that today."

As we approached our family home, I kind of wondered what my Mom's reaction would be. A few days before, I had printed pictures of German Shepherd puppies off the Internet to show her. I was preparing the way for Yuri—sort of like a nine-year-old would. I carried the puppy into the house and immediately placed him into my mother's lap. She instantly fell in love.

As the weeks went on, there was, of course, the very difficult process of trying to housebreak Yuri. For household rubbish, I had always used the huge "contractor" trash bags. Before Yuri stopped defecating in the house, I had filled two and a half of those big bags with his… you know. It's hard to admit it now, but Yuri was a very difficult puppy. Often he would stand in front of me and bark for thirty minutes straight—seemingly for no reason at all. I came home from church one day and my mom was actually hiding in the bathroom because Yuri wouldn't stop yapping at her. Like a parent with a new baby, I again had to eschew Sunday Masses in favor of the much quicker weekday ones. Yet when he reached six months of age, he had to spend the night in the animal hospital after neutering surgery, and with his being absent, both my mom and I were totally miserable. The next morning, when he was brought out of the hospital's back area, he was looking around completely disoriented. I saw him from the waiting room and yelled out, "Yuri!" He turned, saw me, and was so happy he urinated all over the floor.

I would play "ball fetch" with Yuri at least five times every day in our backyard. There had always been a leash out there with a very long rope for all of our dogs. However, Yuri was so fast and energetic that it was becoming too confining for him to play while attached to it. The city had a leash law, so whenever one of our previous dogs got the chance to break free, it was usually hell to chase them down and bring them back. (Except for Jasmine. Probably owing to the fact that she had been kicked out of two previous homes, Jasmine always took a run then promptly returned home.)

Yuri was so incredibly attached to me, following me all over the house, including at times jumping into the shower with me, so I had a sense that if he were allowed off the leash, he would probably stick fairly close to me. One afternoon, I took him out to play without hooking him to the leash and he never left the yard. He would never again wear a leash while playing.

At around seven months of age, the backyard was simply too small an area for Yuri to get his running in. Melrose frowned upon people bringing dogs onto their athletic fields, so I began taking Yuri to a good-sized park in neighboring Wakefield. That town was very reasonable. It was OK to play with your dog in their park as long as you picked up after the dog "relieved" himself. I stopped throwing away plastic grocery bags and instead kept an ample supply of them in my car.

After a couple of months, I began meeting other people who also brought their dogs to the same park. One was a former Marine who had fought in both Iraq and Afghanistan—multiple times. He was a great guy to talk with. He had a small dog that Yuri seemed to like immensely. There was also a woman with a half cocker spaniel, half poodle, as well as a married couple with a boxer. Yuri tolerated the former and disliked the latter. Well, at least all the people were nice, and it was always great to find them in the park, particularly when I was starved for conversation.

# *Two Final Injustices*

Growing up in the 1960s and 1970s, it wasn't entirely uncommon for all the neighborhood kids to, at one time or another, anger one or more of our adult neighbors. Whenever that took place, you could pretty much count on the offended adult to call your parents. It was never a big deal—a snowball fight where an errant snowball accidentally tagged someone's car or the Fourth of July when some of us celebrated our nation's independence with just a few too many bottle rockets. The thing was, no one ever resorted to calling the cops. It was simply never done. Even on the extremely rare occasions when a couple of the adults argued over something, it never caused anyone to call the authorities. However returning home after being away from 1979 to 1987 for both school and work, I quickly became aware that only a few of my former neighbors still resided there.

In 2009, it became obvious that my mom needed someone to be around the house pretty much all the time. I was the only one of her three kids that could actually be there both day and night, the other two being married. And in order to keep the whole enterprise going, we decided that we would need to apply for a reverse mortgage.

Our home was built in 1961, and my family had been its sole occupants, and while the exterior had been repainted a couple of times, a deck added out back and the roof replaced, nothing else had ever really been done to the place. In order to receive the reverse mortgage, we had to basically remodel practically the entire interior. Additionally, all the windows needed replacing. It would be the windows that would lead to problems.

When you're living in a house undergoing extensive remodeling, it's hard to keep up with the pace of it all. Early one warm summer evening after the workers had left for the day and seconds after having taken a shower, the phone rang at my second floor desk. The caller ID merely said, "Mobile caller." When I picked up the phone, a male voice said, "I just thought you should know, your neighbors directly behind your house just called the cops and said you were seen in your bathroom window naked. I just thought you would want to know." Then the caller hung up, but before he did, I detected the unmistakable sound of a two-way radio in the background. Was the caller a "friendly" cop or a neighbor with a police scanner? I'll never know.

I quickly moved back to the bathroom, and of course, the widow's blinds had been taken down by the remodeling crew. Still, I found it hard to believe that the people behind our home would actually call the cops. There's a lot to be said for simply "looking away." Worst-case scenario—how about a neighborly or even not so neighborly personal phone call to say that I should have been more careful seeing that the window no longer had any blinds?

Suddenly I saw a uniformed cop in the kitchen of my (rear) neighbor's kitchen. He was holding a camera with a long telephoto lens. *Those bastards!* I thought to myself. Worse still, the house behind us didn't have a single set of blinds or shades on any of the windows facing *our* house. I guess they felt entirely secure because their home was set on a higher hill, so while they could look down into our windows, we couldn't see into theirs. Or so they thought. Their oldest, high-school-aged, son had a second-floor bedroom in the back of the house and he was seen quite frequently late at night in various states of being undressed, but as any good neighbor, as soon as I noticed him, I would simply look away. Would this incident have taken place absent my false convictions? I sincerely do not believe so.

* * *

For years, St. Athanasius Parish in Reading, Massachusetts, had a reputation. It was easily one of the most liberal, if not theologically and socially *radical*, parishes in the Archdiocese of Boston. It even hosted meetings of the group Voice of the Faithful. That group had sprung up ostensibly in response to the Archdioceses' clergy sexual abuse crisis. However it always seemed that the ultimate goal of that group was to remake the Roman Catholic Church into the image of the Episcopal Church. They constantly sought to "democratize" the Church. The Catholic Church, however, is a hierarchical organization and has been for the last two thousand years. That is also what it will always be. The mistake that many radical Catholics make is that primarily due to the fact that most Catholics are baptized into the church as infants, these folks end up feeling that they were somehow born into the Church and that like being born in America, that gives them a guaranteed lifetime citizenship. That's simply not the case. Being Catholic means accepting the teachings of the Church, and when you can no longer do that, you essentially cease to be a Catholic. If a person goes as far as to reject a dogma of the Church, that person simply excommunicates him- or herself.

Anyway, I ran into an acquaintance from St. Joseph's parish during a daily Mass there and he told me that the music at St. Athanasius was very traditional and without, as he put it, "any weird instruments." When I said that that parish had always been somewhat radical, he told me, "Not anymore. There's a new guy in there, and he even kicked the 'voice of the heretics' out." I was quite surprised, and I definitely wanted to check it out for myself. It took a few weeks before I felt I could safely leave my mom alone at home. Finally, I got there. The music was indeed very good. The new priest seemed to be orthodox, and his preaching was at least slightly above average. Mostly because of the great music, I began to go there on Saturday or Sunday whenever I could.

When I pray at home, following the Byzantine tradition, I pray with sacred icons, and I usually use incense as well. Despite Saint Gregory's Seminary's Father John saying the "Eastern Church priests don't bless candles, they are blessed by their use," I always got a priest to bless my candles. (Strangely, I have had Eastern Orthodox priests who were willing to bless my candles.) So it happened that I had the priest at St. Athanasius, Father Alan (a pseudonym), bless my candles. I was struck by how friendly he was, a quality that I feel is necessary in a priest but unfortunately often lacking.

The second time that I had Father Alan bless the candles for me, I sent him a thank-you card, and I also gave him an icon as a gift. The following week, when I went to Mass, there was a complete reversal of Father Alan's prior "friendliness." Now he wouldn't speak to me. In fact, at the end of Mass when I went to shake his hand at the exit doors, he even turned his back to me. Now one has to be careful not to jump to conclusions about things like this, so I continued to attend Mass at Saint Athanasius for another month. However, it became painfully obvious that Father Alan was outright "shunning" me. I had really come to like that parish, and now, just as at St. Patrick's before, I was forced to leave.

Many years before, when I had experienced the same type of problem at Annunciation Melkite Cathedral, I had written a letter to Melkite Bishop Nicholas Samra. Despite misspelling my name, Bishop Nicholas wrote me an extremely kind letter that he ended by saying, "You are welcome to attend the Divine Liturgy at any of our parishes."

With that in mind and basically boiling over with anger because of the injustice of it all, I wrote a letter to Boston's Cardinal Sean O'Malley. Not only did I completely explain what had taken place with Father Alan, I also reported in detail the incident with St. Patrick's Father Bob, including the very serious crime of his breaking the seal of Confession. I also told him that at neither St. Patrick's nor at St. Athanasius had I ever attended any church social functions, so I was never near any "family events." I shouldn't have had to write that, but by now I knew exactly how some priests think. Knowing that the Archdiocese of Boston is a huge bureaucracy, I sent the letter certified with a requested return receipt. I ended the letter with the words, "If I stop going to Church because of these nasty priests, is the sin mine or theirs?" I received the post office's return receipt; however, neither Cardinal O'Malley nor anyone else in the Archdiocese of Boston ever responded.

What had happened with Father Alan? It is possible that someone from the parish recognized me, knew my "case," and spoke with Father Alan. However, that's highly unlikely. More likely would be that after sending Father Alan the thank-you card, he decided to Google my name. Father Alan often spoke of his computer and being on the Internet, so that was most likely what had taken place. Yet why didn't he speak to me about it? Not in the highly confrontational manner of Father Bob, of course, but why simply launch into a "shunning campaign?" The whole incident reflects very poorly upon the Archdiocese, their two seminaries, and the quality of both their priest's theological and pastoral education. It also speaks volumes about the quality of the people that they accept for ordination. No wonder the Roman Church continues to suffer every year from various priest-induced scandals.

# Time Runs Out

In 2010, life was fairly good. My mom was happily living at home, I had a beautiful new dog that I loved, and I had a decent car and a nice home to live in. With each passing year, however, it became more and more difficult to take care of my mom. Way back in the early 1990s, my mother and I had spent an evening watching a family drama movie on cable. In the film, a woman's adult children basically *force* their mother into a nursing home long before the woman needed to be there. At the time, my mom was in great condition both physically and mentally. The movie greatly upset her, and she said to me, "Please don't put me in one of those awful places." I remember emphatically telling her, "Of course I won't!"

As her condition worsened, I remained determined to do everything in my power to keep that promise. In the summer of 2010, after a hard fall, she was sent to a nursing home simply for physical therapy and to learn how to do everyday things "safely." I too had to go to a few classes at the same facility to learn how to assist her in the safest possible manner—not just to prevent injury to Mom but also to keep from hurting myself. Though as I have mentioned, I would later separately tear both of my rotator cuffs picking her up after falls. What was awful to me was that the longer she was at the rehabilitation facility, the more her mind seemed to be failing her. Yet as soon as she returned home, her memory and other cognitive functions seemed to be miraculously restored. I'm not sure why her mind faltered while she was away from home, but I have a feeling that she was not an isolated case. Then, as now, I firmly believe that an institutional setting has a negative impact on an elderly person's mind.

As 2013 began, however, despite being at home and having me as nearly constant company, Mom's mind began to fail more and more. After two small fires, I had to hide the tea kettle because she would place it on the stove, turn the burner on, then forget all about it. Once the water boiled away, the kettle itself would burn. Thankfully, I was just upstairs and the smoke detectors alerted me. Mom began making her tea by placing a mug of water in the microwave oven to heat it. It was a very old appliance, and it would take about three minutes for the water to heat up. Late one night, the smoke detectors sounded again, waking me up. Mom had gotten up in the middle of the night, placed a mug of water in the microwave, and set the timer for thirty minutes. Then she went back to bed. Using oven mitts, I was able to throw the smoking (and melting) oven into the backyard. I got a new one, but I had to insist on making her tea for her. If I went out or to bed, I had to unplug it. I felt like a total "rat" doing that, but I had no other option.

Mom also could no longer control her bodily functions at all. A woman was now coming in six days a week to wash her, and it just wasn't enough. At times I had to wash her. I figured she had done that for me during my first few years of life, so it was the least I could do. I also had to wash about five loads of laundry a day. They were small loads, but they had to be done at once or the odor would become unbearable.

The most difficult thing of all was her falling. It didn't take place all that often—maybe once or twice a month—and she never hurt herself, but the Melrose Fire Department had to come and lift her back into her chair each time. I could see that they were tiring of coming to our house, though only a couple of them ever overtly registered their displeasure. Far more difficult were the times when the firefighters would insist on taking her to the hospital. The hospital always performed x-rays and sometimes a CT scan, though they never found anything wrong. Then we would have to pay for an ambulance to return her back home. Sadly, trips to the emergency room usually lasted from four to six hours.

My sister Janice and I could see that sooner or later, Mom would need twenty-four-hour care. So it was with the greatest of reluctance that we went and checked out two nursing facilities. One was quite close to home. I had a friend from church who had gone there toward the end of her life. I had visited her on a Saturday, and most of the elderly residents at that time were sitting in wheelchairs just outside of their rooms. It struck me as just plain awful. Most of them were completely asleep in their chairs. Was there nothing better that they could have been doing? Even a good movie in a large room would have been a major improvement. I think the best way to check out a nursing facility is to go there unannounced on a weekend when the administrators are gone.

We checked out another place in Wakefield that was easily a hundred times better. As much as I absolutely hated the idea of her going *anywhere*, Mom was placed on that facility's waiting list. I secretly hoped that it would be a very long wait.

Keeping Mom clean was a major chore, and the woman who came to wash her began complaining to her bosses that it was all "too much." One day, my mom had a tiny cut on her toe—something that would require a Band-Aid at most, but the personal care woman actually called 911 bringing the fire department up. Before I could get a word in, they took her to the hospital. It was an enormous waste. Even the ER doctor was visibly upset. When he confronted me as to why she was there, I just answered, "It wasn't *my* choice." As great as the firefighters were, some of them, usually the EMTs, would basically brow-beat my mom into agreeing to be transported to the hospital. It was just plain wrong. Trust me, an elderly person with dementia will basically agree to anything that a uniformed person suggests.

Finally, in late April of 2014, my mom again fell down. I had just gone upstairs to write a quick letter, and she basically slipped out of her recliner by accident. I knew that with the pressure from her doctor for her to be placed in a nursing facility, if she went to the hospital, she would never come home again. I think she knew it as well because she asked me, "What should I tell the firemen?" I gave her some pointers on how to handle the conversation, but it was no use; the firefighters packed her into an ambulance and drove her to the hospital. Eventually, the facility that had her on their waiting list admitted her to their rehab section.

Mom was OK at first. Fortunately, I was allowed to bring Yuri in to see her whenever I visited. Some of the staff were afraid of him, yet for the most part, he was a virtual celebrity among the elderly residents. One wheelchair-bound woman would always start clapping whenever we got to the second floor, and I would have to spend some time with her as she petted Yuri. I think it was really good for her. I was surprised that Yuri seemed to enjoy her company as well since he seldom wished to make friends with anyone outside of our family.

My mom always excitedly exclaimed, "My big baby!" whenever Yuri entered the room. In the beginning, she didn't ask too many questions about her situation. After a while, she started to ask me, "How long do I have to stay here?" I didn't know what to say, so I always answered, "I'm not sure." That was a lie, and I knew it. I hated myself for not having a better answer. Later, she began saying, "Tell Jannie [my sister Janice] to get me out of here." However, when she finally realized that she was never going to leave the place, she began to withdraw—especially from conversation. Once, during an hour-long visit, while she never said a word to me, she looked at Yuri and said, "My big baby, I have to get out of here and take care of you." After that visit, she would no longer eat or drink. She lost all hope of ever going back to the home she loved, and if you ask me, that would be the "cause of death." In the absence of all hope, an elderly person will simply cease to exist.

Medicare will not pay for nursing home care as long as the elderly person has *any* type of personal financial assets. So as soon as Mom was admitted to the facility in Wakefield, we had to place the family home up for sale. Even if there were anything left after the nursing home got their share, the bank that held the reverse mortgage would certainly get the rest. Within weeks, an offer was made by a potential buyer.

I found out on Wednesday, June 11, 2014, that I, along with Yuri, would have to be out of the house by the following Sunday. Yuri and I had absolutely nowhere to go. Even homeless shelters were discussed—but that would mean losing my dog. On that Thursday, I got a call from a semi-retired independent Anglican Bishop that I had met only once in church one Sunday. He had a small, what he called a "cottage" in northern Vermont. He said that I could stay there for the price of the electricity.

Yuri and I drove up to see the place the very next day. The bishop had said that it was "primitive," and that was an understatement. There was no shower, bath, or toilet—in fact, there was no running water of any kind. There was no television or Internet either. And the place was filthy. The area was surrounded by dairy farms, and it was so rural that the shack didn't even receive mail delivery. I drove home in a state of shock.

Saturday, June 14, Yuri and I arrived at Bear Hill Nursing Facility in Wakefield for what I knew would be our last visit. My mom was sitting in a chair staring at a television that no one had even bothered to turn on for her. I turned the TV on. I had brought her a small Sprite from McDonald's and a pastry from a local bakery. She looked at both but wouldn't touch them. After the longest silence, she reached for Yuri and he went over and licked her hand. He looked up into her eyes, kissed her face, and she quietly said, "My big baby." After another half hour, we had to leave. I gave her a huge hug. When we returned to the car, I just held Yuri in my arms and cried for the longest time. I knew I would never see my mother alive again and that there was nothing I could do to change that.

On Sunday, June 15, with no other available options, Janice and her husband, Jeff, each filled their individual cars with as much of my belongings as would fit. I filled most of my car as well, leaving only enough room for myself and Yuri.

Janice and Jeff did a remarkable job cleaning the shack up while I walked around in a severely depressed daze. Then we all said goodbye. I sat down on what would have to pass as a bed. Yuri jumped up and lay down next to me. In less than a week, I had basically lost everything that I had ever had. My bedroom furniture, most of my books, my television—all hauled away by a modern-day Sanford and Son. (They were paid over a thousand dollars to haul it and the rest of the house's furnishings away and then most likely sold the stuff for a huge profit.) I had my car, my clothing, and thankfully, my beloved dog. I wasn't certain if or how the two of us would survive.

The next day, June 16th, was my Mom's ninetieth birthday. The priest from St. Joseph's in Wakefield came on the eighteenth and, with both of my sisters present, administered the Sacrament of the Sick (Last Rites). On June 19, Mom died.

# *Epilogue*

Yuri and I have been living in the shack now for nearly three months. The roof of the place is not insulated, so during the day, when the sun beats down on the roof, the temperature often reaches over 100 degrees inside. Thus far, the nighttime temperature hovers around fifty-eight degrees. Early in September (2014), there was an overnight frost. The radio forecasted the overnight low to be between twenty-eight and thirty degrees. With help from a local charity, Yuri and I spent the night in a "pet-friendly" motel. When we returned the next morning, the water in Yuri's dish was partially frozen. On some nights, despite wearing a ton of clothing, I shiver throughout the night. The shack will be uninhabitable by the end of October.

Being completely surrounded by dairy farms, finding work has been all but impossible. Back in Massachusetts, the Sex Offender Registry Board places the photographs of Level 3 offenders—considered the most likely to re-offend—on the Internet. They had classified me as Level 2. Here in Vermont, they put *every* offender on the Internet. A McDonald's restaurant thirty-two miles away would not hire me solely because my picture was online. I greatly fear discrimination in both housing and employment.

My father was one of the biggest proponents of higher education that I have ever known. His favorite expression regarding education was "A good education is one thing 'they' can never take away from you." Maybe so, but a false conviction can prevent you from ever being able to put that education to actual use. Despite my hard-earned Master of Divinity, there is no Catholic religious order or diocese, Roman or Eastern Rite, that would touch me with the proverbial ten-foot pole. Teaching at any level is also out of the question.

If I were a wealthy man, I could have the very best attorney appeal my conviction. In my situation, however, my only hope for justice is if the New England Innocence Project decides to take my case. They have been reviewing my case since 2012. As they have told me, "Our case review process is very thorough and can be a lengthy process." I can only hope and pray for a positive outcome.

Ray Swanson, for some unknown reason, set out to destroy me. His weapon of choice was his vicious, lying mouth. Father David once asked me if I had forgiven him. I told him that it was nearly impossible to forgive someone when the injury they have caused simply continues on and on unabated. Yet Jesus does demand that we forgive. I guess I'll have to keep working on it. It may well entail a lifelong process.

One day, an Eastern Orthodox priest said to me, "Considering what you've been through, I'm surprised that you haven't lost your faith." I told him that although I didn't know where the quotation came from, I had learned to live by the words "I don't understand, Lord, but I believe."

# About the Author

Kevin Paul DeCoste was born and raised in Melrose, Massachusetts. He served with the Army Reserve and was both a military police sergeant and campus police corporal. He later worked as a counselor at a treatment program for adolescent males who had committed sex offenses. He received his AS in Criminal Justice from Bunker Hill Community College in Boston, his BA in Political Science from Westfield (Massachusetts) State University, and his Master of Divinity from Boston University. He lives in Boston with his German Shepherd, Koji.

CPSIA information can be obtained
at www.ICGtesting.com
Printed in the USA
FSHW01n0837061018
52705FS

9 781643 504865